INVALID MODERNISM

Invalid Modernism

Disability and the Missing Body
of the Aesthetic

MICHAEL DAVIDSON

OXFORD

UNIVERSITY PRESS

OXFORD
UNIVERSITY PRESS

Great Clarendon Street, Oxford, OX2 6DP,
United Kingdom

Oxford University Press is a department of the University of Oxford.
It furthers the University's objective of excellence in research, scholarship,
and education by publishing worldwide. Oxford is a registered trade mark of
Oxford University Press in the UK and in certain other countries

© Michael Davidson 2019

The moral rights of the author have been asserted

First Edition published in 2019

Published in the United States of America by Oxford University Press
198 Madison Avenue, New York, NY 10016, United States of America

British Library Cataloguing in Publication Data
Data available

Library of Congress Control Number: 2018958826

ISBN 978–0–19–883281–2

In Memory of Tobin Siebers

Preface: Disorientations

My only out of body experience happened when I was giving a talk on my campus to a luncheon group made up of faculty from various departments. My talk was about homosocial alliances and conflicts during the AIDS pandemic of the early 1980s when information about the spread of HIV/AIDS targeted homosexual men as the source of a "gay plague." I was interested in the intersection of gay activists and young men with hemophilia during a period when the latter group became 90 percent HIV positive as a consequence of infected blood.[1] I used my own hemophilic condition to talk about the ways that the Moral Majority positioned hemophilic boys, major carriers of hemophilia, as tragic victims of gay lifestyles, thereby dividing two constituencies joined by a blood-related virus. In the Q&A after my talk a well-known geneticist from my university asked me if it wouldn't have been better if my mother had had genetic testing when she became pregnant so that she could have aborted the fetus when she discovered the presence of hemophilia? I was dumbfounded. To paraphrase Carly Simon, I was so vain; I thought this song was about *me*. Apparently, the geneticist was able to separate the person standing in front of him from the fictive person necessary for his research.[2]

The geneticist who posed the question was echoing the bioethicist Peter Singer who, in his 1993 book *Practical Ethics*, proposes a similar hypothetical about a newborn baby diagnosed with hemophilia. He imagines that the child's parents "daunted by the prospect of bringing up a child in this condition, are not anxious for him to live. Could euthanasia be defended here?" (163). Singer equivocates:

> When the death of a disabled infant will lead to the birth of another infant with better prospects of a happy life, the total amount of happiness will be greater if the disabled infant is killed. The loss of happy life for the first infant is outweighed by the gain of a happier life for the second. Therefore, if killing the hemophiliac infant has no adverse effects on the others, it would, according to the total view, be right to kill him. The main point is clear: killing a disabled infant is not morally equivalent to killing a person. Very often it is not wrong at all.   (163)

Singer's cost–benefit version of personhood assigns a happiness quotient to my family based on my erasure. According to his logic, by surviving with a chronic disease I'd be taking up a happiness quotient that could be had by my replacement, were my parents to have another child. As it turned out, my parents did have another child, my brother, who also has hemophilia and who, like me, has lived to tell about it. Our happiness quotient has been enhanced thanks to the benefits of

---

[1] I discuss these issues in the first chapter of *Concerto for the Left Hand*.

[2] Alicia Ouelette, discussing a meeting of bioethicist Peter Singer and disability rights lawyer and activist, Harriet McBryde Johnson, notes that most "disability experts understandably recoil at the thought of engaging in a debate about whether their own parents would have been better off had they allowed them to die" (133).

strong family and medical support but also to the freeze-dried blood factor by which we can control bleeds. Thanks to the Affordable Care Act, we no longer have a "prior condition" that denies us medical insurance for an ongoing condition whose medical costs are considerable.

What is uncanny here is Singer's separation of two forms of utility, a "prior existence" version that imagines a life worth living, despite disability, and a "total version" that imagines alternate narratives foreclosed by disability. One cringes at the idea that Singer might serve as a witness at a trial involving fetal euthanasia or end of life treatment, weighing the balance between "prior existence" and "totality." As Alicia Ouelette says of this passage, "Singer's argument depends entirely on subjective assessments about an individual's prospects for quality of life. Those assessments do not need to be based on evidence or experience" (104). Nor do they depend, apparently, on any personal acquaintance with bleeders or, needless to say, with disability studies.

This is a book about modernism and disability, not about bioethics, but subsequent chapters will suggest important connections between the two topics. What links issues in modernist aesthetics with bioethical concerns about a livable life is the presence of an absent body—a disorderly, volatile, often unsettling figure haunting a good number of literary works and, as I've indicated, scientific and medical research. In exploring the uncanny body in modernism, I look at a period stretching back into the mid-nineteenth century and continuing into the genomic present. My anecdote suggests that the utopian promises of curative medicine and eugenic improvement of the late nineteenth and early twentieth centuries continue in the current period, albeit under a different set of terms. The erasure of disability and chronic disease to make way for a healthier, risk-free body remains a dream of modernity sustained today in arguments for prenatal testing, innovations in gene therapy, CRISPR technology, and the vast entrepreneurial realm of body modification and "aesthetic" surgery. For the well-intentioned geneticist and bioethicist, personhood is defined as those human characteristics of health, independence, and autonomy shared by most people. Deviations from such a unitary definition of personhood require not only physiological and psychological judgments but aesthetic judgments about how a body or mind conforms to some putative ideal. For persons with disabilities, personhood is relational, subject to varying criteria of ability and agency. Against restricted versions of embodied personhood, a disability perspective considers individuals as part of a network of family members, friends, care-givers, and community that troubles the location of impairment in a single individual.

What I've described as the absent personhood in bioethics is, in some ways, the double of the body absented from aesthetics. Classical aesthetics from Kant to Adorno requires the sensate body to disappear once sensory response has made its impact. The doctrine of artistic distanciation and autonomy, framed formally by serialism in music, abstraction in painting and sculpture, organic form in poetry, is often haunted by a figure whose stutter, chronic cough, paralysis, mad rages, dismemberment, neurasthenia, or blindness are the focal points in *Billy Budd, The Magic Mountain, Lady Chatterley's Lover, Wozzeck, Guernica, The Waste Land,* and

Endgame. My task in *Invalid Modernism* is not only to find examples of disabled characters in modernist literature—they are everywhere—but to understand how physical and cognitive disabilities underwrite the aesthetic function itself as the contingent corollary to non-contingent judgment. As I say later in the book, the body is the ghost in the machine of the aesthetic, necessary for its smooth functioning yet invisible as its source.[3]

In my previous book, *Concerto for the Left Hand: Disability and the Defamiliar Body*, I recognized how standard definitions of modernist formal innovation—alienation effect, defamiliarization, *ostrenenie*, making-strange—have their counterparts in disability experience. When one's body refuses to conform to social requirements of size, shape, independence, behavior, communication, sensory response, or the built environment, it is, in Sara Ahmed's terms, "disoriented" from what most people regard as familiar. We become oriented when our relationships to the lived environment and bodily and sensory functions are thwarted. "It is by understanding how we become orientated in moments of disorientation that we might learn what it means to be oriented in the first place" (*Queer Phenomenology*, 6). At this point we notice orientation as "something we do not have," something of which we were not aware (5). This can occur when we become temporarily disabled and must use crutches or medication, but as my examples here and in my final chapter show it can illustrate how the different body or mind disorients definitions of what it means to be human.

Disorientation also functions as a defining characteristic of the aesthetic insofar as representations of such moments make visible points of tension between a totalizing and a situated judgment. Kant differentiates between judgments of beauty and those of taste on precisely this point: judgments of beauty must be disinterested, detached from any personal intention and subject to universal validation; judgments of taste are more local—judgments about this or that object without regard to any universal appreciation. Or to adapt Carly Simon again, judgments of beauty are not about you; those of taste are. Yet for persons subject to aesthetic judgments, what pertains to "us" matters. The rallying cry of the international disability rights movement, "nothing about us without us," is partly my justification—and that of many of us doing disability studies—to introduce personal anecdote into cultural criticism.

My warrant for stressing a phenomenological and situated approach to disability is provided by Tobin Siebers and others who have faulted the social model of disability for its narrow focus on environmental and societal barriers, to the exclusion of what it means to live with a disability. This is another example of the disappearing act with which I began where the attempt to see disability as a function of external restrictions, prejudices, and aesthetic criteria leaves the disabled body intact.

---

[3] I have been aided in the study of disability modernism by the work of Janet Lyon, Tobin Siebers, Maren Tova Linnett, Lennard Davis, David Mitchell, Carol Poole, Sharon Snyder, Rosemarie Garland-Thomson, James Berger, Susan Schweik, and many others. Their work constitutes, in total, a strong argument for seeing disability's emergence as a social category within modernist aesthetics.

As a consequence, there is little room for understanding what new knowledges and solidarities are created through disability.

To illustrate the experience of disorientation, I look, in my final chapter, through the prism of Emily Dickinson who was not permanently disabled herself but who had a preternatural understanding of how physical and mental disorientation are ways of rethinking what it means to be alive. Her poetry—like that of other authors I discuss in *Invalid Modernism*—often invokes pain, dismemberment, blindness, madness, and deafness as ways of imagining liminal states of awareness. When she figures what it might feel like to become unconscious, she says, "I could not see to see." At one level, she is recalling her own experiences of temporary blindness in her early life, but she is also aware of the difference between sight and the ability to organize sensory information. One might see her double vision as complicating Emerson's famous figure of the transparent eyeball which allows him to experience "the universal currents of being" flowing through him while walking in nature. Emerson's transcendental vision does not see "with" the eyes but "through" them to a larger world of which we are a part. But Dickinson is not content with such merging; rather, she interrogates, as she says in one poem, "internal difference— / Where the Meanings, are—" (153).

Invalid Modernism studies a range of authors, composers, and painters for whom internal difference is embodied in new formal strategies, eccentric characters, and reconfigured bodies. The book also looks at modernist cultural production through a number of different media: novels, short stories, poems, plays, film, opera, performance, and visual art. What I call the "absent body" of the aesthetic is the prohibition against embodied and sensory response—including fallacies of intention and affect—in evaluating and understanding works of modernist art. My occasional forays into personal anecdote are not attempts to claim some special privilege but to give a situated account of what it feels like to be differently human in an increasingly technological, rationalizing world. That world, as my opening anecdote suggests, is one in which I should not have been allowed to write the book I have written.

Acknowledgments

In writing this book I have been fortunate in having a community of friends and colleagues whose generous advice and conversations are woven throughout each chapter. Special thanks is extended to Peter Middleton for his ongoing, generous commentary on all aspects of the book. Thanks in addition to many friends in and out of the field of disability studies, who gave me feedback, read chapters, or indulged my endless queries and concerns: David Lloyd, Rachel Adams, Page DuBois, Rob Kauffman, Susan Kirkpatrick, Cris Miller, Ari Heinrich, Lisa Cartwright, David Bolt, Stuart Murray, Clare Barker, Chris Krentz, Adelaide Morris, Brenda Brueggemann, Nicole Marcotic, Maren Linnett, Amelia Glaser, Susan Schweik, Georgina Kleege, Bridget Bennett, Benjamin Reiss, David Serlin, Brian Goldfarb, Rodney Livingstone, Jeff Brune, Todd Kontje, Alison Kafer, Carol Padden, Robert McRuer, and Ann Fox. Thanks, too, to my graduate students at the University of California, San Diego, whose insights and research helped me think through many issues in the book: Jenni Marchisotto, Gina di Grazia, Mark Kelley, Jason Farr, Amanda Martin-Sandino, and Michelle Stuckey. I would also like to thank my captioners, Comfort Pettis, Jennifer Betancourt, and Stephanie Lorenz who have permitted me to continue teaching.

I am grateful to Ian Davidson and the Leverhulme Trust for providing me with a research grant at Northumbria University. I also want to thank Clark Lawler at Northumbria whose "Fashionable Diseases: Medicine, Literature and Culture" forum provided material for an early version of Chapter 1. Thanks to Stuart Murray and Clare Barker for inviting me to give a presentation at the Centre for Medical Humanities at Leeds University and to David Bolt at the Centre for Culture and Disability Studies at Liverpool Hope University. Other occasions to present portions of the book were generously provided by Rachel Adams (Columbia University), Martin Padget (University of Aberystwyth), Daniel Kane (University of Sussex), Yu-Fang Cho (Miami University, Ohio), Robert McRuer (George Washington University), Carla Freccero (University of California, Santa Cruz), Benjamin Reiss (Emory University), Peter Middleton (University of Southampton), Charles Bernstein (University of Pennsylvania), Sophie Chapuis and Pierre-Antoine Pellerin (Université Jean Monnet Saint-Etienne and Université Jean Moulin, Lyon), and Jean Heuvig (University of Washington, Bothell).

The editorial staff at Oxford University Press has been generous in its support of this project, in particular my editor, Jacqueline Norton and her editorial team, Aimee Wright and Catherine Owen, my copy-editor, Joanna North, and my indexer, Eileen Quam. I also want to thank the two anonymous readers for their scrupulous and careful assessment of the manuscript. Laura Swartz at the University of California San Diego Library provided amazing help in securing images for the book. I am grateful to Susan Smith and Sheldon Nodelman for their advice about images and reproductions.

Earlier versions of individual chapters appeared in several venues, for which thanks are extended to the editors: Kirsty Johnston, *Disability Theatre and Modern Drama* (Bloomsbury, 2016); Nancy Armstrong (*Novel*), Kim Nielsen (*DSQ*), Nick Wolterman (*Modernism/modernity*), Cesare Casarino, John Mowitt, Simona Sawhney (*Cultural Critique*), Rober McRuer (*GLQ*).

The love and support of my family—Lori, Ryder, Sophie, and Shiloh—have been an inspiration and blessing.

Finally, *Invalid Modernism* is dedicated to the memory of Tobin Siebers whose friendship and example are responsible, in good part, for the writing of this book. He will be missed.

[Chapter 2] Copyright © Johns Hopkins University Press. This article was first published in *Modernism/modernity* 22.4 (2015): 609–25. Reprinted with permission by Johns Hopkins University Press.

[Chapter 4] Kirsty Johnson (ed.) (2016) *Disability Theatre and Modern Drama*, Methuen Drama, an imprint of Bloomsbury Publishing Plc.

Excerpts from *Waiting for Godot* copyright © 1954 by Grove Press Inc.; Coyright © renewed 1982 by Samuel Beckett. Used by permission of Grove/Atlantic, Inc. Any third party use of this material, outside of this publication, is prohibited.

Excerpts from *Happy Days* copyright © 1961 by Grove Press, Inc. Copyright renewed © 1989 by Samuel Beckett. Used by permission of Grove/Atlantic, Inc. Any third party use of this material, outside of this publication, is prohibited.

Excerpt from *Endgame* and *Act Without Words* by Samuel Beckett copyright © 1958 by Grove Press, Inc. Used by permission of Grove/Atlantic, Inc. Any third party use of this material, outside of this publication, is prohibited.

Excerpt from Ezra Pound, *The Cantos*, Canto XII, pages 56–7. Used by permission of New Directions Publishing Corp.

Excerpt from William Carlos Williams, *The Collected Poems of William Carlos Williams*, Vol. I: *1909–1939*, pp. 183–4. "By the road to the contagious hospital." Used by permission of New Directions Publishing Corp.

Excerpt from *The Poems of W. B. Yeats*, "Under Ben Bulben," p. 327. Used by Permission of Simon & Schuster, Inc.

Excerpt from Walter Benjamin, *The Writer of Modern Life*, Charles Baudelaire, "A une passante," p. 76. Used by permission of Verso Press.

Contents

List of Figures

Introduction
Disability, Modernism, and the
Embodied Aesthetic

MEETING HAROLD RUSSELL

Theodor Adorno describes attending a party in Malibu shortly after the end of World War II that included, among its guests, Charlie Chaplin. Also in attendance was the actor Harold Russell, best known for his Oscar-winning role as a disabled veteran in *The Best Years of our Lives* (1946). Russell, who lost both of his hands while making a military training film, wore prosthetic hooks on both of his arms. Adorno reports that when introduced to Russell, he experienced a moment of panic:

> When I shook his right hand and it responded to the pressure, I was very taken aback, but realizing at once that I should not let Russell see my reaction under any circumstances, I instantly transformed the shocked expression on my face into a winning grimace, which must have looked even more shocking. Scarcely had the actor departed than [Charlie] Chaplin was already mimicking the scene. So close to horror is the laughter he provoked that only from close up can it acquire its legitimacy and its salutary aspect.   (qtd. Claussen, 165)[1]

There are fascinating elements to this anecdote, not the least of which is Adorno's willingness to admit his discomfort in this awkward interchange. Seeing his anxiety mimicked by Chaplin adds another theatrical layer. One reading of this incident could see his discomfort as a reflection of his general distaste for American popular culture and of his own estrangement in Southern California. For a theorist famous for his critique of the Hollywood culture industry (notwithstanding his admiration for Chaplin's films) Adorno here seems bemused by its intrusion at a Southern California party. The "winning grimace" into which he transforms his shock is the epitome of what Ato Quayson calls "aesthetic nervousness" that the able-bodied person experiences in the face of disability. The fact of a differently configured body short-circuits one's expectations of bodily normalcy producing, in Quayson's terms, a dissonance "that cannot be properly articulated via available social protocols [that] define the affective and emotional economy of the recognition of contingency" (17). Adorno seems particularly conscious of this dissonance when he says "so close to horror is the laughter he provoked that only from close up can it acquire its salutary aspect." The phrasing here is somewhat confusing as he

---

[1] I am indebted to Rodney Livingstone for alerting me to this anecdote.

attempts to contextualize the effect that Chaplin's satiric mimicry gives to the "horror" produced by a prosthetic hand. Close proximity to disability brings one into intimate awareness of bodily contingency for which able-bodied persons are often ill prepared. Adorno seems suspended between affect and emotion, between the sensory impact of bodily difference and subsequent attempts to describe it.[2]

I see this small incident as one of many awkward confrontations between modernism and disability, here narrated by a famous theorist of autonomy aesthetics. Although Adorno never frames it as such, his response to Russell's prosthetic hand illustrates the challenge that the "different" body raises for a period defined by its pursuit of normalcy following the war. As subsequent chapters will suggest, disability is a constitutive feature of modernist art and literature by making visible those bodies and minds that interrupt an ideal of bodily coherence and health. The neurasthenic couple in *The Waste Land*, the shrieking figure in Edward Munch's *The Scream*, Benjy Compson in *The Sound and the Fury*, Joyce's crippled ingénue, Gerty MacDowell in *Ulysses*, Joseph Conrad's developmentally disabled Stevie in *The Secret Agent*, Sherwood Anderson's grotesques in *Winesberg Ohio*, the recombinant bodies of Hans Bellmer's *Poupées*, the deranged woman of Schönberg's *Erwartung* all represent uncontainable bodies and minds of modernism. As with the freak shows on the midways of international exhibitions, such figures offered audiences the comforting feeling that there, but for the grace of some higher power or genetic advantage, go most of us.

This merging of disability and modernism has been admirably theorized by Tobin Siebers in *Disability Aesthetics*, and my debts to his work will be evident in each chapter. He argues that disability "enriches and complicates notions of the aesthetic" and that the non-traditional body has directly impacted modernist art while creating a critical framework by which to rethink the nature of the human (3). As he says, "disability aesthetics refuses to recognize the representation of the healthy body—and its definition of harmony, integrity, and beauty—as the sole determination of the aesthetic" (3). Siebers' examples are taken largely from contemporary visual and performance artists who have used their bodies, often in extreme and punishing ways, to foreground the body's materiality and revise conventional treatments of aesthetic appreciation. In what follows I look at figures from a longer modernist era for whom disability and dependency are formative in generating what I am calling an "invalid modernism," one that exists in the interstices of more canonical versions.

At the same time, I am interested in how disability unsettles modernist aesthetics itself, not only by providing examples of disabled or mad characters such as the ones mentioned above but by challenging the very idea of an autonomous art as it has organized theoretical discourse around this period.[3] Adorno begins his *Aesthetic*

[2] The distinction between affect and emotion is usually described as one between stimulus and subjective response, between the body's neurological registration of an event and one's subsequent attempt to define it. Summarized by Julie Taylor, "we don't weep because we feel sorry...but rather feel sorry because we weep" (7).

[3] Ato Quayson places disability "on a continuum with the sublime in terms of its oscillation between a pure abstraction and asset of material circumstances and conditions. Considered in this

Theory by remarking that "art's autonomy shows signs of blindness," using an ableist metaphor to represent art's refusal of the mimetic, the familiar, the true (1). He recognizes that art must relinquish its reliance on what is already known or self-evident in order to establish a critical distance from it. As he says in a later essay, it is necessary "to make things of which we do not know what they are," a remark that could describe the unsettling effects of Duchamp's readymades as much as Cage's aleatory techniques in music ("Vers une musique," 322). When he uses a metaphor that links blindness to willed unknowing, he suggests that even in the attempt to escape instrumentality in art an embodied figure is necessary to imagine what is unimaginable.[4]

As a related issue, I am interested in exploring the role of affective response in modernist studies, one epitomized by Adorno's reaction to Harold Russell's prosthesis. The recent critical interest in affect has returned the body to cultural theory by emphasizing phenomenological relations among subjects—what Sara Ahmed characterizes as "dramas of contingency," or "how we are touched by what comes near" (*Promise*, 22).[5] It is this close proximity of dissimilar bodies that early diagnosticians of modernity like Georg Simmel saw as the "intensification of emotional life" that characterizes a metropolitan mentality (325). At the same time, this emphasis on sensual response returns aesthetics to its original meanings in eighteenth-century philosophy: *aesthesis* or corporeal perception.[6] Many of the terms that have organized theories of modernism—*ressentiment*, *ennui*, spleen, alienation, shock—derive from the close proximity of others, providing affective realms to protect oneself against the "apparition" of faces in the crowd that Pound observed coming out of the Paris Metro.

Although Adorno seldom refers to the body, his confrontation with disability is elaborated in a famous passage in *The Dialectic of Enlightenment*, written close to the time of his meeting with Harold Russell. He and Max Horkheimer are discussing the Sirens episode of *The Odyssey* as an early anticipation of bourgeois enlightenment. They regard Odysseus is the very type of Enlightenment man who seeks rational authority over the mythic power of nature as embodied by the Sirens. Odysseus' rationality takes the form of an exception: "He must escape the legal

---

way, we can think of the sublime as occupying one end of the spectrum (being a pure abstraction despite generating certain psychological effects of judgment and the impulse to represent it in material forms) and disability occupying the other end and being defined by a different kind of oscillation between the abstract and the material" (*Aesthetic Nervousness*, 23–4).

[4] I am indebted to Robert Kaufman for his discussion of Adorno's ideas in *Aesthetic Theory*. He emphasizes that Adorno's figure of blindness is precisely *not* what Paul de Man means by "blindness and insight," the idea that "all knowledge is purchased at the cost of certain blindness." Rather, for Adorno and Horkheimer, such formulations as de Man's ignore the fact that the artwork seeks to make itself "blind and deaf to ruling versions of knowledge precisely so that it can then go seek to see/hear the reality that would otherwise not be apprehended (by ruling conceptual tools)." I would observe, however, that this formulation still privileges seeing and hearing as the *telos* of the artwork's willed unknowing (e-mail communication, May 6, 2016).

[5] An excellent survey of the material turn in cultural theory, particularly in feminism, can be found in Stacy Alaimo, *Bodily Natures: Science, Environment, and the Material Self.*

[6] Alexander Baumgarten's foundational 1750 work, *Aesthetica*, distinguishes corporeal perception, *aisthetike*, from *noema* or objects of thought. Cf. Martin Jay, "Drifting" (6).

conditions which enclose and threaten him, and which are, so to speak, laid down in every figure" (58). He satisfies these conditions by forcing himself to listen to the Sirens' song while lashed to the mast. He deafens his crew by plugging their ears with wax and thus remains firmly in control of his ship. Adorno and Horkheimer call Odysseus' stratagem his "escape clause": "The bound listener wants to hear the Sirens as any other man would, but he has hit upon the arrangement by which he as subject need not be subjected to them" (59). Commentators on this passage have attended to its account of how bourgeois reason has mastered "the mythic past."[7] Rita Felski has extended this reading to show how their narrative privileges a patriarchal myth of rational authority over nature but also over the seductive lure of a gendered mass culture. Odysseus becomes the "disciplined male bourgeois individual, foreshadowing the repression of the body and the feminine that will determine the development of Western culture" (5). Felski's reading recognizes the effacement of the body in this allegory, but she does not pursue the passage's theme of deafness as a palliative against erotic temptation. Odysseus' "escape clause" allows him both to hear and not hear at the same time while maintaining authority over his crew, deafened against desire. It is one of those moments in the analysis of modern culture where overcoming the *lack* of some bodily function is necessary to *produce* rational order and power.

Controlling "lack" is, of course, a centerpiece of Freudian psychoanalysis as the male subject converts castration anxiety into productive labor, compensating for loss by objectifying woman as other. Kaja Silverman understands *The Best Years of our Lives* and Harold Russell's prosthesis as constructed precisely through this optic. She considers a number of postwar films, including *The Best Years*, that attempt to "shore up the ruins of masculinity" caused by the traumas of the recently completed war and the emergence of a female workforce (52). Wyler's film "focuses obsessively and at times erotically on the physical and psychic mutilation of the three veterans," making the film "almost unwatchable" (53, 67). I would agree that the film focuses extensively on Homer's prostheses, but I would not conclude that witnessing disability makes the film unwatchable, nor would I conclude that castration anxiety is the tenor for this vehicle. Rather, I would agree with Sarah Sahn that the friendship among the three veterans is a powerful counter-motif to postwar trauma through which the shared experience of disability creates alliances that ultimately allow "hurt" men to bond. The problem with Silverman's reading— and a good deal of psychoanalytic film theory—is its reliance on castration and specularity as the only vehicles for understanding bodily difference or masculine psychological trauma. What if instead the "spectacle of Homer's hooks," as Silverman calls them, offered a teachable moment about living with disability and forging a new awareness about the contingent nature of embodiment?[8] If Wyler's film looks obsessively at Homer's prosthesis or Fred Derry's (Dana Andrews) PTSD

---

[7] Kellner, *Critical Theory, Marxism and Modernity* (91).
[8] David Mitchell, Sharon Snyder, and Linda Ware have referred to such teachable moments offered by disability as "curricular cripistemologies" that "offer teachable moments organized around crip/queer content that interrupt normative cultural practices" ("[Every] Child," 296).

or Al Stevenson's (Fredric March) alcoholism as compensatory diversions of emasculation it also looks at the homosocial alliances forged *through* disability.

Controlling lack is hardly limited to Freud but could be seen as a major imperative of modernization as it impacted persons with disabilities. In the USA for example the attempt to create an imagined community out of disparate demographics and across geographic distances in the late nineteenth century necessitated the control of populations whose language, cultural traditions, and non-traditional bodies challenged a national standard. One example would be the imposition of oralist education on deaf children in order to accommodate their deafness to a hearing world. The pedagogical issue here, as Douglas Baynton says in *Forbidden Signs*, is a national imperative to bring minority populations into a common national language and ideological consensus. The same could be said for so-called anti-mendicant or "ugly laws" passed in various cities in the early part of the twentieth century. As holdovers from earlier "Poor Laws," these ordinances were designed to protect citizens from encounters with diseased or deformed individuals. "Unsightly beggar ordinances" were part of Progressive Era reform efforts and city beautification projects whose ends, as Susan Schweik says, involved "identifying, representing, knowing, correcting, and disciplining the 'unsightly beggar'" (2). And as a third example, David Serlin in *Replaceable You* observes the prosthetic hand that Harold Russell extended to Theodor Adorno was part of a postwar consolidation effort that by "engineering masculinity" attempted to bring the wounded veteran into line with a physical ideal. There is a reciprocal relationship between the lacking body and the technologies and governmentality developed to cure, rehabilitate, legislate, and restore. Such cases could be multiplied many times to show the close proximity between ideals of modernization and the enforcement of a standard body and sensorium.[9]

Technology plays a key role in this process by promising more efficient systems, machines, medications, and bureaucracies to restore the presumed "broken" body to wholeness. As Tim Armstrong notes, "[m]odernity, then, brings both a fragmentation and augmentation of the body in relation to technology; it offers the body as lack, at the same time as it offers technological compensation" (*Modernism, Technology*, 3). Such innovations as "electro-therapy, dietary regimes, eye-therapy, manipulation, hormones, surgery" and other body modification procedures return the missing body to its "true" form. And if the private body is in need of restoration, so the social body could be rehabilitated through the hygienic imperatives of eugenic science. Such "progressive" structures imagine a body made whole through wonder-working technologies, rest cures, and institutionalization. Psychoanalysis may control the subterranean libido that erupts into consciousness while progressive reform and social engineering may purge society of its libidinized populations.

---

[9] Amanda Martin Sandino reminds me that in L. Frank Baum's Oz books, characters who "lack" some body part or quality are often positive figures. In *The Wizard of Oz*, the Tin Woodman lacks a heart; the Scarecrow lacks a brain, and the Cowardly Lion lacks courage which, translated into disability terms, could be seen as disabilities. Yet Baum shows them to be affirmative characters who, although they desire a more "normate" existence, nevertheless display qualities of courage, endurance, and friendship. In one case, the Tin man saves a mouse, which challenges his assumption that he lacks charity.

As modern medical and scientific technologies promised cures for the bodies politic, photographic technologies helped make them visible. Nineteenth-century photographic albums and archives created by Francis Galton, Alphonse Bertillon, and Matthew Brady sought to identify the "deviant type," often by using racialized and disabled persons as comparisons. Turn-of-the-century medical photography, as Dana Seitler says, often identified homosexuality by juxtaposing images of "sexual perverts" with persons with physical or cognitive anomalies, thus reinforcing the intersection of moral character with physical difference. Seitler notes that the term "degeneracy" was used rather broadly to create links between various identity positions still undefined at the turn of the century. She refers to the American physician Eugene Talbot who used "degeneracy" as an umbrella term for any number of social ailments—from "alcoholism to hermaphroditism, prostitution, pauperism, moral insanity, 'giantism,' and 'negro degeneracy'—all of which he describes as 'buds of the same tree of degenerate heredity'" (79). By juxtaposing images of persons exhibiting these characteristics medical photography allowed one form of deviance to be defined by another. As Seitler notes, these "queer physiognomies" are produced in a serial fashion, "intelligible only through its affinities and variations with other Others" (83). Paradoxically, the more that photography was enlisted to police and categorize bodies, the more that different bodies became available to the public eye. The sexual invert, Jew, or prostitute and by extension, the feeble-minded or deaf person were intelligible largely through their difference from others, a fact reinforced by medical photographic albums and their side-by-side juxtaposition of exemplary portraits.

INVALID MODERNISM: AESTHETICS, DISABILITY, DIFFERENCE

What has cultural theory had to say about the materiality of the body? Not much, at least until recently. "What about the materiality of the body, *Judy*?" Judith Butler asks in *Bodies that Matter*, a question specifically addressed to critics who worried that her theorization of gender performativity tends to imagine gender as a somewhat arbitrary form of role-playing, something that could be taken on or off like clothing. By rhetorically addressing herself, she attempts to "recall…a bodily life that could not be theorized away" (ix). Although she never addresses disability, her question suggests that theoretical treatments of materiality have treated corporeality largely as the inert mass upon which ideology imposes constraints.[10] Butler does, however, provide a space where disability *could* appear when she speaks of how thinking of the constraints that produce intelligible bodies, produces "as well a domain of unthinkable, abject, unlivable bodies" (xi). The bodies that matter in

---

[10] Butler indirectly mentions disability when she qualifies constructionist definitions of identity by stating that "surely bodies live and die; eat and sleep; feel pain, pleasure; endure illness and violence; and these 'facts,' one might skeptically proclaim, cannot be dismissed as mere construction" (xi). Disability theorists have long made the same point about the limits of a strictly social model of disability that erases the material body of a person who lives with a physical or mental impairment.

Bodies that Matter are gendered or queer, but they could easily be those produced within the discursive arena of disability and without which the "discursive limits of sex" (to appropriate her subtitle) would be unthinkable. Butler's self-critique of constructionist theories of identity belies a critique of the social model of disability.

But what about the materiality of the artwork? To answer this question is to engage the vexed issue of modernism's own materiality and the extent to which formal innovations contest or extend that materiality. Critics often differentiate between modernism and modernity, seeing the former as an aesthetic response to the latter, either as a critique of bourgeois mores or, as in more avant-garde movements, an appropriation of consumer culture to contest the institutional authority of what Herbert Marcuse calls "affirmative culture." James Knapp uses a typically embodied metaphor to make this argument: modernity is "a kind of soul trapped in the gross body of modern industrial society" (22). Rather than see modernity and modernism as discrete entities I see them intimately conjoined *through* that "gross" body. The material forms of modernization mentioned above—photography, psychoanalysis, "ugly laws," film, racial taxonomy, criminology—are symptoms of modernization as well as effects of aesthetic rationalization. The photographic image that interpellated the convict or eastern European "type" contributed to the "reality effect" of the Realist novel or the Imagist doctrine of direct visual presentation.

One might be forgiven for assuming that disability was *invented* in the period that this book covers. A cursory look at historical scholarship on disability suggests that the preponderance of work in this field has been devoted to the late nineteenth and early twentieth centuries. Essays in Paul Longmore and Lauri Umansky's foundational collection, *The New Disability History*, deal exclusively with disability from the postbellum through Progressive Eras. Although, as Douglas Baynton says in that volume, "disability is everywhere in history, once you begin looking for it," the term takes on particular relevance with the rise of industrial capitalism, global war, medical science, and rehabilitation technologies, not to mention psychoanalysis (52). It is within this period that the "medical model" of disability is formed and strategies of "biopower" perfected.[11] The appearance of institutions for disabled persons, residential schools for the deaf and blind, legislation to provide benefits for workplace injuries or wounded veterans, and the beginnings of charity organizations all testify to the growth of an institutional recognition of disability. Deborah Stone argues that disability emerges when it becomes a category for the modern welfare state, a matter of economic distribution as increasing numbers of people require access to public and private facilities. Workers' compensation, sick leave, and medical certification emerge when disability becomes tied to occupational categories. At the same time, because of perceived abuses to the welfare system disability also emerges as a disparaged entity. Persons who require assistance, buildings that need to be retrofitted, jobs that need to be reassigned, moneys that

---

[11] Paul Longmore and David Goldberger discuss the emergence of the medical model of disability in "The League of the Physically Handicapped and the Great Depression." Foucault's notion of "biopower" is not limited to the late nineteenth century but arises with the formation of the modern nation-state. My emphasis here is on the degree to which fin de siècle technologies of medicine and science helped to put into practice the general area Foucault outlined in *The History of Sexuality*.

need to be designated for sick leave and company-provided insurance cast the person with a disability as a drain on the system, a "dependent" who does not contribute to the common weal. Although *Invalid Modernism* will be concerned with the missing body in aesthetic discourse, it is worth mentioning the emergence of what we might call the "welfare state body" in modernity as backdrop to its artistic transformations.

As I develop the theme in Chapter 1, my title contains something of a *double entendre* depending on whether one places the accent on the first or second syllable of "invalid," whether one refers to a "sick" or "ill" modernism—one in a state of convalescence—or a modernism invalidated by elements that challenge artisanal autonomy. The term, in both pronunciations, derives from early eighteenth-century French where it originally referred to soldiers considered unfit for battle. The two versions merge in Nazi *entartete kunst* exhibitions of the late 1930s that displayed the work of Expressionists and Cubists as degenerate and "sick."[12] If the aesthetic function involves judgments, freed from intentions or desires about what constitutes an ideal of beauty and proportion, it also presumes a body that is unacceptable, distorted, or grotesque—inválid, in other words—upon which to base that judgment. The issue here is not only aesthetic but ethical: If one wants to justify slavery, it is useful to define the black body as abnormal or diseased; if wants to justify homophobia, it is useful to define homosexuality as a form of mental illness; if one wants to deny female suffrage, it is useful to think of women as unstable or hysterical. If one wants to restrict immigration, it is useful to think of immigrants as bearers of communicable diseases.[13] In each case, normative identity is produced through bodies deemed invalid according to some standard of physical and cognitive purity.

The process of "enforcing normalcy," in Lennard Davis' terms, is a key component of modernization. Davis bases his account of the emergence of a bodily norm on the rise of statistics and quantification in the early nineteenth century. I would add the importance of aesthetics in interpreting—for better or worse—what statistics discovers about bodies. A pervasive theme in the following chapters is the degree to which disability interrupts a certain aesthetic modality through which an empirical norm is usually seen. Modern aesthetics, since Baumgarten and Kant, has suppressed corporeality from judgments about beauty, judgments that in order to claim validity must be detached and disinterested. But this evacuation of the body from the aesthetic is complicated by the fact that disinterested appreciation begins with sensory response. As Kant argues in the *Critique of Judgment*, aesthetic appreciation is not about the beautiful object so much as the pleasure it inspires in us;

---

[12] In *Prosthetic Gods* Hal Foster notes that the 1937 "Degenerate Art" exhibit drew on reproductions of art created by mentally disabled patients that were collected by the psychiatrist Hans Prinzhorn in *Bildnerei der Geisteskranken* (Artistry of the Mentally Ill, 1922). The work exhibited reflected certain modernist formal tendencies (despite the fact that the patients often had little acquaintance with modern art), thus creating what Foster calls a "reversibility [that] haunts the modernist revaluation of the art of the mentally ill, for if this art could be revealed as somehow modernist in affinity, the art of the modernists could also be branded as somehow pathological in tendency" (*Prosthetic*, 196).

[13] Sander Gilman in *The Jew's Body* notes that hysteria in the late nineteenth century was often applied to Jewish men as a way of feminizing them. Thus it was not surprising that Jewish scientists like Freud displaced Jewish hysteria to women.

it is constituted not in the object but in the perceiving subject, detached from all concepts and interests. But acts of perception are situated in specific regimes of access. The beautiful castle that Kant uses as his example in the opening of his third critique may not be subject to matters of comparative design, possible inhabitants, or usefulness but must be judged on "whether the mere representation of the object is to my liking, no matter how indifferent I may be to the real existence of the object of this representation" (43). This is all very well, say, for an able-bodied or sighted person, but for a person who is blind or in a wheelchair the question of its disinterested beauty is more complicated. Of course there may be *other* forms of pleasure that such a building inspires in a person with a disability, but the apprehension of its "real existence" divorced from its access exists within an idealized representational regime.

This defamiliarizing feature of disability is also the defamiliarizing quality that we identify with modernist art—music that challenges traditional harmony, painting that disrupts single point perspective, narrative that refuses chronological sequence.[14] These disruptions in modernist art are never only aesthetic but betray, as Ato Quayson says, "an active ethical core that serves to disrupt the surface of representation" (*Aesthetic*, 19). Modernist abstraction or atonality are not in any way equivalent to disability, but they share a common root in embodied, sensory experience. The shock of *Sprechstimme* in Schönberg's *Pierrot Lunaire* is only a shock to one who has lived with an acoustic history of song and speech. As I point out in Chapter 2, modern music's chromaticism and harmonic indecidability troubled Nietzsche whose "physiological" objections to the music of Wagner led him to believe that the composer's "infinite melody" could lead to social contagion. What we regard as a key moment in Nietzsche's aesthetic theory also turns out to be a key statement of aesthetic nervousness.

The modern application of Kantian disinterestedness would be the model of aesthetic autonomy that emerges in the mid-nineteenth century with Flaubert's desire to write a "book about nothing" and, later, Symbolism. In its more extreme versions in *art pour art* the important connection between sensuous cognition and the object of contemplation is broken in favor of the artwork itself. This creates a form of what Martin Jay calls "aesthetic separatism" that results in "nonpractical contemplation . . . to fend off at least temporarily, the meaninglessness of the world" (13). In the USA, for example, postwar consensus intellectuals who sought to chasten modernism of its more experimental tendencies reified some version of this ideology in pursuit of an art whose self-reflexiveness and formal complexity forged a barrier to mass culture and commodity society. The linguistic experimentalism of Gertrude Stein or the Futurists, the genre-bending performances of Dada or Surrealism, the Popular Front novels of Michael Gold or Richard Wright could now be replaced by the psychologically complex novels of Joyce, Woolf, and Faulkner or the poetry of T. S. Eliot and Ezra Pound, works whose "spatial form" aspired to the condition of sculpture.[15] For Irving Howe, Clement Greenberg,

---

[14] Michael Davidson. *Concerto for the Left Hand: Disability and the Defamiliar Body*.
[15] On "spatial form," see Joseph Frank, *The Widening Gyre* (3–9).

Richard Chase, Delmore Schwartz, Joseph Frank, and Daniel Bell modernism is characterized by a densely textured, psychologically complex, formally intricate artistic alternative to the sensational elements of popular fiction or the confrontational gestures of the avant-garde. The New Criticism's caveats against fallacies of affect and intention cautioned readers against a literature too dedicated to bodily response or social impact.

The desire to recalibrate modernist experimentation around an auto-telic ideal is underwritten by a more covert worry over volatile bodies. Frankfurt School theory along with Andreas Huyssen's *After the Great Divide* tends to see this worry more in terms of mass culture or a feminized sentimental tradition. But this social volatility had its counterpart in actual bodies that were being categorized, defined, and repaired. The term "inválid" was often identified with the historical condition of disabled people at the end of the nineteenth century who become increasingly the objects of biopolitical monitoring and taxonomic categorization. The eugenics movement drew from the emerging sciences of animal husbandry, statistics, and social Darwinism and subjected them to practical solutions, including the sterilization of criminals, incarceration of the "feeble-minded," sequestration of the "deaf and dumb," and by the time of the Nazi Final Solution, genocide. Martin Pernick has noted the importance of aesthetics in this process and the extent to which a norm of beauty was seen as a necessary feature of racial improvement. Aesthetic criteria of physical beauty were seen as "objective" and "scientific" since based on disinterested observation and ideals of organic coherence.[16]

For African Americans during the Progressive Era, ideas of uplift and assimilation could also be aligned with racial improvement for which aesthetic criteria are paramount. For W. E. B. Du Bois, Booker T. Washington, Anne Julia Cooper, and other reformers, it was necessary to redeem the black body from decades of racist depictions of that body as disabled. Racist medicine infamously imagined African Americans to be susceptible to diseases that caused them to escape enslavement (Drapetomania) or that posited them as lazy and mischievous (Aysaesthesia Aithiopis). Du Bois in *The Souls of Black Folk* notes that such depictions rendered African Americans as a "handicapped" race whose bodies were often regarded as diseased or pathologized. As Stephen Knadler observes, Du Bois dwells extensively on "the unsightliness of the maimed and the diseased as if to add his own anecdotal weight to prevailing statistics about the degeneration of black bodies as a result of their freedom" (104). Du Bois criticizes Booker T. Washington for advocating a gradualist approach to rights, while the latter characterizes the progress of the Negro as "physically and mentally dwarfed" (qtd. Knadler, 109).

African American members of the Talented Tenth contested eugenically tinged treatment of racial character but ultimately adopted some of its principles as a counter discourse to biological racism. Du Bois' most famous pronouncement, "The problem of the twentieth century is the problem of the color-line" in its first incarnation prefaced a display of photographs at the Paris Exposition of 1900. This display, "The American Negro Exhibit," featured 363 photographs of ideal "Negro Types" suggesting that even within the color line there would be gradations of

---

[16] Martin Pernick, "Defining the Defective" (96).

value. Shawn Smith observes that the American Negro Exhibit photographs "collectively function as a counterarchive that challenges a long legacy of racist taxonomy, intervening in turn-of-the-century 'race science' by offering competing visual evidence" (2). But it is clear that similar taxonomies that demonized the black body also demonized that body as disabled, stunted, or diseased. The pairing of frontal and profile photos of these members of the Talented Tenth and their offspring "signified," as Smith observes, on the racial photographic albums of racial science by the founder of eugenics, Francis Galton.

This intersection of racial uplift and eugenics points to one of many contradictions of progressivism, specifically, and modernism more generally with implications for disability. The biopolitical imperative to improve and create a better future was underwritten by fears of an ill, "feeble-minded," or deformed body. In justifying sterilization, eugenic physicians linked "deviant" behavior to any number of categories. The Mental Deficiency Act of 1913 in Britain legitimated institutionalization for "mental defectives" on the basis that they represent a danger to society, requiring, as James Berger points out, "both care and control" and thus excluding them from social polity (63). In the Legislative Record for the state of Iowa, for example, sterilization was justified for "criminals, rapists, idiots, feeble-minded, imbeciles, lunatics, drunkards, drug fiends, epileptics, syphilitics, moral and sexual perverts, and diseased and degenerate persons" (Laughlin, 22). The list might have included immigrants as well. In 1912 the Medical Examiner of Mentally Defective Children in New York's Department of Education, Isabelle Smart, worried about the fate of children with "a serious mental defect": "Ten thousand cases! Ten thousand little human beings so seriously handicapped that they will never be able to enter fully into competition in order to earn a livelihood—so seriously handicapped that the major number should be segregated, and marriage and procreation be absolutely denied them" (Laughlin, 391). Smart notes that the source of this problem is the increase in immigration: "[g]ladly do we welcome the poor amid the downtrodden of other nations, but we must be firm in our exclusion of the mentally unfit" (Laughlin, 392).

Disability was often equated with poverty, illiteracy, or sexuality. Alice Smith, a patient admitted the New Jersey State Village for Epileptics in 1902, was, as the case history says, "classed with and accounted for in the same category with feeble-mindedness." In justifying sterilization (she had conceived a child after being raped) the editors summarized that:

> to discharge such a case as this one as cured, and allow her to return to her usual walks in life would be a crime against society. To withdraw each and every person who has at any time displayed epileptic tendencies, in any degree whatever, from the community, is the only rational course left open. It would be indeed most wasteful to the nation and State to allow this defective to wander about, as it would entail perpetuation of her kind and other evils due to this lack of proper care and segregation.   (Laughlin, 294)[17]

---

[17] The term "defective" derives from early seventeenth-century Poor Law administration to characterize anyone having a deficiency of the senses. It gradually became a more general term for other forms of disability, especially mental illness. On English Poor Law and disability see Deborah Stone, *Disabled State*, 47.

And Harry Laughlin, a proponent of "eugenical sterilization" argues in 1934 that:

> Because America needs no more human seed-stock, she is in a very strong position to set high standards for future immigrants who seek to enter the country. If the country is wise it will admit as future immigrants—i.e. human seed-stock—except those applicants who, in race and numbers, can be promptly distributed over the country and readily assimilated to American ideals and loyalty, and who in hereditary quality are—not barely above capacity 'to keep out of institutions for the insane, and the prisons' but who, by the most searching tests humanly possible, will constitute an asset to America in physical stamina, in mental capacity, and in moral fibre.   (434)

Laughlin's terminology—"seed-stock," "hereditary quality," "distribution," "stamina"—indicates the close relationship between animal husbandry and population control in eugenic thinking. It is not surprising that scientists in the Third Reich in developing policies of sterilization and forced segregation respected the work of Laughlin and other American eugenicists.

It is against this medical and technological background that we might adapt what Tobin Siebers calls an "aesthetics of human disqualification," to characters mentioned in this book: Alexander Zemlinsky's dwarf in his opera *Der Zwerg*, Thomas Mann's Hans Castorp in *The Magic Mountain*, Djuna Barnes' Mathew O'Connor and Robin Vote in *Nightwood*, Samuel Beckett's Winnie in *Happy Days*, F. T. Marinetti's Mafarka, Frida Kahlo's portraits of herself, Henry James' Ralph Touchett in *Portrait of a Lady*, James Joyce's Leopold Bloom in *Ulysses*, and many of Emily Dickinson's self-representations. All are in some way "invalid" members of society whose outlier status is marked by atypical bodies or non-traditional forms of cognition. Unable to define Leopold Bloom's racial otherness in Dublin, Irish nationalists characterize him as a "dark horse," "old sloppy eyes," "mixed middling," and a "half and half…a fellow that's neither fish nor flesh" (263).[18] As a sham gynecologist and abortionist, Dr. Mathew O'Connor is cast as a cross-dressing male who desires to bear children and who haunts the Paris *pissoirs* for religious (and sexual) gratification. Unsatisfied with the redemptive grace of Protestantism or the domestic grace conferred by Victorian marriage, Emily Dickinson imagines an alternate Calvary:

> Rearrange a "Wife's" Affection!
> When they dislocate my Brain!
> Amputate my freckled Bosom!
> Make me bearded like a man!   (132)

Such figures in Siebers' terms are "disqualified" and therein lies their critical ability to unseat what we presume are normative versions of national, gendered, and racial identity. Dickinson understands that for a mid-century woman to imagine an alternative female role is equivalent to having one's brain "dislocated" and one's breast amputated. In short, a masculine woman would be a disabled man.

---

[18] Dana Seitler notes that in the sexological literature of the day, calling someone a "half and half" or "hybrid" was equivalent to "invert" ("Queer Physiognomies," 84).

Within modernist studies there has been an analogous attempt to invalidate the canonical criteria by which the period is often defined. Douglas Mao and Rebecca Walkowitz characterize such subversive elements as a "bad modernism" that lies outside conventional associations with the term. A "bad modernism" would resuscitate those elements that gave the movement its first impulse—its resistance to conventional middle-class values, its rejection of the myth of progress (Futurism notwithstanding), and its critique of "rational" man. "Bad" modernism may also suggest elements within high modernism that queer its psychological explorations of gender, that critique its orientalist or racist depictions or that reveal mass cultural elements in works of high culture. In fact, as Heather Love suggests, in "thinking about *bad modernism* it may be useful to recall that it was modernism itself that gave *bad* a good name" (19).

We can see a "bad" modernism hiding in what is usually thought to be representative, once we discern its embodied metaphors. The appeal of progressive reform leaks into the rhetoric of poets like Ezra Pound in his plan to "resuscitate" English verse as a "cure" and "hygiene" and who, in *The Cantos*, represents decay through the metaphor of infection. In "Canto 45" he describes the corrosive effects of Jewish usury which "hath brought palsy to bed, [and] lyeth / between the young bride and her bridegroom / CONTRA NATURAM" (230). When his Imagist colleague, H.D. wants to render the ugliness of cities against the spare beauty of classical nature, she imagines

> ...in these dark cells,
> packed street after street,
> souls live, hideous yet—
> O disfigured, defaced,
> with no trace of the beauty
> men once held so light.   (41)

And Yeats' *Under Ben Bulben* urges Irish poets to "learn your trade" and

> Sing whatever is well made,
> Scorn the sort now growing up
> All out of shape from toe to top,
> Their unremembering hearts and heads
> Base-born products of base beds.   (327)

Mina Loy, in "Songs to Joannes" (1917), worries that "Unnatural selection / [will] Breed such sons and daughters / As shall jibber at each other..." and relates racial mixing to what she calls "mongrelization" (66). In her "Feminist Manifesto," Loy attacks the institution of marriage and compulsory reproduction, arguing for the "unconditional surgical destruction of virginity" at puberty, thereby eliminating the "principal instrument of her subjection" as commodity (156). Her call for sexual liberation, however, contains a troubling eugenicist subtext: "Every woman of superior intelligence should realize her race-responsibility, in producing children in adequate proportion to the unfit or degenerate members of her sex" (157). The use of eugenic rhetoric to imagine a cleansed, improved, or better future suggests how pervasively progressive social reform influenced progressive artistic innovation.

Anxiety about "base born products of base beds" fuels popular media as well during the same period. Since I have already invoked Charlie Chaplin, let me elaborate this point by reference to the 1927 silent film *Old San Francisco* in which disability serves to finesse a story of racial passing. Warner Oland plays a conniving Chinese entrepreneur, Chris Buckwell, who cross-dresses as a white business mogul in early twentieth-century San Francisco. His masquerade allows him to bilk his Chinese countrymen out of their property while posing as an upright pillar of the white community. He becomes interested in appropriating the rancho of an old Californio whose daughter, Dolores (Dolores Costello) becomes the object of Buckwell's lust. The protagonist of the film is a plucky Irishman, Terrence O'Shaughnessy (Charles Mack) who protects Dolores from Buckwell's designs, both material and erotic, and saves her father's rancho from Buckwell's acquisitive greed. The film rehearses historic conflicts in San Francisco between Chinese, Irish, and Hispanic cultures, each minority population seeking to claim a more authentic American identity by racializing another. In the film's rather spectacular denouement the 1906 San Francisco earthquake conveniently destroys the evil cross-dressing Buckwell along with the Chinatown ghetto and permits a new "white" city to be rebuilt on the ruins of old San Francisco.

We might see the film as an amalgam of terms already discussed: Progressive Era worries over "dysgenic" populations; uplift ideology and "fitter" citizens; popular genres annexing nativist fears of amalgamation and immigration. As Michael Rogin has pointed out, *Old San Francisco* is one of numerous early films that merged the trope of racial passing with fears of the Yellow Peril. He notes that these films were often made by Jewish film moguls who sought to establish their claim to Americanness by creating narratives of successful cross-racial alliances while, at the same time, marginalizing other racial types.[19] In *Old San Francisco* Warner Oland as a white actor cross-dressing as a Chinese man passing as white, participates in an elaborate form of racial masquerade that threatens to upset the clear delineation of racial categories. Moreover his desire for the film's Hispanic heroine introduces the threat of miscegenation across racial lines. But there is a disability narrative that serves to cement the various strands of the film.

At one point, after he has successfully coerced a group of Chinese businessmen to sell their property to him, Buckwell goes through a secret passage in his luxurious San Francisco home and down a winding staircase into the basement below. Here he dons a ceremonial cap and kimono, lights incense and prays before a giant statue of Buddha. Behind him in a cage is his "Mongolian brother," Chang Loo (Angelo Rossita) a dwarf who mocks Buckwell's religious pretensions and condemns his treatment of his Chinese brethren.[20] Buckwell angrily goes to the cage, opens it, and threatens to kill his dwarf brother who replies that he would be better

[19] In another early film made by the same director, *The Jazz Singer* (1927), Jakie Rabinowitz (Al Jolson), son of a Jewish Cantor puts on black face to become Jack Robin the jazz singer. (The father in *The Jazz Singer* is also played by the racial cross-dressing Warner Oland.)

[20] Angelo Rossita, who plays Chang Loo in *Old San Francisco*, appeared in many films between 1927 and 1985, but his most famous appearance was in Todd Browning's 1932 film *Freaks* where he plays a member of a freak show.

off dead than caged in this dungeon. Why he is kept in a cage is never revealed, but it becomes clear that as such he represents the subterranean threat of the Yellow Peril.

Old San Francisco demonstrates how film as a key technology of modernism deployed disability to illustrate the dangers of racial mixing. Although Chang Loo is a positive figure who aids the protagonist in rescuing the Californio daughter, his short stature helps to mark the villain's hidden "Mongolian" character. One might say that Chang Loo embodies racial threat as much as his deceitful, cross-dressing brother. While he knows the labyrinthine tunnels and warrens of Chinatown and upholds the "true" morality of Confucian teaching his different body ensures that his racial character will never be equivalent to that of the Irish hero. *Old San Francisco* was made shortly after the passage of the 1921 Immigration Act, the Emergency Quota Act of 1921, and the Immigration Act of 1924 and could be seen as a commentary on the anxieties these acts sought to quell, but the presence of the dwarf figure caged in an orientalist dungeon reinforces those anxieties by metaphorically presenting Chinese as literally sub-human.[21]

BIOFUTURITIES

Old San Francisco illustrates that one of the more problematic aspects of any consideration of modernism is in its formation in concert with pseudo-scientific ideas of biological perfection and racial purity that promise a better life through an improved gene pool—what we might call "biofuturity." Many authors and intellectuals took seriously the writings of Francis Galton, Otto Weininger, Charles Davenport, and Max Nordeau who applied Darwinian ideas of natural selection and animal breeding to humans. Among the most obvious adherents were Charlotte Perkins Gilman, Helen Keller, W. B. Yeats, Gertrude Stein, Virginia Woolf, T. S. Eliot, D. H. Lawrence, Ezra Pound, Margaret Sanger, Jane Addams, F. T. Marinetti, and Thomas Mann. What inspired such vanguard thinkers to endorse eugenics is perhaps aligned with their aesthetic interest in repudiating past models to "make it new."[22] But making it new involves a revision of temporality that reflects the discontinuities and dislocations of the age. As Tim Armstrong summarizes, "Modernism works, then, with notions of temporality which overlap, collide, and register their own incompletion" (*Modernism: A Cultural History*, 9). Innovative narrative experiments or the collage techniques of Pound and Eliot attempt to imagine a fragmented present based not on Hegel's progressive history but one based on the variable body.

Or the variable mind. Fears of dysgenic or degenerative futurity were particularly acute in the case of mental disability or what was then called "feeble-mindedness." The 1927 Supreme Court decision in *Buck v. Bell* upholding the sterilization of

[21] One could say much the same thing about the representation of Jews during this period. Sander Gilman in *The Jew's Body* notes that at the turn of the century, "the Jew" was defined as effeminate, hysterical, and diseased, often linked to other racial minorities.

[22] The best overview of modernists' relationship to eugenics is Donald J. Childs' *Modernism and Eugenics: Woolf, Eliot, Yeats, and the Culture of Degeneration.*

Carrie Buck is the most obvious example of an attempt to secure a better future by managing reproduction in the present. Chief Justice Holmes in his majority opinion summarized the court's justification for controlling Buck's future: "Three generations of imbeciles are enough" (qtd. Kevles, 111). Whereas Romantic poets could celebrate the simple fool or mad prophet, modernist writers tended to treat mental disability as pathological counterpart to cultural decay. The developmentally disabled Benjy Compson, in Faulkner's *Sound and the Fury* (1929) embodies in his fragmentary narrative the South's capitulation to entrepreneurial capital and cultural sterility. William Carlos Williams' mentally disabled servant Elsie expresses with "broken brain" modern America's dedication to cheap "gauds" and excitements. Joseph Conrad's anarchists in *The Secret Agent* all appear to be derived from one of Bertillon's criminal catalogues, especially the innocent Stevie who is variously described as a "slobbering idjut," "crazy," "degenerate," half-witted," and "weak-minded."[23] John Steinbeck's indictment of Depression era economic powerlessness is figured in *Mice and Men* (1937) by his mentally disabled character, Lennie Small, whose act of inadvertent violence justifies euthanasia by his fellow migrant worker, George. In each case, mental disability is equated to biological degeneration and social disorder that the narrative seeks to contain.[24] Benjy's castration, Stevie's incineration, and Lennie's euthanasia mark thematic treatments that mirror larger social attitudes toward the mentally "unfit."

We could think of two obvious sites for considerations of biofuturistic thinking in modernist literature, the first in utopian fiction of the late nineteenth century and the second in the Futurist movement of the 1910s. Speculative fiction of the late nineteenth and early twentieth century often configured utopian futures around a eugenic basis with a world purged of disability and disease. From Edward Bellamy's *Looking Backwards* (1888) to Charlotte Perkins Gilman's *Herland* (1915), authors idealized future societies free of disability and disease. And where disease still lingers, as in Samuel Butler's *Erewhon* (1872), persons so afflicted are criminalized or incarcerated. In H. G. Wells' *The Island of Dr. Moreau* (1896) the titular scientist performs experiments that transform animals into humans in a parody of Darwinian evolutionary science. According to the novel's narrator, Edward Prendick, who is shipwrecked on Moreau's island, the results of his experimentation do not create, as Moreau says, "a rational creature of my own," but rather a series of "crippled and distorted men" (78, 35). Gilman's *Herland* imagines a feminist utopia in which reproduction has been removed from heterosexual alliances and children are born parthenogenically, creating an Amazonian race of "wise, sweet, strong women" and in which

> ...physiology, hygiene, sanitation, physical culture—all that line of work had been perfected long since. Sickness was almost wholly unknown among them, so much so that a previously high development in what we call the "science of medicine" had

---

[23] On Conrad's representation of Stevie as "idiot" see Joseph Valente, "Modernism and Cognitive Disability," 390–5.

[24] Joseph Valente provides a thorough summary of mental disability in modernism, drawing extensively on the influence of Max Nordau's "degeneration" theory as an aspect of modernist art.

become practically a lost art. They were a clean-bred, vigorous lot, having the best of care, the most perfect living condition always.   (72)

As I will elaborate in subsequent chapters, parthenogenic reproduction and male pregnancy become central tropes for imagining a non-heteronormative futurity.

Among artists of the avant-garde, as I point out in Chapter 3, representations of biofuturity are figured through utopian bodies forged in an ideal of technology, speed, and athletic prowess. F. T. Marinetti's first Futurist manifesto celebrates a new human type, "the man at the wheel who hurls the lance of his spirit across the Earth" and who excoriates "the city of Paralysis with its henhouse cackle, its impotent prides of truncated columns, its bloated domes that give birth to mean little statues" (*Selected Writings*, 41, 47). There is little room in the Futurist program for bodies incapable of "aggressive action...the racer's stride, the mortal leap" (41). Marinetti's most notorious proposal, his glorification of war and militarism, is directly tied to a "scorn for women" and by implication feminine associations with Catholic Italy (42). In Marinetti's rhetorically bombastic manifestos, Futurism promises a world free of domestic obligation and religious authority and imagines a new physiology modeled on the machine. Futurist manifestos, needless to say, do not trade in reasoned debate or nuanced distinctions; their function is to cajole and declaim, imagine a collective future that did not yet exist. The movement's eventual alliance with Italian Fascism made concrete the social implications of a purified body politic.

Against the machinic modernism of the Futurists the Vorticism of Ezra Pound and Wyndham Lewis was founded on dynamic energies in the present. If the Futurist body was a machine, the Vorticist ideal was a whirlpool, a swirling fluid force around a stable center. Machines wear out, but the Vortex, in Hugh Kenner's words, "is a circulation with a still center; a system of energies drawing in whatever comes near" (239). Against this dynamic view of the present Lewis scorned the "time cult" that he identified with the philosophy of Bergson and the literary experimentalism of Stein, Joyce, Pound, Eliot, Lawrence, and Hemingway. For Lewis the various narrative attempts to render a "continuous present" or *durée* or "stream of consciousness" dissolve history into an inert lump. The chief danger of the "time cult" was its reduction of any form of historicity or agency into a formless relativism. When Lewis attempts to particularize the effects of this dissolution in the work of Gertrude Stein, he shows the degree to which his critique is founded on that "aesthetic nervousness" that disability invokes. Stein's early writings in *Three Lives* and *The Making of Americans* (which Lewis admits he never read) are the products of a childlike imbecile:

> Gertrude Stein's prose-song is a cold, black suet-pudding. We can represent it as a cold suet-roll of fabulously reptilian length. Cut it at any point it is the same thing; the same heavy, sticky, opaque mass all through and all along...mournful and monstrous, composed of dead and inanimate material. It is all fat, without nerve.   (59)

> The monstrous, desperate, soggy lengths of primitive mass-life, chopped off and presented to us as never-ending prose-song, are undoubtedly intended as an epic contribution to the present mass-democracy.   (60)

> It is in these occasional pieces [he is referring to the stories in *Three Lives*] that the *child-personality* of Miss Stein is discovered in its acutest form. But *the child* with her is always overshadowed by the imbecile. (60)
>
> That, very briefly, is Miss Stein's role in the child-cult, and the kindred one (Freud-inspired or not) of *the demented*. (61)

Lewis' invective includes a host of embodied metaphors that he associates with Stein: fatness, reptilian, imbecility, dementia, childhood, and, most damning for Lewis at this stage in his career, mass-democracy. Stein's "continuous present" or Joyce's mythic method or Woolf's stream-of-consciousness reduce consciousness to a series of undifferentiated moments, a depthlessness or irreality that can only be compared to regression and disembodiment. The vortex transmutes a deracinated consciousness into focused energy that, in its more extreme version in the later Lewis and Pound, is called Fascism.

If Lewis' complaint against Stein's fracturing of temporality is, obliquely, an attack on her body and gender, it is more generally an attack on forms of relative modalities of time. Fredric Jameson summarizes this aspect by suggesting that Lewis' critique of *durée* reduces modern man "to a bundle of disparate moments, discrediting abstraction in the name of sheer physiological and phenomenal sensation, and in the process giving rise to the compensatory mechanisms of all the false gods, nationalisms, and collective hysterias, through which the individual vainly attempts to repossess a measure of substantiality" (*Fables of Aggression*, 124). What Jameson characterizes as Lewis' fear of an unreality that leads to "collective hysterias" could be rewritten as an anxiety over a temporality loosed from its chronometric, developmental function in producing a unified subject.

These alternate temporalities that Lewis lumps under the phrase "time cult" anticipate contemporary debates around queer or crip time—the idea that non-traditional bodies and sexualities require "a different time and place," to adapt terms developed by Jack Halberstam, from normative ideas of embodiment and sexuality. I probe the implications of biofuturity in later chapters but want here to stress the degree to which current reconsiderations of time were being raised in utopian or futurist elements of modernism. Imagining futures purged of disease and disability involved imagining a world where reproduction no longer depends on heterosexual intercourse, where genetic monitoring has eliminated certain genetically inherited diseases, where the fusion of human and machine produces a new cyborg species. The current recognition of such utopian possibilities is viewed through the lens of the Genome project, but there is a darker undertone expressed in Lewis' nervousness about Gertrude Stein's repetitions and iterations.

The issue of biofuturities marks an important convergence between modernism and disability insofar as reconsiderations of temporality are both threatening, as in Lewis, and liberatory, as in Pound's belief that a new poetry would provide a "freedom from time and space limits" ("A Retrospect," 4). Imagining alternative futures involves rethinking time around the variable body and cognitive apparatus. When we think of the need for disability access we often think only of accommodations of a spatial character—ramps, signage, parking spaces—but we forget the need for accommodation of the varying temporalities of the body, temporalities first visited in the philosophical writings of Bergson and James and in the stream of consciousness novels of Joyce, Faulkner, and Woolf.

NEGATIVE INTERSECTIONALITY

As I indicated with regards to the film *Old San Francisco*, racialization occurs when the threat of one kind of body is articulated through a different kind of body, one that foregrounds qualities not immediately visible in the former. The Yellow Peril of the late nineteenth century was represented by a body deemed diseased or stunted, whose racial identity threatened the purity of the white race and was therefore unequal to claims of belonging and citizenship. The intersectional analysis of identity complicates a melting pot or multicultural definition of identity constructed around a plurality of discrete identities. Developed initially by critical race theorists, intersectional analysis challenges the idea of unitary identity by pointing out that individuals are multiply constituted through race, class, sexual orientation, national origin, gender, and, not insignificantly, embodiment. Most of the works covered in this book exemplify the idea that disability is often the modality through which these categories are lived. But disability itself is by no means a single identity. Gay activists during the early AIDS crisis had to negotiate twin sets of disqualification based on blood-borne disease and homophobia. Polio survivors in the 1950s were often feminized, if male, and desexualized if female. Deaf persons often consider themselves a linguistic minority and reject the descriptor "disabled," yet rely on federal assistance under the Americans with Disabilities Act (ADA) for interpreters or captioners. As I develop the theme in Chapter 4, Samuel Beckett's characters are often disabled as individuals, but they are equally co-dependent on care-givers, family members, and, most importantly, each other. These are not contradictions but conditions of complex embodiment that make unitary definitions of disability untenable.

What I am calling "negative intersectionality" occurs when one component of complex embodiment is used to define and disempower another. The canonical version of this phenomenon would be the Third Reich's conflation of Jewishness with disease. Hitler's 1939 memo that empowered physicians to euthanize those patients "judged incurably sick by critical medical examinations" led inexorably to the same logic applied to Jews (Proctor, 171). But it was first necessary, as Sander Gilman and Robert Proctor have observed, to regard the Jewish race as diseased in order to justify a policy of extermination in the name of national health. The various ghettos erected to contain Jews in Lodz, Krakow, and Warsaw were justified as a way of containing infectious diseases associated with Jews. As a consequence of this incarceration and deprivation, disease did spread in the ghettos, thereby validating Nazi doctors' warnings.[25] What Robert Proctor calls "the medicalization of

---

[25] On disease and the Warsaw Ghetto, see Proctor, "The Destruction of 'Lives Not Worth Living'" (176).

anti-Semitism" that led to the Holocaust of Jews, Slavs, homosexuals, and Romany people began as the "mercy killing" of 70,000 disabled persons in the notorious T-4 program (174). Intersectionality does not occur in a vacuum, nor is it free from misuse. It is produced within discourses of health, natural selection, and progress that however salutary for some permit the exclusion of others.

Despite the advantages that intersectionality poses for understanding disability, we have seen an increasing use of provisions established by the ADA to deny women access to abortion and health providers, restrict homeless populations, and curtail reproductive technologies. Reports indicate that 95 percent of cases brought under the banner of the ADA are thrown out of court. According to Lennard Davis, employees who sue companies under the ADA are now being told that "an employer wants the right to determine for an employee if the job that employee wants is a danger to his or her health" (*Bending*, 2). In such cases, the employer denies appropriate coverage using the argument that the individual would be doing "possible harm" to him or herself if such accommodation were made. This negative intersectionality uses disability rights in isolation so that it can deny the rights of a category with which it is associated.

Negative intersectionality appears at a moment when tensions between reproductive and disability rights over issues of abortion and genetic testing have reached a crisis point. A 2015 Ohio bill, HB 135, being pushed by anti-abortion advocates, would prohibit a doctor from performing an abortion if a woman decides to terminate her pregnancy to avoid having a child with Down syndrome. The National Right to Life Committee supports the bill. "We all want to be born perfect, but none of us are, and everyone has a right to live, perfect or not," says Mike Gonidakis, the president of Ohio Right to Life. He quotes parents of children with Down syndrome who tell him "how fortunate they are to have those children" (Nossiter, 17). Feminists have decried the law as an attack on *Roe v. Wade* and on women's right to choose, claiming as does Kellie Copeland, the executive director of Naral Pro-choice Ohio, "for us, it comes down to who makes the decision and who's going to have to live with it" (Nossiter, 17). Disability rights advocates have criticized the bill for its assumption that "we all want to be born perfect" and for what that says about the non-traditional child. HB 135 could be expanded to include debates surrounding "fetal personhood," raised by 2008 vice presidential candidate Sarah Palin whose son has Down syndrome or the case of Ashley X who underwent growth attenuation treatments to prevent her from achieving puberty due to "static encephalopathy" which retards growth and maturation.[26] We could add to these examples the way that arguments for disability access have been used to open up federal wilderness areas to off-road vehicles, civic legislation that draws on wheelchair access to remove homeless populations from city streets, and bills that have weakened provisions of the ADA by excluding non-visible or preventable disabilities.[27]

---

[26] Alison Kafer discusses Ashley X in *Feminist, Queer, Crip* (47–68).
[27] On the use of disability legislation to remove homeless populations, see Susan Schweik, "Kicked to the Curb: Ugly Law Then and Now."

Disability studies has reached an intersectional moment, aligned with a much broader critique of identity politics, but it is worth pointing to what happens when legislation to protect one social group is used to disempower another.[28] I raise this issue in a book about modernism only to indicate that the origins of this intersection of categories occurs when ideas of progressive reform to protect the health of workers or racial minorities collide with regressive attitudes about what constitutes a healthy body. *Old San Francisco's* treatment of urban renewal and mixed-race marriage coincides with a narrative about Asian sexual predation and miscegenation. In this intersectional moment, we might remember a longer history of disempowerment in the name of progress.

CONCLUSION

Invalid Modernism covers the "long" modernist period that begins in the late nineteenth century and continues in the present day. The first six chapters explore a variety of sites where volatile bodies meet modernist innovation. Beginning with an exploration of fin de siècle aestheticism and concluding with works by Djuna Barnes and Samuel Beckett, these chapters offers a number of ways to read disability in modernist cultural production through poetry, fiction, film, theater, opera, and painting. The last two chapters bring the missing body in aesthetics into the present day by looking at the legacy of classical aesthetics as it is deconstructed around the political realities of disappeared bodies. The book's final chapter, "Cleavings," is my personal account of incipient deafness as a test of the limits and advantages of what has been called "disability gain."

Chapter 1 begins by looking back into the nineteenth century for a moment when the aesthetic and the disabled body were aligned around the figure of the "invert." "Invalid Modernism" discusses representations of the aesthete and convalescent as seminal figures in the formation of modernist art and literature. Unlike the more fashionable treatment of disease in the Victorian period, embodied often in the figure of the female invalid, modernist representations of disease or illness were more likely to be considered pathological, subject to increasing medicalization, diagnosis, and incarceration. The figures of the male aesthete and the convalescent offer a more transgressive model to ideals of health and improvement by which modernity is measured. By looking at several writers—Friedrich Nietzsche, William Carlos Williams, John Addington Symonds, Henry James, Virginia Woolf, and Thomas Mann—this opening chapter seeks a correlation between the aesthetic and the wasting body, between autonomy and contagion.

Rather than seeing disability as a series of tropes for cultural and psychological malaise, Chapter 2, " 'The Rage of Caliban': The Mirror of Recognition," regards conditions of physical and cognitive difference as foundational for the aesthetic itself. By focusing on works that mark the transition from fin de siècle aestheticism to works of high modernism, I investigate the changing fortunes of embodiment

---

[28] I discuss the intersectional moment in disability studies in "Cripping Consensus."

in modernist aesthetics, specifically as it appears in music. The chapter looks at several works based on Velázquez's *Las Meninas* (1656) in which the figure of the court dwarf represented in the painting becomes a site for anxieties about bodily and sexual difference. Alexander Zemlinsky's opera *Der Zwerg* (The Dwarf) from 1922 is the principal focus, based on Oscar Wilde's story, "The Birthday of the Infanta" (1891). The libretto for Zemlinsky's opera by George Klaren transforms Wilde's story of recognition and betrayal into an allegory of dysgenic characterology founded on the work of Otto Weininger. What Wilde perceived as a story about the noble soul beneath the grotesque body, Zemlinsky transformed into a eugenicist allegory of man's fatal alliance with the femme fatale. As a work that embodies elements of late Romantic chromaticism as well as modernist atonality, *Der Zwerg* is a site for studying musical representation of bodily difference.

Chapter 3, "Exquisite Corporeality: Detachable Bodies of the Avant-Garde," considers the representation of disability in avant-garde art and literature. In Futurism, Dadaism, and Surrealism, the introduction of everyday life practices and objects into the artwork offers a critique—or satire—of autonomy aesthetics. But "everyday life," in my reading, must include the material body which in all three movements is subjected to deformation, disaggregation, and reassignment. Against the integrity of the classical body, Futurist writers like Marinetti imagined a new form of human, detached from biological reproduction and amalgamated with industrial technology. Tristan Tzara's satiric play, *The Gas Heart*, creates a cast of characters based on sensory organs whose discontinuous speeches and unmotivated actions challenge theatrical conventions and bodily integrity alike. Frida Kahlo's self-portraits challenge Surrealism's fetishization of female bodies and disjointed body parts by representing her own physical pain and life with disabilities. Through readings of F. T. Marinetti's novel *Mafarka the Futurist*, paintings by René Magritte, sculpture by Raoul Hausmann, Tristan Tzara's *The Gas Heart*, and the self-portraiture of Frida Kahlo, "Exquisite Corporeality" shows various ways that disjointed, injured, or recombined bodies in avant-garde cultural production imagine different, transgressive forms of sensation, bodily coherence, and sociality.

Chapter 4, " 'Every Man his Specialty': Beckett and the Dialectics of Dependency," discusses the dialectics of dependency, the interplay between a social contract based on free, equal agents and one that recognizes contingent interrelationships. The recent theorization of care-giving by Eva Kittay, Martha Nussbaum, Rachel Adams, and others has complicated the independent living ethos of the early disability rights movement. By acknowledging the realities of dependent relations among persons with disabilities, these authors have questioned whether a social contract needs to be rethought around the actual matrix of dependencies upon which we all rely—familial, social, medical, institutional.

Samuel Beckett challenges liberal theories of autonomy and independent agency by creating scenes of "abject dependency." Most of Beckett's characters are, in some way, disabled, whether blind like Hamm or crippled like Clov or immobile like Winnie in *Happy Days*. But they also exist in tragi-comic relations of co-dependence that seem to mock communitarian ideals of charity and mutual aid while exposing the limits of liberal individualism. Since Beckett's work is often seen as a commentary on Ireland's long history of colonial dependence on England, I turn to another version of dependency, that embodied in Frantz Fanon's *Black Skin, White Masks*, to see if parallels between the disabled body and the disempowered colony and racial subject are, in any way, analogous. By looking at *Black Skin, White Masks*, written close to the time of Beckett's later plays, we may perceive important links between two models of dependency set in a postcolonial context.

When Stephen Dedalus in *Portrait of the Artist as a Young Man* sets out his aesthetic theory to his friend, Lynch, he imagines the creative act as one of male reproduction, freed from heterosexual contact. In this manner he may not only produce his own progeny through art but reinvent his biological paternity. This turns out to be a common theme in a number of modernist works. Chapter 5, "Pregnant Men: Biofuturity in Djuna Barnes and Virginia Woolf," investigates the idea of biofuturity, focusing specifically on the figure of male maternity in Djuna Barnes' *Nightwood* (1936) and Virginia Woolf's *Orlando*. Although representations of male pregnancy can be found in ancient and classical literature the trope surfaces significantly among modernist works—Apollinaire's *Les Mamelles de Tiresias*, Joyce's *Ulysses*, Marinetti's *Mafarka the Futurist*, Freud's Schreber case—at a moment when biological life was being reimagined through the optic of eugenic science and comparative anatomy. The chapter extends Lee Edelman's critique of reproductive futurity in *No Future* to suggest that dystopic biological futures were being imagined around figures such as Dr. Mathew O'Connor whose desire, as he says, to "boil some good man's potatoes and toss up a child . . . every nine months" reinforces his queer identity and annexes the importance of disability in many of the novel's characters. In the case of *Orlando* pregnancy occurs in a biological woman who was born as a male. This transgendered scenario permits Woolf to deliver a witty critique of a legal system that insists on economic succession and inheritance through the birth of a male child. By creating a character who changes from male to female Woolf suggests that the biological child born through heteronormative sexuality is, in fact, the product of a masculinist legal body. Modernist cultural representations of the pregnant male foreground reproduction divorced from the female body and displaced elsewhere, including the novel. This displacement is both a queering and cripping of normative attitudes toward reproductive health and the futures that such embodiment implies. It also warps traditional *narrative* attitudes toward biological futurity when the family romance no longer reproduces the heterosexual body.

The recent turn to affect has not included a substantive discussion of disability, despite its focus on the body and sensation. Chapter 6, "Uncanny Encounters: Dramas of Contingency in Modernism," attempts to remedy this absence by exploring embodied response to dynamic historical changes in modernity. Works by Charles Baudelaire, Sigmund Freud, Frank Norris, and Henry James illustrate stages in what Sara Ahmed calls "dramas of contingency" by which world historical changes are registered through quotidian moments of attention and embodiment. Drawing on Raymond Williams' "structure of feeling," this chapter explores the ways that the aesthetic registers traumatic historical change through moments of shock, surprise, and ambiguity. Freud's theory of the "uncanny" is a test case for representations of affective responses that unsettle familiar, daily experience and for which there are no adequate narratives.

Modernist fiction provides such narratives by its microscopic focus on quotidian moments when characters encounter, as in Norris, a new form of technology or, as in James, a ghost of a possible queer identity. Such novels imagine new futures that begin in the "shock" of encounter. Rather than regard modernism through Freud's theories of mourning and melancholia and the politics of trauma and loss, this chapter studies possible futures through contingent relations in the present.

Chapter 7, "Missing Bodies: Disappearances in the Aesthetic," moves the historical period into the present to explore the relationship between bodies erased from the socio-political sphere and the missing body in aesthetics. Since 9/11 we have seen the increased visibility of queer, racialized, transgender, and disabled bodies, but we have also witnessed the concomitant disappearance of bodies in wars, forced migrations, incarcerations, or through the suspension of rights. The chapter brings the aesthetic and historical disappearances together by arguing that the absent body, particularly the absent disabled body, is foundational for the aesthetic insofar as judgments about the beautiful and grotesque are often based upon an idealized or disparaged body. I adapt Foucault's idea of biopolitics as the absorption of power in and through the body to examine *biopoetics* as the reinscription of the missing body in aesthetics. The chapter focuses on the novelist Indra Sinha's *Animal's People*, neurodiversity activist Amanda Baggs' film *In my Language*, Rachel Zolf's *Neighbour Procedure*, and M. NourbeSe Philip's *Zong!* These works look back at modernist formal precedents of appropriation, fragmentation, and displacement to examine contemporary arguments about species identity, neurodiversity, citizenship, and racial identity.

My final chapter, "Cleavings: Critical Losses in the Politics of Deaf Gain," offers a more personal account of this author's own hearing loss, set against the backdrop of changes in disability theory. My example for observing these changes is the poetry of Emily Dickinson, many of whose poems confront the loss of sight as a metaphor for the limits of consciousness. She represented the loss of sensation for its expression of what is most familiar—and thereby invisible. Using poems by Dickinson and recent work in cultural and queer theory, this chapter explores the fine line between "gain" and "loss" in disability studies. Recent claims for "deaf gain" have vaunted possibilities of cultural inclusiveness to the exclusion of affective realms of frustration and failure that are seldom acknowledged experiences of deaf and hard-of-hearing persons. While endorsing the general thrust of deaf gain and its implications for the larger context of disability, the chapter argues for a more critical understanding of loss in the politics of gain.

My last chapter is, in fact, the first chapter in my relationship to disability studies. Gradual hearing loss that began some years ago prompted a deeper consideration of what it means to "hear" in literature and led, ultimately, to a rethinking of a speech and text based poetics. It also gave me permission to incorporate my own experience of disability into critical projects. Most of us who work in the field of disability studies have a story to tell about our own—or that of a family member, lover, friend—experience of how an illness, paralysis, sensory loss, or chronic disease changed one's life narrative. In Arthur Frank's terms, such an interruption is a story in its own right, one that complicates the seeming natural standpoint of health and embodiment.[29] In my case, this interruption was productive in thinking about modernism and its representation of bodies such as that described in my opening anecdote. When Theodor Adorno winces at the pressure of a prosthetic hand, he registers the difference disability makes in the narrative of autonomy—that of the artwork and that of the individual. *Invalid Modernism* attempts to provide a new story about a modernism we thought we knew and an autonomous subject we never were.

---

[29] Frank's focus, and to some extent mine in the final chapter, is on illness that occurs during a life that already has an ableist narrative. For someone born with a congenital condition, this model is inadequate. A person who is deaf from birth and who lives in a community of sign-language users differs radically (and culturally) from a late-deafened person whose life has been spent among hearing persons. A person born with cerebral palsy has learned to negotiate movement, space, and language early in life whereas a person who contracts a neurological disorder late in life must reinterpret the built environment quite differently.

1

Invalid Modernism
A Diseased Aesthetic

In *The Great Gatsby* Nick Carraway reflects on the difference between the wealthy, athletic Tom Buchanan and the anemic garage owner, George Wilson whose wife is Tom's mistress: "...and it occurred to me that there was no difference between men, in intelligence or face, so profound as the difference between the sick and the well" (124). In a novel so dependent on distinctions of class, race, and ethnicity, its narrator's contrast of "intelligence or face" to that of health articulates the Progressive Era's conflation of the two realms in the interests of reform.[1] The cultural logic of disease in this era often involves a scenario in which social threats to the body politic are represented through references to contagion and infection. Immigration health inspections, anthropometric photography, and eugenic scrutiny of "dysgenic" bodies are only the most obvious instances of a biopolitics of health and character that emerges in the latter nineteenth century and continues in the first decades of the twentieth. In literature this logic is embodied in the ways that metaphors of illness, wasting, invalidism, and contagion provide a story for what society wants to expunge. As Athena Vrettos says, "to be ill is to produce narrative" around anxieties connected to modern life—the shock of the crowd, the wasting of cultural values, epidemics brought by those "hooded hordes" T. S. Eliot in *The Waste Land* imagined invading London (2).

Such narratives (what I am calling a cultural logic) are not merely stories we tell about specific diseases but frames for situating illness in a biocultural context. Carraway's attempt to link character to health is a frame through which he understands his own relationship to others—including Gatsby—in a highly competitive, racialized environment. The problem with using the term "frame" is that in the interest of contextualizing where illness begins and discourse takes over, it becomes a static trope, extrinsic to the intersectional relationship between, say, pain, and its articulation in language and diagnosis.[2] We should distinguish between disease—the immunodeficiency virus, HIV, for example—and illness, the lived experience

---

[1] Nick's tendency to racialize others confirms his sense of bodily integrity against the "small flat nosed Jew," Meyer Wolfsheim or the "modish negroes" he encounters entering New York City.

[2] Charles Rosenberg prefers the term "frame" to social constructionist definitions of disease, feeling that the latter tend to foreground "functionalist ends and the degree of arbitrariness inherent in the negotiations that result in accepted disease pictures" (307). He notes that by its focus on the twin determinates of knowledge and power social constructionist definitions remove the biological and somatic aspects of disease and treat "purveyors as ordinarily unwitting rationalizers and legitimators of an oppressive social order" (307).

of gay men in the early 1980s. The first is usually thought to be the province of doctors and the second that of patients, yet every "objective" medical diagnosis contains its own set of subjective assumptions. It is for this very reason that I sometimes conflate them in the interest of showing their interdependent character.

As Clark Lawlor argues, the term "narrative" might be more useful than "frame" since "it suggests illness as an aesthetic object that is in process rather than static, dialogic rather than monologic" (6). And it is precisely this incomplete character of all disabilities that complicates "frame" as an adequate term for the various conditions of embodied life. Lawlor's idea that the aesthetic is never static but "in process" helps us understand how the artwork, although historically specific, may constitute a structure of feeling around conditions that have yet to appear. The aesthetic could be considered an *anaesthetic* against those conditions, an attempt to create a story or objective correlative as palliative against pain, both personal and historical.[3]

Romantic literature often figured death from consumption as a beautiful, even aesthetic moment.[4] As Dana Luciano observes, "[if] one aspires to play a pivotal role in a nineteenth-century novel, perhaps the best qualification that one can acquire is a mortal illness" (196). Increased medical knowledge of diseases and their origins, combined with an expanding medical professionalism—diagnostics, epidemiology, therapeutics, transfusion, and vaccination—made aestheticizing disease more difficult. Victorian literature, as Luciano, Athena Vrettos, Martha Stoddard-Holmes, Diane Price Herndl, Maria Frawley, Ann Jurecic, and others have testified is replete with references to disease, offering an important bridge between the fashionable and the pathological. That bridge is embodied in a new modernist type that appears in the late nineteenth century, the male invalid aesthete, whose inertia and passivity are the antithesis of modern mobility and progress. On the one hand, his confinement offers a feminized contrast to masculine models of action, physical labor, and circulation that are requirements for what Gail Bederman characterizes as "civilized manliness" (23). His cultivation of sensation, beauty, and reflection embody an alternative labor to that of capitalist exchange (it is no small irony that the term for the period's most devastating illness, consumption, was also the term for a new consumer society satirized by Thorsten Veblen).[5] When, in significant cases, the invalid leaves his sickbed, he experiences renewed vigor and clarity of vision that allow him, in the case of Nietzsche's Zarathustra, to forge a new lyre.

I want to situate modernist aesthetic illness within the broader field of disability studies but before proceeding would observe that the study of disease is often excluded from theoretical work in this field. For disability activists, the idea that a physical impairment is analogous to disease challenges the goals of independent

[3] As Terry Eagleton argues, autonomy aesthetics, as described in Kant's third critique, is also an "anaesthetic" against sensuousness, but I would add that it is no less an anaesthetic against racial infection and social amalgamation (171).

[4] On romantic attitudes toward illness see Hermann J. Weigand, "Disease."

[5] Jean-Christophe Agnew notes that "[it] is at the point where consumption converts its meaning from a disease into a cure that we may begin to speak of a consumer culture in the sense we experience it" (74).

living. Susan Wendell describes the problematic relationship between the two areas, noting that chronic disease seems fatally linked to a medical model that considers disability as an individual misfortune. As Wendell argues, "some people with disabilities *are* sick, diseased, and ill," and require medical intervention (162). Furthermore, there is no firm line between sickness and physical impairment, between someone with smallpox and blindness, between diabetes or polio and orthopedic impairments, between cardiovascular disease and heart failure. To create a rigid separation between illness and disability is to perpetuate the very medical, taxonomic model that the disability rights movement has attacked.[6] This blurring of the boundary between chronic disease and physical disability is especially acute during the Progressive Era when reform of the social body is enacted through the perceived threat of disease and racial degeneracy among immigrant and racialized populations.

By looking at disease as a discursive system rather than an epidemiological problem we may understand the processes by which the ill body becomes a cultural sign that could be deployed, for good or ill, to explain or rationalize the unruly or volatile body. My primary example, the invalid aesthete, is a disabled person who produces his illness as a work of art, a hedge against modernity's imperatives of health, reproduction, and independence. To this extent, he offers a camera obscura on modernity—a non-productive, dependent, retiring figure for whom passivity is a kind of cultural style. But the aesthete is only one half of the equation; he is the corporeal version of the autonomy aesthetics to which he aspires, an embodied version of the work of art detached from historical causality and biological growth. Dorian Gray remains eternally young through a painting that depicts his decrepitude; Eschenbach, in Mann's *Death in Venice*, pursues an Apollonian purity that is challenged both by his desire for the beautiful Tazio but also by the cholera that eventually causes his death. The close proximity of illness and the aesthetic is not simply one of content and form, disease as the context behind (or before) the literary work. Rather, disability is foundational for the aesthetic, linking the vulnerable body to its representation and organizing sensations around values of order, social coherence, and bodily integrity. The disabled or ill body insinuates itself into discourses of ideal beauty and formal perfection, causing ruptures that mimic the fragmented, discontinuous works of modernism. When the Third Reich paraded examples of decadent modernist art (*entartete kunst*) before the German public in the late 1930s the descriptive placards on the wall made sure to conflate the "diseased" and "sick" elements of paintings by Kandinsky, Nolde, or Dix with their Bolshevist and Jewish qualities. For Nazi ideology, somatic and racial infections were coterminous features of a diseased aesthetic.

---

[6] Catherine J. Kudlick asks whether the fields of disability studies and medical history are "rival siblings" or "conjoined twins" (qtd. Linker, 500). Beth Linker suggests that perhaps a better model for the relationship between disease and disability would be Wittgenstein's idea of "family resemblances" rather than conjoined twins (500). Linker provides an excellent overview of the debate between the two areas.

Thus far I have been speaking of the aesthete using the masculine pronoun, but there were many female aesthetes who contributed substantially to the movement.[7] In some respects there was an inverse relationship between masculine aestheticism, with its cult of passivity, sensation, and languor, and its female counterpart. For male modernists, the aesthetic woman became the prototype of cultural dilettantism, satirized as such in Ezra Pound's "Portrait d'une femme" or T. S. Eliot's "Portrait of a Lady." While these portraits did not imagine aesthetic women as ill, their depictions of a society woman's arid and deracinated life represented what Pound described as a "Sargasso Sea" of scattered ideas and opinions (61). But as Elaine Showalter, Talia Schaffer, Margaret Stetz, Regenia Gagnier, and others attest, the female aesthete of the 1890s who published in decadent periodicals like *The Yellow Book* was often a New Woman, feminist and author herself. Elaine Showalter notes that, "New Women and decadent artists were linked together as twin monsters of a degenerate age, sexual anarchists who blurred the boundaries of gender. The decadent art was unmanly and effeminate, while New Women's writing was unwomanly and perverse" (x). The works of Lucas Malet, Florence Farr, Ouida, Rosamund Marriott Watson, and other women aesthetes were read by male and female readers alike and in large numbers. Where male aesthetes adopted (perceived) effeminate characteristics of languor, wasting illness, and detachment, female aesthetes wore masculine clothing, stressed health and exercise, and pursued activism on behalf of suffrage. To some extent the inverse relationship between cultural styles reflected the degree to which the aesthetic became a window through which new gender roles and non-traditional bodies were made visible.

THE *PHARMAKON* OF CONTAGION

> By the road to the contagious hospital
> under the surge of the blue
> mottled clouds driven from the
> northeast-a cold wind. Beyond, the
> waste of broad, muddy fields
> brown with dried weeds, standing and fallen
>
> patches of standing water
> the scattering of tall trees
>
> All along the road the reddish
> purplish, forked, upstanding, twiggy
> stuff of bushes and small trees
> with dead, brown leaves under them
> leafless vines-
>
> Lifeless in appearance, sluggish
> dazed spring approaches   (183)

---

[7] On female aesthetes, see Talia Schaffer, *The Forgotten Female Aesthetes* and essays in Talia Schaffer and Kathy Alexis Psomiades, *Women and British Aestheticism*.

In one of his best-known poems, William Carlos Williams witnesses the emergence of "dazed spring" while on the road to the contagious hospital. Why is it, my students ask, that Doctor Williams muses on the appearance of spring in the shadow of contagion? Is this a *hospital* for contagious diseases or is the hospital itself contagious in some way? Is the *poem* contagious in its desultory chronicle of dead nature—"dried weeds," "muddy fields," and "twiggy / stuff of bushes"—that emerges like a convalescent from a long winter illness? As a doctor, Williams understands that just as disease spreads in a riot of microbes, so spring awakens in a proliferation of tendrils, buds, and leaves, the natural equivalents of the prepositional phrases that spread through the poem's opening lines searching for an independent clause.

In the poem's conclusion the metaphor of contagion changes to that of parturition:

> But now the stark dignity of
> entrance—Still, the profound change
> has come upon them: rooted, they
> grip down and begin to awaken   (183)

Williams may have tapped into a powerful *pharmakon* of modernism—the inextricable relationship between disease and growth, illness and rebirth, contagion and social organization, first diagnosed by Edmund Wilson in *The Wound and the Bow* and given its more theoretical elaboration in Derrida's *Dissemination*. In Greek, *pharmakon* may refer both to a remedy and a poison, a doubling that Derrida exploits in his reading of Plato's *Phaedrus*. In the dialogue, Socrates quotes King Thamus of Egypt who compares writing to a *pharmakon*—a remedy—whose power can be alternately healthful or fatal: "...this invention [writing] will produce forgetfulness in the souls of those who have learned it because they will not need to exercise their memories, being able to rely on what is written, using the stimulus of external marks that are alien to themselves...rather than, from within..." (102). Plato uses Thamus' remark to suggest that writing is a delusory remedy for erring memory and a diversion from speech's primary access to truth. Derrida regards the ambivalent character of the *pharmakon* as the very condition of difference, the play of presence and absence, content and inscription that Plato's valorization of speech tends to reify. Writing contains its own opposite and thus fuses the presence that words hope to stabilize through a material medium that embodies presence's absence.

Applied to Williams' 1923 book, *Spring and All*, in which the poem appears, the word "contagious" permits the poet to exploit the close proximity of spring's transformation of dead nature and the representation of this process through syntax that defers closure and defies grammatical agreement. For Williams, the oxymoronic joining of spring and contagion offers a subtle riposte to Eliot's darker version in the opening lines of *The Waste Land*: "April is the cruellest month / mixing memory and desire" (37). For Williams spring's violent rupture of winter's stasis produces new life—and not incidentally, new forms of writing of which the fragmented syntax of his poem is exemplary. In 1923, one year after *The Waste Land* first appeared, Williams throws down the gauntlet to Eliot's chronicle of cultural decay by mixing infectious disease with the pangs of birth.

Williams was not alone, in representing illness as a disruptive force and generative metaphor. Contagion and disease are everywhere in modernist literary works; consumption (tuberculosis), neurasthenia, hysteria, syphilis, shell shock, silicosis, cholera, and influenza occupy prominent roles in various literary works. Illness is prominent in Charlotte Perkins Gilman's "The Yellow Wall-Paper," Edith Wharton's *Ethan Frome*, Marcel Proust's, *A la recherche du temps perdu*, Henry James' *Daisy Miller* or *Wings of the Dove*, Ford Madox Ford's *The Good Soldier*, Joseph Conrad's *Secret Agent*, Dostoevsky's *The Idiot* and *The Underground Man*, Ibsen's *Ghosts*, André Gide's *L'Immoralist*, Thomas Mann's *Death in Venice* and *The Magic Mountain*, James Joyce's "The Dead," Katherine Ann Porter's "Pale Horse, Pale Rider," and Muriel Rukeyser's *Book of the Dead*.[8] Alexandre Dumas' tubercular heroine, Marguerite Gautier in *La Dame aux Camélias* spawned a number of theatrical and operatic romances, including *La Traviata*, *Camille*, and, more distantly, *La Bohème*. One must include in this list the residual effects of trauma caused by World War I in the poetry of Wilfred Owen, Rupert Brooke, and Siegfried Sassoon or characters such as Jake Barnes in *The Sun Also Rises*, Clifford Chatterley in *Lady Chatterley's Lover*, and Septimus Smith in *Mrs. Dalloway*.[9] The most famous chronicle of modern diseased society, *The Waste Land*, features an ill king, neurasthenic women, and desiccated prophets, pub patrons, and merchants, written in a sanitarium by a poet undergoing his own cure for nervous exhaustion.

Foundational theories of modernity often rely on metaphors of illness to describe the affective register of a culture in transition. Max Nordau's mammoth indictment of the modern era, *Degeneration* (1895), describes "the effect of diseases in these fin-de-siècle literary and artistic tendencies and fashions, as well as in the susceptibility of the public with regard to them, and we have succeeded in maintaining that these diseases are degeneracy and hysteria" (34). Matthew Arnold in "The Scholar Gypsy" speaks of "this strange disease of modern life with its sick hurry, its divided aims" (993). Søren Kierkegaard describes modern secularism as a "sickness unto death," while Dostoevsky's Underground Man regards "excessive consciousness [as] a...genuine absolute disease" (6). Walter Benjamin refers to Baudelaire's description of the shock of the modern metropole as a type of nervous disorder ("On Some Motifs," 185). The artist capable of capturing its effects must be a perpetual "convalescent" (7). In a letter, Proust celebrates illness as a pre-condition for writing: "I believe that, even if it were due only to the creative value of suffering, physical illness (in our degenerate days) is almost a precondition for any intellectual force that has a touch of genius" (qtd. Bragg and Sayers, 180). As I point out in Chapter 2, Nietzsche in his later writing on Wagner's music

---

[8] In the opening of *Illness as Metaphor* Susan Sontag provides an extensive list of late nineteenth- and early twentieth-century examples of the literature of illness in modernism.

[9] See Laura Salisbury and Andrew Shail, *Neurology and Modernity: A Cultural History of Nervous Systems, 1800–1950*.

speaks of it as "contagious" and "unhealthy."[10] Georg Lukács feels that modernism reflects "the nebulous consciousness of an idiot... its obsession with the morbid and the pathological" (qtd. Berger, 67). If representations of cultural change and innovation in the nineteenth century could be rendered by reference to social revolution, that same function for the early twentieth century could now be served by reference to a wasting body.

This emphasis on modernist illness is usually described as a manifestation of biopolitical regimes of medicalization, comparative anatomy, and eugenics that emerge in the nineteenth century. Michel Foucault in *The History of Sexuality* describes the ways that bodies are produced discursively through disciplinary regimes that attempt to rationalize populations and contain difference. As a consequence, a vast taxonomy of new diseases was created to diagnose and represent somatic conditions that had previously been invisible—or irrelevant to the social order.[11] Priscilla Wald notes that the rise of communicable diseases during the early twentieth century was both a medical and a social problem that infected cultural discourse generally: "The growth of cities gave rise to what [public health officials] saw as 'promiscuous' social spaces; people literally and figuratively bumping up against each other in smaller spaces and larger numbers than ever before" (15). As Gustav Le Bon indicated in 1895, the emergence of crowds created possibilities for the spread of microbes. Nor are germs the only thing distributed: "in a crowd every sentiment and act is contagious, and contagious to such a degree that an individual readily sacrifices his personal interest to the collective interest" (7). The cultural manifestation of infectious social contact can be read in any number of literary texts from Baudelaire to Pound and Eliot in which the "apparition of these faces in the crowd" elicits anxieties about infection—and by extension fears of social and racial pollution. William Carlos Williams' reference to a contagious diseases hospital would have been particularly acute in the early 1920s, following the disastrous outbreak of influenza, the "Spanish flu," in 1918 that killed, by some estimates, a hundred million persons worldwide.

Reforms in the first decades of the twentieth century attempted to mitigate the effects of communicable diseases, workplace injuries, and sweatshop conditions, but these accomplishments were marked by a eugenic subtext. Charlotte Perkins Gilman's progressive views about the medicalization of the female body, as narrated in her fiction, stand in contrast to her rather retrograde views on birth control. She reflects a common view of her era that saw birth control not only as a method of family planning but also as a means of controlling society from the "unfit" and "defective." In an article published in 1932, "Birth Control, Religion and the Unfit," Gilman writes that she is "mortified at our moronic average, alarmed at the increasing numbers of those far below it. Further, we find that the unfitter they

---

[10] "This does not mean that I consider [Wagner's] music healthy... My objections to the music of Wagner are physiological objections: why should I trouble to dress them up in aesthetic formulas? After all, aesthetics is nothing but a kind of applied physiology." "Nietzsche contra Wagner" (664).

[11] In Conrad's *The Secret Agent*, Stevie, the cognitively disabled brother of the novel's main female character, is endlessly defined by the anarchist cabal through references to Cesare Lombroso's criminal characterology.

are, the more lavishly they fulfill what some religionists assure us is the divine command to increase and multiply and replenish the earth." She notes the benefit of birth control "does not interfere with the pleasures of the unfit but saves society from their reduplication." Seen in light of this essay, "The Yellow Wall-Paper's" feminist polemic against the masculine medical establishment may be tainted by its class and racial optic, its eugenicist belief that birth control and family planning may help control "undesirable increase by the simple device of sterilizing the unfit." In such remarks the promises of biofuturity are infused with backward-looking attitudes about persons deemed earlier on some evolutionary or cultural scale.

AESTHETIC INVALIDISM:
THE UNPRODUCTIVE LIFE

I have been speaking of illness as a negative descriptor for various social transformations, but as I hope to develop the theme, illness, disease, and convalescence could be equally enlisted to support a more positive, even subversive set of identity categories. The form of subversion with which I will be concerned is the aesthete's refusal of normative attitudes toward nature, reproduction, and health. Heather Love refers to the aesthete's withdrawal and political quietism as a "politics of refusal" manifest in the writings of Walter Pater (27). His representation of characters who are "indecisive, shrinking, transparent" in *The Renaissance* permits Pater to create a "'counterimage' of the paranoid world of the late nineteenth-century . . . [whose] language of suggestion indexes the diffuseness and suggestibility of male homo-erotic subcultures on the eve of the invention of the homosexual" (29). Like Huysmans' des Esseintes, the aesthete prefers the glories of the past to the dynamic energies of the present, cultivates synthetic surfaces over natural, organic growth, and avoids the social conformism of heterosexual domesticity. One might call any one of these conditions a kind of social illness that blurred the boundaries between physical enervation and societal transformation. By looking at the ill or weak aesthete as a transgressive figure according to the models of late Victorian masculinity we may see an alternative modernism to more familiar versions.

The aestheticism that we identify with Pater, Huysmans, or Proust may seem the most obvious instances of aesthetic illness, but one may observe it organizing the psychological complexities of realist fiction:

> . . . it would have been nice if he could have been taken with fever all alone at his hotel, and she could have come to look after him, to write to his people, to drive him out in convalescence. *Then* they would be in possession of the something or other that their actual show seemed to lack.   (429)

In Henry James' story, "The Beast in the Jungle" (1903) John Marcher imagines he is reserved for some exceptional, transformative experience. He figures his heroic destiny throughout the story as a romantic confrontation with a lurking beast, but his egotism, manifested in remarks such as the one above, prevents any such encounter. In Marcher's imagination, illness and convalescence would afford him the illusion of sociality—provided by his companion May Bartram—thus giving him the "something or other that their actual show seemed to lack." Marcher's inability to name the "something or other" that would define a heteronormative masculinity is, as Eve Sedgwick has said, an example of rhetorical preterition or deferral that marks his proximity to the closet of unspeakable sexualities. Convalescence becomes for Marcher (and for James whose entire family lived with a number of ailments) not a site of painful solitude but an alternative form of social intercourse, one that his solipsism denies him. If the flâneur is the first of the major modernist types, botanizing on crowds and consumerism, the convalescent is the second.

Being ill, as Virginia Woolf says, is a cultural trope that applies not only to the author's own history of mental breakdowns and depression but to nervous disorders experienced by many modernist artists. In the late nineteenth century, the phrase "nervous disorders" was applied to a variety of psychological and physical conditions whose clinical diagnoses often referred to the stress and complexities of modern life. American writers such as Kate Chopin, Theodore Dreiser, Henry Adams, Henry James, Frank Lloyd Wright, Alice James, Charlotte Perkins Gilman and many others suffered from what George M. Beard first defined as "neurasthenia." Symptoms varied from individual to individual and across genders, but appeared variously as exhaustion, sick headaches, nausea, depression, and psychosis. To some extent neurasthenia was regarded as an inevitable, perhaps honorific, product of modern civilization, appearing specifically among "brain workers" and educated, independent women. According to Beard, "no age, no country, and no form of civilization, not Greece, nor Rome, nor Spain, nor the Netherlands, in the days of their glory, possessed such maladies" (qtd. Lutz, 6). Beard utilized economic metaphors, appropriate to an age of expanding capitalism, to explain how neurasthenia manifested itself. When one's quotient of "nerve force" is expended through overwork or stress, the individual becomes "bankrupt," requiring him to "reinvest" nervous energy either through bed-rest or vigorous exercise. Tom Lutz notes that dissipation "eventually led to 'decadence,' the death and decay of nerve centers in the individual and the death and decay of civilization at the social level" (4). Therapeutic solutions to neurasthenia were differently applied to women and men. The physician S. Weir Mitchell prescribed a "rest cure" for women, requiring bed-rest and complete and total elimination of all stimulation, whereas overworked males were instructed to engage in manly activities of hunting, hiking, and horseback riding—the infamous "West cure" enjoyed by Theodore Roosevelt, Thomas Eakins, and Owen Wister. Clearly neurasthenia was viewed as a marker of one's success in a highly competitive marketplace, legitimating a reinvigorated pursuit of masculine values.

Female hysteria, while pathologized, had its own fashionable element that permitted a kind of agency in the sickroom. Diane Price Herndl's *Invalid Women* describes the ways that female illness and identity were collapsed during the mid to late nineteenth century. While hysterical symptoms were the most obvious female maladies, Herndl's title encompasses much more than nervous illness. On the one hand, the female invalid may have verified cultural attitudes about her frailty and vulnerability; on the other hand, as in the case of Alice James (and perhaps

Emily Dickinson), she used her illness as a negotiation of agency. The figure of the invalid woman

> focuses on the play of power and desire in the narrative, the family, and the culture. The woman who becomes sick is portrayed as a figure with no power, subject to whims of her body or mind, or as a figure with enormous power, able to achieve her desires through the threat of her imminent death or her disability.   (4)

The latter case certainly represents the situation of many figures in American fiction—from Little Eva to Milly Theale to Lily Bart to the narrator of "The Yellow Wall-Paper." Speaking of Alice James, Herndl notes that she "writes repeatedly in her *Diary* of 'achieving' illness and of 'getting herself dead' as a feat equal to or surpassing Henry's and William's writing" (126). Feminist scholars such as Carol Smith-Rosenberg, Jane Tompkins, Ann Douglas, and others have read feminine illness as both an embodiment of women's subordinate position under patriarchy as well as a form of resistance to it. Smith-Rosenberg goes so far as to suggest that hysteria "may have served as one option or tactic offering particular women, otherwise unable to respond to these changes, a chance to redefine or restructure their place within the family," a remark that rather stints the role of activist women in early suffrage or abolition movements (200). Hysteria was less a disease than a social role through which gender among bourgeois women was experienced. If hysteria was endemic, it reflected the tension between the ideals of womanhood demanded of Victorian women and the realities of living up to those ideals.[12]

Virginia Woolf, who shared some eugenicist views with other writers of her day, similarly regarded illness as a state of acute awareness in which "undiscovered countries" are disclosed and one's own mortality is revealed.[13] For Woolf, who lived with many illnesses, besides neurasthenia, illness challenges the privileging of the mind over the body and brings the latter into a proper relation with intellectual endeavor. She wonders at the absence of novels and epic poems devoted to influenza, typhoid, or pneumonia, but acknowledges, "literature does its best to maintain that its concern is with the mind; that the body is a sheet of plain glass through which the soul looks straight and clear…" (*On Being Ill*, 4). Given my earlier list of works that *do* figure illness, Woolf might have repressed the extent to which works about the pains of consciousness (*Death in Venice* would be the type) are underwritten by a body in pain. Woolf's essay is less about illness than the acute awareness that illness brings.

This new consciousness produced through convalescence becomes an important link between the sick body and the aesthetic sphere. As I will develop the theme later in this chapter, Hans Castorp, the protagonist of Thomas Mann's *The Magic Mountain* develops his sensuous and intellectual abilities by convalescing for seven years in an alpine sanitarium. Among early modernist writers the aesthetic and invalid state are elided as paired "cures" for social ills. They are not ends in themselves

---

[12] The definitive account of Victorian female invalids is Maria Frawley's *Invalidism and Identity in Nineteenth-Century Britain*, which chronicles the omnipresence of invalidism as a positive social role, often supported by evangelicalism and serving as "an emblem of sensitivity and insight" (17).

[13] On Woolf's relationship to eugenics, see Childs, *Modernism and Eugenics* (22–37).

but stages on the way to cultural and physical recovery. In different ways, they contest the productivist mentality of capitalist accumulation as the convalescent defers, detours, pauses, elaborates, lingers, and watches where others, like the factory workers in Fritz Lang's *Metropolis*, move in lock step to replenish the machine of Mammon. Against dystopic industrial futurity, aesthetes and invalids pursue what John Addington Symonds calls "emotional fermentation":

> At Harrow and Oxford I was always on the verge of falling into invalidism, irritable nerves and a morbid condition of the reproductive organs, due to the peculiar erethism of my sexual instinct and the absurd habit of antenuptial continence, rendered me physically a very poor creature. Then I continuously overworked myself...by the strain of emotions combined with my specific tendency to approach knowledge from the aesthetical and literary side. I lived in a perpetual simmer of intellectual and emotional fermentation.   (230)

In this ornate passage Symonds identifies his sexual continence as a kind of invalidism for which dedication to "aesthetical and literary" pursuits becomes a form of compensation. Maria Frawley points out that "Symonds came gradually to reject aestheticism as a source of sexual self-understanding and health," recognizing that it served only as a kind of "false memory" or deferral of his sexual instincts (105). In a post-Freudian context we would probably identify Symonds' dilemma as a form of repression, the aesthetic as diversion of his "peculiar erethism" (stimulation of the sexual organs), but his remark makes concrete the role that the aesthetic plays in such displacement. Indeed, Symonds calls his fusion of consumption and aesthetical pursuits, "hyperaesthesia" (230). Since for Symonds this displacement concerns his homosexual desires, artistic pursuits help him divert "the coarse and hard vibrations of sex" (qtd. Frawley, 105). His "aesthetical and literary side" offers an alternative to the "sickness" of sexual abstinence for which his acknowledgment of homosexuality could redeem. Despite such confident assertions, Symonds continues to conflate his physical illness with sexuality: "And yet I carry within me the seeds of what I know to be an incurable malady—not merely the disease of the lungs, which is always ready to appear—but that more deeply rooted perversion of the sexual instincts" (qtd. Frawley, 106). We do not tend to think of the aesthetic as an affliction yet as my example of Symonds suggests there was a close relationship between the sick body and the attempt to divert its wastage into art.

A more overt representation of aesthetic illness occurs in Oscar Wilde's *The Picture of Dorian Gray*.[14] Dorian's gradually wasting image in Basil Hallward's painting is both an image of physical and moral decay, but also a manifestation of art's presumed ability to transcend the vicissitudes of bodily decline. Dorian as the representative of decadent new hedonism pursues a world of immorality and sensuality, and because he remains eternally beautiful and youthful, his pursuits have no mortal consequences, at least to himself. By the novel's end, however, it becomes clear that the aesthetic promise of arrested time is a delusion. The painting that the

[14] Tobin Siebers observes: "We are all playing at Dorian Gray, so confident that the self can be freed from the dead weight of the body, but we have forgotten somehow to read to the end of the novel" (*Disability Theory*, 7).

artist, Basil, keeps in the closet is the suppressed record of Dorian's actual decay, the site of vulnerable mortality of which Dorian's outward beauty is the displacement. In order to restore the "natural order" of life to art, Dorian destroys both the artist and the painting, and in the process becomes the wasted figure depicted on the canvas. The sickness of the aesthetic is figured as the diseased, wasted body in a cautionary tale about the risk of killing nature by preserving it in art.

We tend to look upon aesthetes like Dorian Gray, des Esseintes, Pater's Marius, Proust's Marcel, or Evelyn Waugh's Sebastian Flyte through their cultivation of exquisite sensations that provide a barrier against modernist progress and bourgeois rationality. The aesthete's ennui is embodied in the term "languor," a word derived from the French to refer to conditions of wastage and lassitude but which is revived, as Ellis Hanson says, among fin de siècle decadents to suggest a mood of "immoral and voluptuous bittersweetness of erotic fatigue, often with a degree of ironic detachment" (548). Not quite an illness, not quite an affect, languor captures certain qualities of decadent writing, evident in Pre-Raphaelite painting and Symbolist poetry. The term also captures the way that physical wastage is linked to erotic desire—an excess that cannot be expressed in heteronormative terms. In the idealized futurity of the middle-class family, expressions of non-reproductive sexuality must be seen as a pathological illness for which society seeks a cure.

As the title and subject of one of Verlaine's most famous poems (1883) "Languor" encapsulates the late nineteenth century's mood of exhaustion and cultural loss through an expression of personal malaise. The poet describes himself as "*l'Empire à la fin de la décadence / Qui regarde passer les grands Barbares blancs*" (the Empire at the end of decadence / Watching the great white Barbarians pass [349], 100). As such he is both the observer and embodiment of decline, comparing present-day France to late Roman civilization as it is invaded by Germanic "barbarians." Against such decadence, poetry can only be regarded as idle wordplay ("*acrostiches indolents*") in a mood of intense boredom ("*ennui dense*" [100]). Battles may rage, drunkenness and gluttony prevail, and poems might as well be thrown on the fire ("*Seul un poeme un peu nisis qu'on jette au feu*" [100]). Subsequent poets who appropriated languor as the mood of their own early poetry like Pound, Yeats, Eliot, and Stevens made voluptuous despair an objective correlative for personal insecurities. The "*style d'or*" embodied by Symbolism is both a sign of the age's illness and yet the reparative condition for its renewal. What Symonds called aestheticism's "emotional fermentation" is here represented in a poem that chronicles its inutility while exploiting its affective realm as a therapeutic.

SIGNIFYING NOTHING

A good deal has been written about nineteenth-century invalidism among female characters—what Catherine Beecher called "women's complaints."[15] What often

---

[15] Quoted in Ann Douglas Wood, "'The Fashionable Diseases': Women's Complaints and their Treatment in Nineteenth-Century America" (38). "[Among many nineteenth-century women] ill

differentiates women invalids in literary works from their male counterparts is that in most cases, the former die or go mad, whereas male invalids often rise like Lazarus from the sickbed and write with renewed vigor. It is not in sickness that the aesthete is defined so much as in his convalescence, and convalescence implies a temporal triumph over inertia. Symonds' invalid aestheticism empowers his coming out as homosexual; Huysmans' des Esseintes in *À Rebours* begins his sybaritic journey into sensations after recovering from a long illness; the young poet whose awakening to love inspires Kierkegaard's narrator to discover the meaning of time in "Repetition," does so when "the rage of fever is over, and [he is] like a convalescent" (207); the northern entrepreneur in Charles Chesnutt's story "The Goophered Grapevine," brings his convalescent wife to the south for her health where he discovers the possibility for developing a grape-growing industry on former plantations. Perhaps the prototype of the endlessly convalescing aesthete is Proust's Marcel, who uses his bedridden state as a lure to secure his mother's and grandmother's affection but also as an occasion to indulge his infantilism, a combination vividly depicted in the famous madeleine scene.[16] In these several examples, the convalescent figure, however weakened, becomes the occasion for a redemptive moment of insight and growth and, in the case of Proust, for creative expression.

The paradigmatic case for redemptive convalescence occurs in Nietzsche's chapter of *Thus Spoke Zarathustra* entitled "The Convalescent."[17] The titular narrator gathers the animals of nature around him to hear his prophecy but promptly falls into a seven-day illness during which time, "pale and trembling...he would neither eat nor drink." When at last he rises, the animals question him: "Did perhaps a new knowledge come to you, a bitter, grievous knowledge? Like leavened dough lay you, your soul rose and swelled beyond all its bounds." Whereupon Zarathustra delivers his sermon on the myth of eternal return:

> Everything goes, everything returns; eternally rolls the wheel of existence. Everything dies, everything blossoms forth again; eternally runs on the year of existence.
>
> Everything breaks, everything is integrated anew; eternally builds itself the same house of existence. All things separate, all things again greet one another; eternally true to itself remains the ring of existence.   (237)

After this speech, he remembers his sickness with disgust, but the animals prevent him from dwelling on the past: "Do not talk further...rather, you convalescent prepare for yourself first a lyre, a new lyre!" That lyre—the lyric of eternal return and cyclic time—would inspire subsequent modernists, from Bergson and William James to Proust, Eliot, and Stein to imagine different modalities of time, but its strings were strung in a sickbed.

---

health in women had become positively fashionable and was exploited by its victims and practitioners as an advertisement of genteel sensibility and an escape from the too pressing demands of bedroom and kitchen" (27).

[16] On Proust and illness see Bragg and Sayers, "Proust's Prescription: Sickness as the Pre-condition for Writing."

[17] For a more thorough treatment of Nietzsche and disability, see David Mitchell and Sharon Snyder's chapter three of *Narrative Prosthesis: Disability and the Dependencies of Discourse.*

The idea of convalescence as a form of alternate productivity is elaborately developed in Henry James' *Portrait of a Lady* through the figure of Ralph Touchett, the son of a wealthy American businessman living in England who is dying of consumption. Although he is not an artist, he is described throughout the novel as one who uses his recumbent state and income to fashion a fictive life for others. He becomes entranced with his cousin, Isabel Archer, who comes to visit. Although he is not erotically interested in Isabel, Ralph sees her as a type of independent, Emersonian American, and he desires to "put wind in her sails," as he explains, by diverting a large portion of his considerable inheritance to her upon his—inevitable—death. His long, lingering illness is to some extent the necessary inverse of Isabel's youth, beauty, and imagination. But as it turns out the wind he puts in *her* sails at the expense of the wind draining from his lungs, becomes her downfall. Instead of using her new wealth to achieve the independence Ralph believes she deserves, she marries the Machiavellian aesthete, Gilbert Osmond and becomes ensnared in a diabolic plot between her husband and his lover, Madame Merle. While Ralph's illness is not the centerpiece of the novel it facilitates several important features of the narrative's sexual politics, not the least of which is to finesse his lack of heterosexual desire for Isabel on the basis of his "condition." It also serves as a link between consumption as a bodily infirmity and consumption as an economic disease that destroys self-reliance and independence. It is James' subtle critique of the cash nexus to make Ralph's disease the source of Isabel's imprisonment.

James elaborates on the Victorian era's treatment of invalidism as a form of labor among the wealthy. Ralph's illness becomes, in Madame Merle's terms, his career:

> But the men, the Americans; *je vous demande un peu*, what do they
> make of it over here? I don't envy them, trying to arrange themselves.
> Look at poor Ralph Touchett: what sort of a figure do you call that?
> Fortunately he has got a consumption; I say fortunately, because it
> gives him something to do. His consumption is his career; it's a kind of
> position. You can say, "Oh, Mr. Touchett, he takes care of his lungs,
> he knows a great deal about climates." But without that who would he
> be, what would he represent? "Mr. Ralph Touchett—an American
> who lives in Europe." That signifies absolutely nothing—it's impossible
> that anything should signify less. (171)

Madame Merle articulates something important about the gendering of disability. Ralph's invalidism prevents him from "signifying" as a productive male. Being "[an] American who lives in Europe" and has no profession signifies nothing, but as Merle observes, having an illness removes Ralph from the usual expectations of masculine agency. As Dana Luciano says, "If Ralph can't have a regular career because of his lungs he can still have an alternative career, a "'kind of' career *in* his lungs" (182). In *Portrait of a Lady* James is explicit about this association of illness with career. When Ralph becomes ill, he had to "give up work and embrace the sorry occupation known as taking care of one's self" (37). Madame Merle joins the energetic journalist, Henrietta Stackpole, in deploring Ralph's inactivity as a specifically

"American" failing. But Ralph does have an important function thematically by occupying a homologous relationship to his nemesis Osmond, who is positioned as an arid aesthete, a collector of fine china and bibelots. And just as Ralph capitalizes on what he imagines to be Isabel's autonomy, freeing her to exist outside of economic dependency, so Osmond seeks to turn her into an artwork. He compares her at one point to a new acquisition in his collection of fine china. Isabel is necessary to hide his former sexual relationship with Madame Merle and secure a mother for their illegitimate daughter, but his collecting, belief in social proprieties, and sedentary boredom are the aesthetic equivalent of Ralph's invalidism. Both are joined by the capitalist desire to turn Isabel into a profit, of which Ralph's wasting body is a marker.

THE CONVALESCENT SUBLIME:
THE MAGIC MOUNTAIN

In Thomas Mann's *The Magic Mountain* (*Der Zauberberg*) Hans Castorp, an "ordinary young man," arrives at the International Sanatorium Berghof high in the Swiss Alps to visit his cousin, Joachim, who is convalescing for tuberculosis. Hans plans to stay for three weeks and ends up staying seven years, a period culminating with World War I. Initially he insists he is not ill himself, differentiating his condition from that of residents who are living with tuberculosis and other respiratory ailments. But it is not long before he is slowly interpolated into the Berghof's medical routines and social rituals. And what's not to like? The scenery is beautiful, the food excellent, and the conversation stimulating. He may rest during the day, smoke one of his imported cigars, and count on a good discussion with his doctors and patients. The longer he stays and the more often he visits the sanitarium's director, Dr. Behrens, the more he extends his sojourn. One of Mann's more subtle ironies is to leave the reality of Hans' tuberculosis vague—a "moist spot" the doctor calls it—thus leaving his disease a matter of conjecture and speculation. He comes as a healthy, rather fastidious bourgeois and ends up an invalid. After seven years, Hans' convalescence abruptly ends as the war begins, and we last see him marching into battle for what will be a likely death.

The vast critical literature on *The Magic Mountain* tends to focus on its "big themes": love, death, and time. Tuberculosis links the three terms in various ways and serves, more generally, as a metaphor for European malaise in the prewar period.[18] Written during the same period as other documents of cultural decline— *The Waste Land*, "Hugh Selwyn Mauberley," *Civilization and its Discontents*, *The Decline of the West*, *The Great Gatsby*, *Mrs. Dalloway*—*The Magic Mountain* is

---

[18] Mann spent three weeks at the Davos sanitarium on which the novel is based while visiting his wife who was convalescing there. Like Castorp he submitted himself to a doctor's examination and based much of the novel on his observations of daily life among its inmates. On Mann's biographical relationship to the novel, see Hans Rudolf Vaget, "The Making of *The Magic Mountain*." For an excellent account of the novel's relationship to Germany in the post-World War I period, see Todd Kontje, *Thomas Mann's World*.

unique in its extended focus on the vicissitudes of the body and the calibration of cultural to physical degeneration.[19] If, as most critics observe, it is a novel about the "sickness" of prewar Europe, it chronicles that history through the "sick" bodies of its cosmopolitan bourgeoisie. Illness serves as backdrop for Castorp's reflections on death and mortality, but it is also a formative influence on his knowledge about his body and sensations. Although he is not an aesthete, in the terms already developed, his detachment from the world, his fastidiousness in dress and comportment, and gradual education into sensual pleasures place him in similar company with my more literary examples.

Mann thought of his novel as a kind of *Bildungsroman*, albeit one in quotation marks. In the classic versions of that genre, the protagonist abjures a world of youthful sensation and pleasure to settle for marriage, a profession, and middle-class values. Mann's novel inverts this model by taking his protagonist out of the *via activa* and placing him recumbent in a lounge chair, wrapped in blankets. As Todd Kontje says, "we first meet Hans Castorp at the point where the protagonist of the *Bildungsroman* usually ends: he has weathered some early childhood trauma, chosen his future profession, and is about to enter the working world after a brief visit to his ailing cousin" ("Modern Masculinities," 81). Intellectual growth, assisted by extended conversations with various guides, expands in direct proportion to the presumed decay and withering of the bourgeois body. His long sojourn permits him to experience the pleasures of the flesh (a brief sexual encounter with one of the inmates) and the attractions of new intellectual endeavors—astronomy, psychoanalysis, gramophones, music, parapsychology, botany, medicine—and physical exercise (walking, skiing). The novel's sheer length allows the reader to accompany Castorp on his various forays into these pursuits and watch in some detail his daily regimens of temperature taking, eating, resting, and conversing.

Castorp's "education" is provided by several teachers, the most prominent of which are an Italian humanist Ludovico Settembrini and the religious mystic and Marxist, Leo Naptha.[20] They provide Hans with contrasting theories of social and moral life, based on their attitudes toward embodiment and illness. The former disputes the reign of sickness and death that pervades the sanitarium, preferring the life of the mind, and a kind of eugenic progressivism. Naptha, modeled loosely on Georg Lukács, feels that "Illness was supremely human... because to be human was to be ill" (456). Settembrini feels that an overemphasis on illness "sent a person back to his own body" distracting him from "the worthiness and dignity of man to

---

[19] Many have seen the novel as a narrative of Mann's own transformation from a conservative defender of German nationalism into a supporter of the Weimar Republic and one of Hitler's most vehement opponents.

[20] He is offered a third form of instruction in the form of Minheer Peeperkorn, the companion of Clavdia Chauchat. He is a large, boisterous and sensuous inmate who offers, by example, the pleasures of the flesh and appetites, saying at one point, "it is our duty, our *religious* duty to feel. Our feeling, you see, is our manly vigor, which awakens life" (594). As a "colonial Dutchman, a man from Java, a coffee planter" with a Malaysian servant, Peeperkorn's career has been in international trade in colonial outposts (189). He brings to the novel (and Castorp's imagination) an orientalist view of primitive cultures and sensuality. To some extent he represents the other, colonial end of Hans' own background in maritime shipping in his native Hamburg.

the point of annihilation" (446). As a member of "The International League for the Organization of Progress," Settembrini embraces a eugenic program of rational progress and genetic purity: "the problem of our health as a race and the means for combating the degeneration which [accompanies] our increasing industrialization" (241). Naptha, on the other hand, looks back to medieval religious traditions in which the mortification of the body, epitomized by Christ's stigmata, is the necessary portal into knowledge of spiritual life. Hans must find his way between these two intellectual tempters, and although he tends to prefer Settembrini's more democratic vision, he is tempted by Naptha's willingness to accept bodily infirmity as a form of knowledge.

He also receives an education into the flesh by his obsession with a Russian inmate, Clavdia Chauchat, whose improprieties, sexual promiscuity, and strong-willed actions shatter his middle-class conventionality. He carries her image with him, not by means of a photograph in a locket, but by an X-ray of her bodily interior that he procures from Dr. Behrens. His one night of passion with Clavdia occurs during Mardi Gras, a time of shape-shifting and masquerade, fueled by champagne, that offers a ritualistic version of the X-ray's negative image. All of these inversions reflect Castorp's conflicted sexuality that began when he was thirteen and developed a crush on a male school friend, Pribislav Hippe. Having loaned Hans a pencil, Hippe says "be sure to give it back to me after class," which serves as a leitmotif through the novel for Hans' unresolved homoerotic affections. When Clavdia invites him into her room for their late-night tryst she reminds Hans to return a pencil she has loaned him, thereby cementing the relationship between the two objects of desire. She is, as Todd Kontje observes, "also a man, or at least the reincarnation of a boy," who holds the phallic pencil (*Cambridge*, 68). Mann's own closeted homosexuality is narrated through Castorp's desire for a woman who substitutes for homoerotic experience. We could call this an example of moral panic or repression of homosexual desires, but as Kontje says, we could "leave the matter unresolved, in keeping with what Freud and Otto Weininger described as the essential bisexuality of human beings" (69).

If the *Bildungsroman*'s pedagogical purpose is somewhat turned on its head, so is the romantic concept of the sublime. The sanitarium's alpine setting, surrounded by towering peaks and vast vistas could be seen as a stage set for theories of the sublime, now adapted to the condition of convalescence. Eighteenth-century philosophers often used their perilous passage over the Alps to illustrate the sublime condition as "an agreeable kind of horror" (Addison, 261), or one that "operates in a manner analogous to terror" (Burke, 86). Unlike Kant's aesthetic treatment of beauty, based on the bounded object, the unbounded power of nature defies description. Caspar David Friedrich's painting (*Wanderer über dem Nebelmeer*) of a man standing on a craggy perch looking out into the fog is often used to illustrate the concept.[21] But whereas theories of the sublime invoke the awe and wonder

---

[21] Friedrich's painting adorns the covers of Stephen Dowden's *A Companion to Thomas Mann's Magic Mountain* and Terry Eagleton's *The Ideology of the Aesthetic*, among other works dealing with the sublime.

produced by nature's inexplicable power Hans Castorp experiences similar sensations by pondering the vast interior of his own body. What one might call the "convalescent sublime" refers to the way that extended periods of illness and rehabilitation release temporal boundaries and social proprieties, opening the body to sensations that Kant calls "negative pleasure" (*Critique of Judgment*, 91).

In a key chapter that illustrates this point, Castorp leaves the confines of the Berghof "to enjoy a freer, more active, more intense experience of the snowy mountain wilderness" by skiing in the alpine regions above the sanitarium (464). He witnesses "the towering statues of snow-clad Alps...[that awaken] feelings of the sublime and holy" (462). The awe he experiences by the silence and solitude of this wilderness sends him back to childhood experiences at the seashore where ocean waves produced the "thrill of brushing up against powers whose full embrace would destroy you" (467). When he becomes lost in the snow, he takes shelter under the eve of an abandoned hut. He escapes his confused state with a dream or fantasy of some sunny Mediterranean landscape, surrounded by a fair field of folk, "beautiful, young humanity, so fair to gaze upon." This bucolic return to childhood memories turns into a nightmare as the classical landscape devolves into a scene out of *Macbeth* with witches "busy at a ghastly chore" of dismembering a child. These fantasies of childhood summers and sun-filled landscapes attempt to configure the threat of oblivion in the snow with something familiar. The nightmarish intrusion shatters this attempt at naturalizing strangeness and brings him back to his initial sense of vulnerability. When he finally awakens from these fantasies, he realizes that he has achieved a perspective on death as well as on the experience of convalescence itself:

> I have experienced so much among the people up here about kicking over the traces, about reason. I have passed on with Naptha and Settembrini into these dangerous mountains. I know everything about humankind. I have known flesh and blood. I gave Pribislav Hippe's pencil back to ailing Clavdia. But he who knows the body, who knows life, also knows death. Except that's not the whole thing—but merely a beginning pedagogically speaking. You have to hold it up to the other half, to its opposite. Because our interest in death and illness is nothing but a way of expressing an interest in life... (486)

We could see this as an extended version of Nietzsche's confession to the animals in "The Convalescent" where a prolonged period of sickness awakens his mind to a new sense of the body's relationship to time. Castorp acknowledges the benefits of his stay—the sanitarium community, the relinquishment of homosexual to heterosexual desire, the daily proximity to bodily infirmity. He notes that his experience of convalescence has taught him to get "used to not getting used to things" and begin to live a more spontaneous life (476). His final remark before escaping his snow-bound hut summarizes his "birth" into a new consciousness: "I will keep faith with death in my heart, but I will clearly remember that if faithfulness to death and to what is past rules our thoughts and deeds that leads only to wickedness, dark lust, and hatred of humankind. *For the sake of goodness and love, man shall grant death no dominion over his thought*" (487).

The Magic Mountain offers a significant disability studies perspective on that realm that Susan Sontag has called "the Kingdom of the sick." "Everyone who is born holds dual citizenship, in the kingdom of the well and the kingdom of the sick...Sooner or later each of us is obliged, at least for a spell, to identify ourselves as citizens of that other place" (3). Sontag's metaphor aptly describes the sanitarium as an alternate *polis* made up of expatriates from various countries, engaged in frivolous pursuits and rituals while anticipating impending death. The end of empire, in Verlaine's poem mentioned earlier, was to be realized in the period of *The Magic Mountain*'s composition, a period that begins in 1912 and ends in 1924. It was a period in which Mann's own nationalist leanings changed, and we could read the novel's long period of composition as itself a form of narrative convalescence during which the author, like Hans Castorp, gained his own form of social *bildung*. The war into which Hans Castorp marches at the end of the novel promises to take the aesthete and sensualist out of his sickbed and into the trenches for a different kind of education.

ANAESTHETIC MODERNISM

By considering the motif of illness during a long modernist period, I want to situate its formations in that period Foucault saw as inaugurating a biopolitics of power relations through the body. The period introduces a characterological type that begins to appear in a good deal of early modernist writing, both as exemplar and antagonist. The figure of the enervated or ill aesthete often becomes a stereotype from which modernist authors sought to differentiate themselves. Eliot's Prufrock is the obvious version, but Ezra Pound's Hugh Selwyn Mauberley is the most developed. Pound's titular figure is an artist much like the early Pound, creator of Browningesque masks and medievalist pastiches, whose response to the modern age is "the obscure reveries / Of the inward gaze" and "an art / In profile" (198). Critical consensus regards Mauberley as the fin de siècle figure Pound might have become had he not struck out on the epic ship of *The Cantos*. The same could be said for James Joyce who turned from his portrait of the artist as a young aesthete, unable to forge in the smithy of his soul the uncreated conscience of his race, to the considerably more fleshly and sexual Bloom in *Ulysses*. Although neither Mauberley nor Stephen Dedalus are necessarily ill, their aesthetic experiments are characterized as weak and insubstantial. Yet they represent an important stage on the way to "forge Achaia," as Pound hoped, in the modern age (198). The aesthete convalescent throws off the covers of inertia to enter history.

My focus has been on a specific form that aesthetics takes in the modernist period, the autonomous work as an "anaesthetic" against cultural trauma and historical pain. The decadent artist or aesthete embodies the close proximity of disease and aesthetics that forms an important component of early modernism. As I've suggested, the aesthetic could be described as a *pharmakon*, a remedy for modern malaise and trauma by existing outside of instrumental reason and rationalized production. The promise of progress embodied in fin de siècle ideas of health and rehabilitation produced the invalid as its doppelgänger, one who refuses the lure of medical cure and rehabilitation and makes of that refusal a new art form. Like the invalid narrator of "The Yellow Wall-Paper" who reads on the wallpaper of her sickroom an alternate story of liberation from medical confinement, the invalid aesthete turns the mirror of modernity back on itself to find a more transgressive story: "to be ill is to produce narrative." And similar to the emergent spring that Williams observed growing in the shadow of the convalescent hospital, new forms are born out of decay. To convalesce and remove from the sickbed is to realize the force of this double-edged figure and make out of it a story of eternal return, of repetition as growth. The invalid aesthete, like Plato's *pharmakon*, is the body as artwork, living in order to die, disabled because all too human.

2

"The Rage of Caliban"
The Mirror of Recognition

In my introduction I invoked the absent body in the aesthetic, a corporeal presence necessary to its functioning but forced to remain out of sight in providing the illusion of detached appreciation. Walter Benjamin uses a related image of this phenomenon in his first "Thesis on History" when he invokes Edgar Allan Poe's account of a chess-playing automaton in "Maazel's Chess-Player." The story concerns a puppet in Turkish costume, flanked by a hookah, that plays chess with members of the audience.[1] The orientalized puppet is manipulated by a "wizened" dwarf hidden in the machine who as an expert chess player guides the puppet's hands over the chessboard. Benjamin sees the story as an allegory of the relationship between historical materialism and a desiccated theology:

> One can imagine a philosophical counterpart to this device. The puppet called "historical materialism" is to win all the time. It can easily be a match for anyone if it enlists the services of theology, which today, as we know, is wizened and has to keep out of sight.   (253)

In Benjamin's account, the puppet as materialist history is the external manifestation of progress, human agency reified into the commodity form and produced as spectacle. Since theology is "wizened" during the modern period it must be kept out of sight like the unsightly body of the dwarf. The latter does not control events from some abstract or metaphysical realm; rather as Rolf Tiedemann says, theology "is the servant who must do the work—who must take care of the thinking, so to speak" (190). The metaphor of the dwarf is of little concern; he is simply a device to create the illusion upon which the automaton depends. Dwarf and puppet are fatally linked components of secular modernity, but one might say that they are also components of the aesthetic function itself.

Among the recent "turns" in cultural theory (linguistic, spatial, narrative, transnational, affective) the recent turn toward the aesthetic may seem more of a retreat than an advance. What could be more antithetical to critique than the pursuit of universalizing standards of beauty, detachment, and autonomy?[2] The difference in

---

[1] "Maelzel's Chess Player."
[2] The best-known recent attack on an autonomous aesthetics is Hal Foster's 1983 anthology, *The Anti-Aesthetic*. Foster argues that despite Adorno's view of the subversive elements of the aesthetic, such criticality "is now largely illusory," its forms and procedures having been absorbed into mass culture (xv).

what Michael Kelly calls the recent "hunger for aesthetics" is an outgrowth of these other discourses such that criteria of aesthetic appreciation must now be situated as a discourse, within specific communities, produced in geopolitical spaces, against the backdrop of institutional purposes and validation. Disability studies, as one such cultural turn, occupies a particularly important role in this context since it confronts the various and variable bodies around which aesthetic discourse revolves. In the Poe story, the puppet's non-human body makes visible outwardly what the dwarf's non-standard body represents internally. Classical aesthetics, as we have observed in Chapter 1, is often seen as a rejection of embodied response, a "flight from corporeal existence," as Terry Eagleton says (171). What begins as sensory pleasure derived from and lodged within the body ends in a triumph over bodily contingency. How might the body be reinstated to the aesthetic, not as that reflected in the mirror of art but as the foundational fact of aesthetic discourse? Or to adapt my initial example, how might the dwarf in the automaton be revealed as its genius?

The claim of disinterestedness central to autonomous art presents a problem for disability studies since it attempts to legitimate judgments of taste by removing the body that makes such responses possible, or more precisely by diverting bodily responses onto objective forms. Terry Eagleton describes this diversion in terms of Lacan's mirror stage. Just as the infant discovers a "plenitude lacking in its own body" in his mirror image, so the observer faced with a beautiful form "discovers in it a unity and harmony which are in fact the effect of the free play of its own faculties" (87). The mirror stage of recognition occurs when the viewer projects onto the object subjective potentialities heretofore invisible or repressed.[3] Judgments of taste are always framed by social attitudes and cultural contexts that *become* the mirror into which the subject looks. Such values create forms of cultural capital in the reinforcement of class privilege—and ability—and thus restrict competing views of beauty, sensory satisfaction, and human variety. An aesthetic of disinterestedness is never far from a formalist desire to project the work of art as a *cordon sanitaire* against bodily difference and corporeal mutability.

What happens when the aesthetic object stages its own act of mirroring—when a painting represents the absent body as its principal subject? This is what happens in Velázquez's 1656 painting, *Las Meninas* (Fig. 2.1). In this work, as I will develop it later, the artist's subject is missing. The painter looks out from his canvas not at the King and Queen of Spain, his putative subjects, but at us, the present viewers of the canvas upon which he works and whose surface is hidden from us. The centerpiece of *this* canvas—the one upon which we gaze—is the Spanish Infanta who occupies the central position, flanked by two court dwarfs to her left—a contrast, perhaps, to her youthful perfection. As I will point out with reference to several modernist works inspired by this painting, the figures at the margins of classical representation are often foundational for those at the center.

I want to extend Velázquez's canvas into later works that reframe its problematics of representation around problematic identities. My examples include Oscar

---

[3] Ato Quayson discusses Lacan's mirror stage with specific reference to disability in *Calibrations* (109–20).

Fig. 2.1. Diego Velázquez, *Las Meninas* and detail.
© 2018 Art Resource, New York.

Wilde's "The Birthday of the Infanta" (1891) and Alexander Zemlinsky's opera, *Der Zwerg* (The Dwarf [1922]), works that condense several strands of modernism around the representation of non-traditional bodies. Wilde's story has been read as an attack on aestheticism's cultivation of surface beauty; the "ugly dwarf" belies a noble soul while the beautiful Infanta reveals a superficial glamor. Zemlinsky's opera, based on Wilde's story, foregrounds the short statured body as the site of sight, the protagonist discovering his otherness in a mirror in a moment of recognition that frames both his embodied and (perhaps) sexual difference. As a musical composition that stands on the divide between late Romanticism and modernist atonality, *Der Zwerg* combines the ocularcentric regimes of modernist aesthetics with sonic and dramatic elements in which mental and physical difference play a major role. From Verdi's Rigoletto and Violetta, to Puccini's Mimi, to Wagner's Alberich and Mime, to Berg's Wozzeck and Schönberg's Moses and Pierrot, to Gershwin's Porgy, to Britten's Peter Grimes modern opera curates a gallery of stunted bodies, mad dreamers, and consumptive heroines whose bodily and cognitive infirmities are reinforced by new harmonic and tonal dissonances.[4]

As my previous discussion might suggest, modern aesthetic theories have a categorical function that attempts to organize and rationalize sensory experience. This taxonomic quality parallels in many ways the rationalizing of bodies in modern medical science, the marking, naming, and sequestering of populations that Michel Foucault subsumes under the term "biopolitics." Eighteenth- and early nineteenth-century aesthetic treatises contribute to biopolitics by providing subjective validation for the kinds of authority claimed by empirical evidence. Yet the criteria for judgment often presuppose an ideal of physical embodiment. Johann Joachim Winckelmann seeks artistic perfection in classical sculpture based on the perfect body, preferably that displayed in classical antiquity. He regards ideal beauty as a "state of health" embodied in proportion, smoothness, and balance:

> These masterpieces [of classical art] show us a skin which is not tightly stretched, but gently drawn over a healthy flesh, which fills it out without distended protuberances and follows all the movements of the flesh parts of the body in a single unified direction. (37)

In contrast Gotthold Lessing feels that certain emotions—such as pain—can be better expressed in poetry, while bodily infirmity and variety may be the ideal subject for painting since they create a challenge for the artist's mimetic potentiality:

> 'Who will wish to paint you, when no one wishes to see you?' says an old epigrammatist concerning an extremely misshapen man. Many a more modern artist would say, 'Be you as misshapen as is possible, I will paint you nevertheless. Though, indeed, no one may wish to see you, people will still wish to see my picture; not insofar as it represents you, but insofar as it is a demonstration of my art, which knows how to make so good a likeness of such a monster.' (63)

For Lessing, realistic depiction of a "misshapen man" is less important for its fidelity to the original than its demonstration of artisanal superiority. What is clear in both Winckelmann and Lessing is that the ability of aesthetics to define affective and sensory response depends on—indeed, would be unthinkable without—bodily difference.

An alternate approach to such categorical imperatives around artistic perfection is provided by Jacques Rancière who understands the aesthetic as a political sphere in which sensory experience is organized around social imperatives made visible in art. The politics of aesthetics inheres in "the ways the practices and forms of visibility

---

[4] Joseph N. Strauss has devoted considerable attention to this possibility by looking not only at disabled composers or dramatic works featuring disabled figures but also at the formal features of music itself as a body, against which certain fracturing and deformations disable it.

of art themselves intervene in the distribution of the sensible and its reconfiguration"
(25). For Rancière, the politics of aesthetics (unlike the aestheticized politics
Benjamin observed in Fascist spectacles) is to create new possibilities for common-
ality and "render visible what had not been, and to make heard as speakers those
who had been perceived as mere noisy animals" (25). The pursuit of an autonomous art in modernism, however aligned with biopolitical regimes, often created
the conditions by which "noisy animals" could be seen as human. If we regard
autonomous art merely as a formal repudiation of mass culture or a reflection of
bourgeois taste we may miss its revelation in that form of abjection or otherness
that lurks in bourgeois *moeurs*.

Examples of what we might call a "biopoetics" in literature could be joined by
comparable developments in late nineteenth- and early twentieth-century music in
which human disqualification would be registered through a decisive break from
Western harmonic conventions, a break that Nietzsche experienced as a "physiological response" to the music of Wagner. "Why should I trouble to dress up [my
objections] in aesthetic formulas? After all, aesthetics is nothing but a kind of
applied physiology" ("Nietzsche contra Wagner," 664). Nietzsche is reacting to the
loss of the physical aspects of music ("walking, striding, leaping and dancing")
against Wagner's "infinite melody" (664, 666). The philosopher worries at the
"contagion" and "unhealthy" quality of Wagner's theatricality that is reinforced by
its appeal to the crowd. In Nietzsche's mind, if Wagner represents the future of
German music then the "Germans themselves have no future," a plaint that links
fears of modern music, its chromaticism and lack of tonal center, with a eugenicist
fear of national degeneration (669). Nietzsche came to his disappointment with
Wagner due to the latter's anti-Semitism and conversion to Christianity, but we
may read between the lines of his attack a residue of those elements of cultural
degeneration that drew philosopher to composer in the first place.

THE INFANTA VARIATIONS

Although several of Oscar Wilde's works have been adapted to music (*Salomé*,
"A Florentine Tragedy," *Lady Windermere's Fan*, *The Picture of Dorian Gray*), no
work of his has been so extensively used as his short story, "The Birthday of the
Infanta."[5] In this tale, the daughter of King Philip IV of Spain (the Infanta depicted
in Velázquez's *Las Meninas*)[6] is given a dwarf as a present for her twelfth birthday.
The dwarf is the son of a rustic coal burner whose father is "well pleased to get rid
of so ugly and useless a child" (192). As the dwarf dances and capers about the

[5] "The Birthday of the Infanta" first appeared as "The Birthday of the Little Princess" in *Paris
Illustré* and subsequently as "The Birthday of the Infanta" in *A House of Pomegranates* (1891). It is
available in *The Complete Shorter Fiction of Oscar Wilde*, ed. Isobel Murray (185–202).

[6] Many artists have painted variations on *Las Meninas*, the most famous series of which is Picasso's
fifty-eight paintings from 1957. In this series, the Infanta is the centerpiece of each canvas, along with
her maids, while the dwarfs are eliminated or, in at least one case, reduced to a cartoon sketch The dog,
however, remains.

court, it becomes clear that he is oblivious to his diminutive state, never having seen himself in a mirror. The impish princess convinces the dwarf that he is a handsome cavalier and gives him a white rose from her hair. While her playmates gaze and giggle at the grotesque visitor, the flowers in the garden complain at having to share their paradise with his visage. The dwarf misunderstands the Infanta's cruel flirting as affection and falls in love with her. Wandering about the palace, he accidentally sees himself in a mirror, "a monster, the most grotesque monster he had ever beheld. Not properly shaped, as all other people were, but hunchbacked and crooked-limbed with huge lolling head and mane of black hair" (200). The Infanta enters and, oblivious to his despair, insists that he continue to dance and entertain her. His heart is broken, and he dies, leaving the Infanta to declare: "For the future let those who come to play with me have no hearts" (201).

This rather simple story (Wilde called it a "fairy tale") inspired an extensive number of ballets, musical adaptations, and at least one opera by an international cast of composers that includes Franz Schreker, Bernhard Sekles, Miklos Radnai, John Alden Carpenter, Elisabeth Lutyens, Franz Tischhauser, Nikola Hercigonja, Mario Castelnuovo-Tedesco, Pierre Auclert, Jean Hubeau, Wolfgang Fortner, Harry Partch, Ivan Semenoff, Maurice Ravel, Douglas Johnson, Ron Nelson, Richard Stoker, Malcolm Seagrave, and Alexander von Zemlinsky.[7] The fascination exerted by this story on modernist composers is striking by any standard, but what it says about modernism's obsession with the grotesque has implications for the period's anxieties about racial degeneration and bodily difference. The confrontation of beauty and beast, princess and dwarf, self and double, marks the era's fear of dysgenic amalgamation that would result in racial pollution. At the same time, "The Birthday of the Infanta" advances this fear into the aesthetic realm as a question about the nature of Nature, whether it exists in the mirror of science or is improved through the mirror of art. The dwarf's image of himself as a "normal" heterosexual male is an illusion while his "grotesque" reality, in the sexology of Wilde's day, is that he must be homosexual. Rather than reinforce this compulsorily heterosexual model, Wilde sees the true grotesques as members of the court while the dwarf, "deformed" in their eyes, emerges as the noble, if tragic, hero.[8] Far from simply inverting the moral compass of Wilde's fairy tale, these later works embody an anxiety at the heart of modernism's desire on the one hand to cure social ills by rationalizing health and space and, on the other, to cure society of unfit and unredeemable types.

We could extend this imperative to include the period's anxiety about Oscar Wilde himself whose works often staged a character's uncertain sexuality through a confrontation with a mirror or a portrait.[9] His widely publicized trial and subsequent imprisonment made him a spectacle and scandal throughout Europe, not excluding fin de siècle Vienna where Zemlinsky would have encountered him. Wilde

---

[7] For a thorough discussion of the musical versions of "The Birthday of the Infanta," see Tine Englebert, "Mad, Scarlet Music."

[8] To the extent that this is an allegory of Wilde's sexuality, the story—a "fairy tale" as he called it—offers a rebuke to the court that would, within a few years, ultimately place him in Reading jail.

[9] Lional Croy in E. M. Forster's *Maurice* speaks of himself as "an unspeakable of the Oscar Wilde sort." See Eve Sedgwick, *Tendencies* (77).

fuses the two meanings of the term "decadent"—aesthetic and eugenic—which often substitute for homosexuality. A good example of what we might call "Wilde panic" can be seen in the opening chapter of Joyce's *Ulysses* where Buck Mulligan mocks Stephen Dedalus' unkempt appearance by quoting an aphorism from *The Picture of Dorian Gray*: " 'The rage of Caliban at not seeing his face in a mirror,' he said. 'If Wilde were only alive to see you!' "[10] The remark refers to one of the epigrams that Wilde uses as preface to *The Picture of Dorian Gray* that describes the nineteenth century as divided between a dislike of Realism ("the rage of Caliban seeing his own face in a glass") and Romanticism ("the rage of Caliban *not* seeing his own face in a glass" [3]). Stephen is being positioned as the grotesque primitive of Shakespeare's *Tempest*, denied his image in the mirror of Romantic idealism and forced to see himself in the "cracked mirror" of Irish history. But he is also being positioned in front of Wilde's queer mirror ("If only Wilde could see you!") as held by Mulligan whose theatrical performances and dandyish manner threaten Stephen's cloistered heterosexuality throughout the novel. Mulligan often foregrounds Stephen's queer self against the latter's aestheticized desire to create an Irish epic.

This alliance of grotesque and queer bodies lies behind the thematics of monstrosity and doubling in many Victorian works, from *Frankenstein*, *Dr. Jekyll and Mr. Hyde*, and *Dracula* to Freud's essay on "The Uncanny." *Dorian Gray* is perhaps the best example. His eternal beauty, as Judith Halberstam says, is "all form and no content; Dorian is in some sense plotless because his life is not written upon his body but upon his portrait" (*Skin Shows*, 98). In this scenario, mimesis is inverted; art *embodies* reality whereas reality aspires to the condition of Greek sculpture. One could alter this formulation to say that the "secret" of the artist's desire for his male subject is also etched on the monstrous painting that he sequesters from public display. When Dorian stabs the artist who created him and then destroys his portrait, the aesthetic poles are reversed; the painting reverts to Dorian's youthful image while its subject lies dead on the floor, an old man, "withered, wrinkled, and loathsome of visage" (188). Here at the end of *The Picture of Dorian Gray*, art and life assume their "normal" ratios having been shown in the inverted mirror of Wilde's gothic tale the disabled body hidden in the picture of homosexual desire. Something of the same reversal occurs in "The Birthday of the Infanta" only now the painting is a mirror based on a painting.

In Velázquez's *Las Meninas*, the portrait that inspired Wilde's story, two court dwarfs occupy a triangular relationship to the main grouping surrounding the Infanta Margarita Theresa in the center of the painting. The achondroplastic Maria Bárbola appears on her left flanked by a second dwarf, Nicolas Pertusato, and in front, by a dog, which we might call the twin determinants of her status: not quite grown, not quite human.[11] Bárbola's dark dress contrasts with the light-colored gown of the Infanta, suggesting an affinity that is then erased when we realize that unlike the royal child, the dwarf is only an imitation female. She looks out at the

---

[10] Joyce, *Ulysses* (6).
[11] Anne Finger has created a vivid fictional portrait of Bárbola in her story "The Artist and the Dwarf."

absent subject of the artist's painting with the same degree of attentiveness that painter and Infanta do, completing the trinity of figures that regard us as we look back at them.[12]

Michel Foucault sees *Las Meninas* as a paradigm of the classical episteme by focusing on the complex mirroring between painting and viewer, the complicated—almost vertiginous—representation of the process of representation itself. As viewers of the painting, we occupy the position of the would-be subject of the painter's work; the painter's rendering is hidden from us, and we only see the back of his canvas. At the same time, the literal subject of Velázquez's painting is reflected in a mirror at the back of the studio, revealing that the objects of the artist's gaze are the King of Spain, Philip IV and his wife. Although the monarchs are not "present" in the painting, they are nevertheless ubiquitous, biologically through their daughter at the center of the painting and institutionally through the attendants, chaperones, and bodyguards that populate the canvas. Their reflection in the mirror mirrors the absent presence of court power, of which the Infanta's maids in waiting are the representation. Foucault observes, "in this picture, as in all the representations of which it is, as it were, the manifest essence, the profound invisibility of what one sees is inseparable from the invisibility of the person seeing—despite all mirrors, reflections, imitations, and portraits" (*Order*, 16).

Foucault does not elaborate on the court dwarfs (he calls them "fools") because in his reading of the classical age they do not exist as distinct identities. Rather, they are components of a *combinatoire* of positionalities and relations that contribute to the structure of knowledge. Just as they anchor one side of Velázquez's canvas, so they contribute to the "order of things" that controls all resemblance in the classical system. It is not until the modern period, marked for Foucault by Cuvier and Darwin, that such figures become visible as distinguishable types or categories. The light that floods the canvas from the artist's left falls equally upon the dwarfs as it does on the painter's canvas. As collective subject, we, the viewers, exist within this specular system. In a sense we are the subject of this painting, the painter's model and yet the absence that haunts mimesis.

So, what are dwarfs doing in this and many other early paintings? We know that Maria Bárbola was one of several short statured persons in the Spanish court at this time. Velázquez made several portraits of court dwarfs, the most famous being the portrait of Sebastian de Morra, which hangs in the Prado. Velázquez painted nine other portraits of dwarfs in the court of Philip IV who retained 110 short statured retainers.[13] Velázquez was not the first to represent these subjects. In painting from the fifteenth to eighteenth centuries, dwarfs often appear as decorative elements in

---

[12] Kenneth Clark evinces a certain anxiety about the dwarfs and attempts to explain their presence in the painting: "Her ladies-in-waiting, known by the Portuguese name of meninas, are doing their best to cajole her, and have brought her dwarfs, Maribárbola and Nicolasito, to amuse her. But in fact they alarm her almost as much as they alarm us, and it will be some time before the sitting can take place," *Looking at Pictures* (31).

[13] Dale Brown remarks, since "so much depended on his personal favor, [Philip IV] could pamper a dwarf without arousing the envy of the courtiers who were in constant attendance upon him...a dwarf's life was irrelevant." Quoted in Adelson, *The Lives of Dwarfs* (149).

painting, often flanking the central subject. One could point to Botticelli's *Adoration of the Magi* (1465–7) or Veronese's *The Discovery of the Infant Moses* (1570–5). In Vasari's *Marriage of Catherine de Medici to Henry of Orleans* (1556–9), a male and female dwarf flank the wedding couple, and in Rubens' portrait of Altheia Talbot (1620) a court dwarf stands to her left. Perhaps the most striking structural use of the dwarf figure occurs in Tiepolo's fresco *Henri III reçu à la villa Contarini* (1745) in the Musée Jacquemart-André in Paris. This large work displays the French King greeting the Doge of Venice in 1558. The representation of an alliance between French monarchy and Italian papal authority is marked by another alliance being conducted on the right side of the fresco. There, an African page greets a court dwarf who lies in a recumbent posture with his hand on a dog. The dwarf's legs extend outside of the frame of the fresco, cut into the marble frame of the museum's wall. As in *Las Meninas*, the dwarf and dog mark their species affinity, just as dwarf and African mark their racialized identities. They are both part of the court yet, like the dwarf's legs, outside of the frame of the court.

The more interesting question about Maria Bárbola (also known as Maribárbola Asquin) in *Las Meninas* is how she participates in the representational politics of the painting—why is she necessary to mimetic as much as to sovereign power?[14] In disability studies, we tend to refer to the cameo appearances of disabled persons as prostheses for narrative coherence and closure; the dwarf is not at the center of the painting because she must support the theme of gendered, national power that is hidden from us but whose position we, as viewers, occupy. Although *Las Meninas* precedes the usual dates for the emergence of biopower, yet we see in the painting's infinite regress the founding of a world based on a rationalized body. In order to do so, we must be able to distinguish, say, between a dwarf and a girl or a dog; we must understand the categories of humanness that the court reifies into law. In short, the grotesque body is foundational for the court body, just as we, as the absent subjects of the painting, replace the King's body.

In his story, "The Birthday of the Infanta," Wilde transformed this scene into a fable about recognition.[15] The dwarf, instead of serving as an architectural element of the canvas becomes a tragic hero. Instead of the young girl depicted in Velázquez's painting, the Infanta is transformed into an older adolescent, her innocence perverted into erotic demonism. The ladies in waiting—*las meninas*—who attend the Infanta become chattering harpies who reinforce and encourage the Infanta's cruel

---

[14]　Janet Ravenscroft says that Maribárbola was "part of this household for nearly 50 years, becoming *Enana de la Reina* (The Queen's Dwarf) on the death of her previous employer, a countess, in 1651. She eventually returned to Germany on 30 March, 1700... when all the dwarfs and entertainers were expelled from the court by the new Bourbon king, Philip V, as part of the French monarch's modernizing reforms." Janet Ravenscroft, "'Who Are You Looking At?' Picturing Difference in Early Modern Spain."

[15]　In her definitive article on Zemlinsky's opera version of the story, Sherry Lee sees the composer's adaptation as a drama of recognition. Drawing on the classical trope of *anagnorisis* in Aristotle, along with Paul Ricoeur's *The Course of Recognition*, Lee sees the opera expanding beyond the mirror motif of self and other "to encompass the moral and ethical issues of the politics of recognition, the struggle of marginalized subjects for social recognition of their worth and dignity" ("The Other in the Mirror," 203). I am indebted to Lee's framing of the opera's multiple cultural and musical frames.

treatment of the dwarf. The would-be grotesque sees himself mirrored in the eyes of the Infanta who becomes, in a sense, his creator, while we are able to see his true—if tragic—character within. When the dwarf sees himself in an actual mirror, he recoils in horror and dies at the Infanta's feet. Wilde was obviously fascinated with the specular power of reflection in validating reality while exposing our all-too-human bodies. Instead of the body grown old, as in *The Picture of Dorian Gray*, the dwarf's body in "The Birthday of the Infanta" is reflected against court splendor and sumptuary display. Zemlinsky's adaptation of the story used its tale of abjection and recognition to frame his relationship to his own body.

THE TRAGEDY OF THE UGLY MAN

By all accounts Alexander Zemlinsky was an ugly man. The emphasis here should be on "by all accounts" since the phrase appears in almost every reference to the composer's physiognomy, the most famous being Alma (Shindler) Mahler's characterization of her lover as "a horrid little gnome, undersized, chinless, toothless" who "cuts the most comical figure imaginable—a caricature, chinless and short with bulging eyes."[16] And this from his mistress! Most commentators explain Zemlinsky's interest in Wilde's story as reflecting an obsession with his own body, and perhaps with his Jewish and Turkish-Sephardic background. *Der Zwerg* does permit such an autobiographical reading, but the circumstances of its composition offer a more complex relationship to his era's fascination with racial and sexual purity. He commissioned the libretto from Georg Klaren who had recently finished a monograph on Otto Weininger, infamous author of *Sex and Character*, a work that influenced many modernists, including Charlotte Perkins Gilman, James Joyce, Gertrude Stein, Ludwig Wittgenstein, Franz Kafka, and Arnold Schönberg.[17] Its misogyny and anti-Semitism make it an unlikely influence on vanguard modernists, but as Slavoj Žižek says, it "hauled into the light of day the 'sexist' fantasmatic support of the dominant ideology" (97). Zemlinsky's deployment of Klaren's libretto is symptomatic of a tendency among many modernist artists to create novelty through racial and sexual difference, mocking bourgeois pretensions by adopting the primitive mask, urban demotic, and folk idiom.

Der Zwerg would hardly be the first opera in which very little happens. Alban Berg felt that there was not enough action to sustain the drama, and Theodor Adorno, despite his admiration for the music, notes that Wilde's story only "provides enough material for a single situation and whatever goes beyond that necessarily degenerates into dramatic padding" ("Zemlinsky," 125). But the non-action here serves a particularly significant function in reinforcing Weininger's racial sexology. Rather than move the action forward, characters exhibit what Gertrude Stein

---

[16] Quoted in Robert Tanitch, *Oscar Wilde on Stage and Screen* (364–5).

[17] Klaren's adherence to Weininger's views is clear in his prospectus for the libretto: "A man comes into contact with his fellow men, unaware that he is *different*…and is destroyed by a woman who, instead of seeking his *innermost* depths, does not tell him *how* he differs, but simply plays with him" (qtd. in Beaumont, 300).

might have called their "bottom natures," unchanging character traits expressed musically through a liberal use of Wagnerian leitmotifs. Ladies in waiting flutter about, gossiping while waiting for the arrival of the Infanta on her birthday. The Infanta poses and primps while receiving her birthday presents. The court chamberlain admonishes the maids to stop their chattering and chastises the Infanta for uncovering her presents. Action is reduced to the bare minimum, allowing the music to bear the weight of narrative movement.

In the most dramatic moment in a rather undramatic opera, Moorish litter bearers appear and present the Infanta with a dwarf dressed in oriental finery, a gift from an eastern sultan. The chamberlain mockingly describes the dwarf to the court as "a gift from a distant land, a knight as handsome and well proportioned as Narcissus. Apollo looks upon him with favor, for as a singer, his music is powerful; it hallows and transfigures all those who hear it" (Klaren, 77). Urged by the Infanta, the dwarf sings a love song that he accompanies on his lute. His obvious infatuation with her becomes the subject of much merriment among the ladies of the court, and the Infanta flirts with him, encouraging his ardor by giving him a white rose from her hair. The Infanta's favorite maid, Ghita, gradually becomes offended by this cruel treatment and encourages the dwarf to see himself as he is, but her attempts are futile. It is only in the last scene that he finally comes upon a mirror and realizes, for the first time, that he is not the noble knight he has been led to believe he is and that the Infanta has only been playing with his emotions. He cries out at his reflection and demands to know the truth from her. She dismisses him with a shrug, and he, after much agonizing, dies clutching the white rose. The drama of *Der Zwerg* is directed almost entirely toward this last recognition scene; all else serves to reinforce court rituals and deference. As in baroque operas, staging offers sites for sumptuous costuming, gilded casements, formal dances, and balletic positioning of the court attendants.

Such static staging provided a backdrop for Weininger's schematic treatment of gender and race, about which a brief introduction is in order. Weininger believed in a permanent bisexual condition in every individual of which each has varying fractions of male or female traits. Masculinity is at the top of the scale and femininity at the bottom. The pure male is all intellect while her sexuality and body dominate woman. Man is active, woman passive. Since in Weininger's infamous phrase, "woman is nothing," the man who falls in love with her is in actuality in love with himself.[18] Man projects his "ideal of an absolutely worthy existence, an ideal that he is unable to isolate within himself" onto woman (244). In terms developed earlier, she becomes the aesthetic object that indirectly reflects his disinterested, rational self. Were he to realize this fact—to see his desire in a mirror for example—his idealization would be shattered, his sexuality revealed as a biological imperative to reproduce. And as in Kant's aesthetics, the apprehension of beauty uncovers the potential of the Subject's creative powers; "beauty is really more a projection, an emanation of the requirements of love" (242). Man gives woman

---

[18] "Women have no existence and no essence; they are not, they are nothing." Otto Weininger, *Sex and Character* (286).

existence by turning from his inner essence toward sex. If man could overcome his sexual urges, woman would cease to exist. The Jewish male was similarly disparaged as feminine, linked in Weininger's mind with excessive reproduction and sexuality. As a self-hating Jew and homosexual himself, Weininger was unable to live the idealized categories he theorized and committed suicide aged twenty-four in a room once occupied by Beethoven.

In Klaren's libretto, Weininger's theme of projection is realized through the mirror motif that dominates the opera. When the dwarf sees himself in a mirror, he sees his uncanny double, the libido writ large in the small body. As in Freud's theory of the uncanny he recognizes something familiar about his reflection: "this is my wicked foe, who likes to mimic me. I can't destroy him" (Klaren, 109). He is no longer able to see himself reflected in the Infanta's eyes but as the world sees (and represents) him. His exotic costume, the opera's setting in a Moorish loggia, his captivity by the eastern sultan, orientalize and reinforce his Semitic associations. Although he is a positive character, in contrast to the Infanta, his devotion to the femme fatale ultimately proves his ruin.

The music of *Der Zwerg* is rather distinct from Zemlinsky's more expressionist work such as the Second Quartet or his Lyric Symphony. Sherry Lee sees the opera as divided between two tendencies, the "Infanta" element characterized by ornamental, neoclassical passages that dominate the first half, and an expressionist, more dissonant "Dwarf" motif that increases in the second half. The opera's opening is, for the most part, harmonically conventional, featuring dance motifs and ceremonial music that reinforce the archaic quality of the Spanish court and the formal preparations for the birthday celebration. The "Moorish" elements that assist in orientalizing the dwarf are marked harmonically by the sustained use of fourths and instrumentation that includes tambourines, cymbals, and triangles. In the second half, however, the gradual movement toward the dwarf's recognition is characterized by shifting key signatures and sudden transitions between major and minor keys. The extensive use of chorus in the first half gives way to duets between the Infanta or Ghita and the dwarf, which reinforce the inward, self-revelatory elements of the opera. As an allegory of Zemlinsky's physical appearance and failed relationship with Alma Mahler the opera serves as a musical autobiography of his shift from Strauss and Mahler to the Second Viennese school with which he is usually associated.

We can hear the transition between these two modes vividly in the first appearances of Infanta and dwarf. The former is represented by a triumphal entry (*Die Stunde der Gratulaton*) announced by the chamberlain. The Infanta's appearance among her retainers is sustained by a delicate dance that emphasizes the decorative formality of the presentation and the court's reinforcement of her beauty. When the dwarf is finally brought on stage on a litter his theme is marked by dotted rhythms, ominous glissandi, and what Antony Beaumont calls "frog-like hops" that imitate his physical gait (307). His theme is followed by a corolla of laughter and gossiping among the maids in waiting responding to his grotesque shape, a chorus that, however playful, nevertheless interrupts the straightforward "Infanta" motif. We could see this music as the *court's* representation of difference; we see the dwarf through conflicting musical rhetorics of decorum and imbalance.

When the dwarf sings his lute song, however, we see difference through *his* eyes and voice, anticipating as it does his ultimate apotheosis and defeat:

> O maiden, take the radiant orange that has ripened in my garden, take it! I am poor, and my garden has but one little tree. This radiant orange ripened on it, take it! The maiden lets out a proud, hard laugh, takes the silver needle from her soft hair and stabs it before throwing the radiant orange to the ground, with a deeply wounding laugh. Maiden, ah! your laughter and the needle did not pierce a blood orange—your sharp needle and sharp laughter struck me. See, I am dying, for the blood orange was my heart... (Klaren, 85)

As a kind of *liebestod* this romantic aria summarizes the tension between erotics and death that haunts the opera. The lover offers his beloved a blood orange, symbol of his heart, which she cruelly pierces with a pin. This reverse penetration of the male by the phallic female reinforces the dwarf's feminization, reflecting Weininger's description of female sexuality as the active use of coitus as a means to an end. The woman is "the missionary of sexual union...she is willing to be used by man as a tool, as a thing, as an object, to be treated as his property, to be changed and modeled according to his good pleasure" (337). As the opera progresses, such reversals increase. The dwarf increasingly abases himself before the Infanta, curling up in fetal positions clutching her white rose, kneeling before her, and in one moment of fetishistic abandon, kissing her chair.

The latter third of the opera leads up to the dwarf's recognition scene. A good deal of it is taken up with a duet between the dwarf and Ghita, the Infanta's chief chambermaid, who desires him to "see himself." She becomes the opera's therapist, asking the dwarf questions designed to prompt self-knowledge and scolding the Infanta for her deception: "You hurt him and I am supposed to heal him?" (Klaren, 103) When asked by the ladies-in-waiting what she would do if she were the Infanta, Ghita claims that she would "make all the joyless and ugly people happy through my love" (59). Ghita's compassion offers a contrast to the Infanta's cruelty, although ultimately her nurturing sustains the dwarf's infantilization and leads to his death. As she proffers a small hand mirror, the dwarf queries, "Mirror—what is that?" To which Ghita replies:

> A shining object that speaks the truth, nothing but the truth. If you have a friend, do not believe him—believe the mirror. You hold this solid, wondrous object before your eyes and observe the person that is you. (109)

The dwarf can only understand the small representation in the mirror as a deceptive "monster" that torments him. Unlike Wagner's Siegfried, whose innocence is ultimately his power, the dwarf remains in a state of narcissistic ignorance, refusing to recognize the otherness in the mirror as himself. Mimicry and mirroring are represented musically as well. Ghita and the dwarf trade a repeated ostinato figure as if to reinforce through repetition what the dwarf's refusals negate verbally. Sherry Lee summarizes the ways that Zemlinsky utilizes leitmotifs to "reflect dramatic oppositions [that] recognize each other in their musical similarities" (215). She shows, for example, how the dwarf's entrance in the early part of the opera is announced by a somber English horn solo that is repeated later when he demands to be told that the image in the mirror isn't true (217). Two moments of the dwarf's awakening, one before the court and one before himself, are joined by the same descending theme, reinforcing musically the drama of recognition in two different psychological arenas.

Klaren's libretto extrapolates from Weininger's thesis that the dwarf's fate is not that he is deformed but that he has linked his fortune to a woman. What he sees in the mirror is the emasculating power of the femme fatale. Instead of being the knight he thinks he is, he is the child to which the Infanta (herself a child) has reduced him. The dwarf, in Klaren's summary:

> is intended primarily...to represent an abstract idea: the confrontation of *every* man with *every* woman; his ugliness should be interpreted in a wider context, as representing that sense of inferiority which—as Weininger teaches...overcomes every eroticist when confronted by the object of his idolization, his lack of self-knowledge; likewise the fact that only a woman who loves can teach us that self-knowledge.
>
> (qtd. Beaumont, 301)

We may hear in Klaren's synopsis a concrete version of narrative prosthesis; the dwarf is not significant in himself except as a representation of what the librettist calls "inferiority" but which Freud would call castration. He is a sign of a lack that, as Weininger says, only a woman's love can teach us. Yet as the hero of the opera, he is not an adjunct to the narrative but its *telos*, that which must be revealed to himself. If Klaren infantilized and feminized the protagonist through a schematic application of Weininger, Zemlinsky's score—somewhere between Strauss and Schönberg—gives him a degree of tragic scale.

THE GHOST IN THE MACHINE

In my opening I spoke of the aesthetic turn as part of an ongoing reconsideration of the humanities and social sciences that has brought the body back into cultural theory. Disability studies has contributed to this turn by raising the issue of what constitutes a normal body and cognitive register: whose body speaks and by what standards of sensual pleasure? But activists were there long before disability studies entered the curriculum, crawling up the steps of the US Capitol in support of the ADA, demanding deaf administrators in education, inventing independent living accommodations, and protesting the care in institutional venues. Claiming disability, in Simi Linton's terms, is a matter of recognition—seeing the body that is not there and the body that is.[19] In our turn toward disability studies we must remember that aesthetics is not merely a branch of philosophy but a series of acts and practices that make sensible what society would prefer not to see. Of course the disabled body missing from recent turns in cultural discourse has never been missing but like the picture of Dorian Gray, hidden in disciplinary closets. The spatial turn includes universal design and architectural access; the narrative turn incorporates

---

[19] Simi Linton, *Claiming Disability: Knowledge and Identity.*

personal accounts of impairment; the linguistic turn includes the politics of American Sign Language (ASL) and Braille; the transnational turn incorporates global poverty and healthcare; the affective turn, as Tobin Siebers describes the aesthetic, treats the "sensations that some bodies feel in the presence of other bodies" (*Disability Aesthetics*, 1). My claim here has been that disability is foundational for judgments of taste, contributing to that "distribution of the sensible" that Rancière sees as the function of the aesthetic. In numerous modernist works, the figure of the dwarf has been especially prominent in raising the question of scale and recognition, fueled in many cases by eugenic ideas of sexuality.

In the process I may have reified the "natural standpoint" of the viewer by speaking of the dwarf as the "subject" of the artist's gaze rather than the agent of his own voice. What happens when the dwarf looks back and denaturalizes the natural standpoint? An increasingly visible cohort of short statured artists, activists, and performers—Peter Dinklage, Thomas Quastoff, Tom Shakespeare, Corban Walker, Colleen Fraser, Danny Woodburn—are turning the mirror back on viewers, listeners, and cultural theorists. Instead of occupying the margins of classical paintings—as decorative or architectural elements of court portraits—they occupy center stage as activists, actors, vocalists, sculptors, and disability theorists, who subject mimesis to a different optic. In one of his installations, Corban Walker appears in a video that displays his four-foot frame staring back at us through a flat screen monitor that resembles a mirror (Fig. 2.2). As Amanda Cachia says in a catalogue commentary, he adjusts and fits "into the built environment through this hyper-sized piece of technology but he has inserted himself into its very frame" ("What Can a Body Do?" 19).

In her book *Staring*, Rosemarie Garland-Thomson reminds us of the curious fact that we cannot see ourselves, that "we can only see the very particular self that we are through the mediation of images or reflections, which reverse our appearance so that what we see is a slightly distorted mirror image of how we look to others" (51). As we have seen with the multiple versions of Wilde's works, modernist authors were particularly anxious about this mediated self-knowledge. The inability to see the other condemns us to the fate of Narcissus, drowning in his own reflection. Narcissus is one of the foundational myths of modernism, a cautionary tale about the dangers of solipsism. It is a specifically masculinist phenomenon that haunts many modernist works. Buck Mulligan's outing of Stephen Dedalus' rage "at not seeing his face in the glass," turns him, in Wilde's epigram, into Caliban, a monster—but also an aesthete. We may not think of solipsism as a disability, but its manifestation in wasting invalids, neurotic husbands, tubercular convalescents, and shell-shocked veterans are variations on the theme. In the figures I have just named, solipsism is paralysis, yet it is also the lived version of the aesthetic, the *flâneur*'s detachment from the crowd, the aesthete's investment in sensation, Prufrock's fear that that "human voices [will] wake us and we drown."

Many of Wilde's works, including "The Birthday of the Infanta," enact the mirror stage of self-objectification against the background of the aesthetic, manifested in the artist's dream of an ageless portrait. Such tropes always hide or displace the material body ("The apparition of these faces in the crowd") onto an ethereal plane

Fig. 2.2. Corban Walker, still from *TV Man*, 10 May 2010, LCD monitor 65.
Copyright Corban Walker, courtesy Pace Gallery.

("Petals on a wet, black bough") released from time and space limits.[20] So long as the dwarf sees himself through the theatrical gaze of the court, he is a knight and hero, condemned to endless childhood like Peter Pan. When he sees himself as a category—*der Zwerg*—he detaches himself from the *Real* and enters the social Symbolic. Human voices wake him and he drowns. Writers and composers who looked into Velázquez's painting of the Spanish court looked, as well, into the variable body that could not be contained by the rage of Caliban at the mirror of modernity.

[20] Ezra Pound, "In a Station of the Metro," *Personae*, 109.

3

Exquisite Corporeality
Detachable Bodies of the Avant-Garde

HEADLESSNESS

The 1936 inaugural issue of the surrealist magazine *Acéphale* featured a drawing by André Masson of a headless male body holding a dagger in one hand and a flame in the other (Fig. 3.1).[1] His entrails are visible on the surface of his stomach and in the place of his genitals is a skull. Georges Bataille, the magazine's editor, interprets Masson's figure as a new form of human, neither man nor god:

> It is time to abandon the world of the civilized and its light. It is too late to be reasonable and educated—which has led to a life without appeal. Secretly or not, it is necessary to become completely different, or to cease being...Beyond what I am, I meet a being who makes me laugh because he is headless, a steel weapon in his left hand, flames like those of the Sacred Heart in his right. He reunites in the same eruption Birth and death. He is not a man. He is not a god either. He is not me but is more than me: his stomach is the labyrinth in which he has lost himself, loses me with him, and in which I discover myself as him, in other words as a monster. (181)

Representations of a headless body—or in some cases, a bodiless head—are common in Dada or Surrealist art as an attempt to imagine corporeality separate from mind, or in Bataille's terms a way of becoming "completely different, or to cease being." Masson's design offers an inversion of Leonardo's *Vitruvian Man* as the epitome of physical perfection, a male figure whose extended arms and legs inscribe a perfect circle.[2] The acephalian man, on the other hand, is a "monster," lacking the head that since Descartes signifies human autonomy and rationality. Masson's variation could be extended to other examples of avant-garde art in which the fragmentation of body parts permits new conceptions of the human. Whether figured in the metalized bodies of F. T. Marinetti's Futurism, the recombinant dolls ("poupées") of Hans Bellmer, or the separated body parts of Tristan Tzara's *The Gas Heart*, avant-garde artists and writers subjected the human body to deformation and recombination in ways that challenged modern society's pursuit of a bodily norm. They were not thinking of disabled bodies, but they were using disability and madness as windows on exquisite corporealities.

---

[1] The image reproduced here is from the July 1937 edition, numbers 3–4. Masson's design was on the cover of each issue.

[2] It is worth pointing out that the Vitruvian Man has four arms and four legs, a disfiguration that is often overlooked in favor of the figure's harmonious physical features.

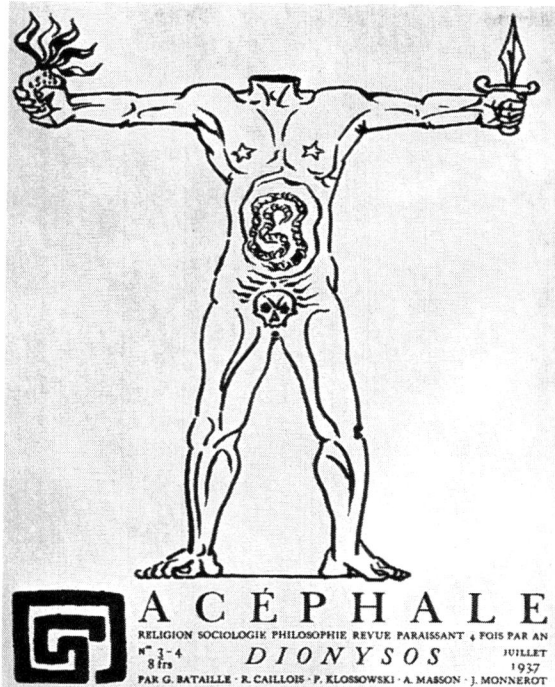

Fig. 3.1. Andre Masson, design for *Acéphale*.
© 2018 Artists Rights Society (ARS), New York / ADAGP, Paris.

In keeping with my interest in describing an *invàlid* modernism that unseats autonomy through an embodied aesthetic, I want to turn to the historic avant-garde in its various attempts to disable bodily viability.[3] In Dada, as Stephen Thomson says, "[body] parts recombine in odd ways to form bodies that are surely not viable, but may be in some way whole, at least in the sense that they compose something" (86). It is this non-viable "something" that will be the focus of this chapter, a body that challenges the presumptive naturalness of the human, a mind whose cognitive functions do not conform to intellectual norms. Imagining this post or non-human entity implicates the means of representation where the naturalized human body is a product of specific aesthetic regimes, genres, and media. Masson's variation on Leonardo is both an aesthetic and social commentary on Enlightenment notions of bodily integrity. While aesthetic dismemberment may not be a response to disability per se, it nevertheless testifies to a crisis of embodiment made salient by the rise of medical science, industrialization, and global war.

The latter—the impact of World War I—is the most obvious influence on representations of fragmented and distorted bodies in modernism with special

---

[3] I use the phrase "historic avant-garde" to differentiate it from its more general use as a descriptor for any vanguard or innovative work and to situate it in its specific timeframe from 1909 into the 1930s.

applicability to the avant-garde.[4] The massive carnage of trench warfare, the effects of sulfur gas, facial lacerations, amputations, and the psychological effects of shell shock exposed bodies traumatized by new chemical and military technologies. The poetry of soldier-poets such as Wilfred Owen, Siegfried Sassoon, and Rupert Brooke provided harrowing accounts of life in the trenches. Their accounts were matched, on the German side, by the paintings of Otto Dix, George Grosz, and Max Beckmann whose own battlefield experiences influenced their brutal depictions of war-ravaged bodies and faces.[5] A significant number of artists, musicians, and writers saw battle or witnessed its effects in hospitals or sanitaria, including Paul Wittgenstein, Paul Éluard, Umberto Boccioni, Franz Marc, Egon Schiele, Isaac Rosenberg, Gertrude Stein, Ford Madox Ford, May Sinclair, Ernest Hemingway, Max Ernst, Apollinaire, Henri Gaudier-Brzeska, and many others. Ezra Pound's elegy for the "myriad" that died "For a botched civilization" in "Hugh Selwyn Mauberley" summarizes the postwar mood of cultural loss (191). A good deal of criticism has reviewed the affective impact of the war expressed in Pound's lines but less how battlefield carnage and medical remediation might have forced artists to reconsider the body itself.[6]

While linking artistic innovation to modern warfare offers an important historical backdrop for avant-garde experiment in Europe, it needs to be placed in the context of a much larger focus on the body through medical and scientific discourse beginning in the mid-nineteenth century. As I have pointed out in my introduction, modernity's attempt to rationalize the body through comparative anatomy, "ugly laws," eugenics, racial science, and visual displays in freak shows, police photography, better baby contests, and international exhibitions contributed to the production of an aesthetically acceptable body. The term "aesthetic" itself, as Sander Gilman has noted, was applied to reconstructive surgery developed in the 1890s as part of an eugenic imperative to restore or improve the wounded or flawed body. The rise of aesthetic surgery coincided with a post-Enlightenment epistemology based on the idea that the body's surface betrays moral conditions within: "in the Enlightenment ideology of nineteenth-century medical science, the hygiene of the body became the hygiene of the spirit and that of the state. [The aesthetic surgeon] provided a type of surgical eugenics, a means of improving the individual and, through the individual, the state" (*Making*, 21). Aesthetic surgery and prosthetics played vital roles in restoring the wounded soldier in World War I, but the impulse behind these technologies can be found in earlier forms of national consolidation.

If the body is missing in classical aesthetics it erupts in multiple forms in avant-garde experiment. It may be that the repudiation of autonomous aesthetics requires

---

    [4] I am here making a distinction between modernism as a general historical phenomenon and the avant-garde as a set of specific movements within modernism that challenged ideas of autonomy. Significant research on the impact of World War I on modern literature can be found in Sara Stich, *Anxious Visions*; Paul Fussell, *The Great War*; and Maud Ellmann, "More Kicks than Pricks."

    [5] Carol Poore has provided a definitive account of such artists and the impact of German warfare in her book *Disability in Twentieth-Century German Culture*.

    [6] Maud Ellmann addresses this close connection between war and new forms of narrative. Speaking of a scene from Woolf's *Between the Acts* she observes "[it] suggests a sinister complicity between the fracturing effects of modernism and those of aerial bombardment" ("More Kicks than Pricks," 255).

a sensate body as a libidinal response. This formulation repeats a familiar binary opposition made prominent by Peter Bürger, Matei Calinescu, and Andreas Huyssen, for whom modernist autonomous art is seen as a rejection of an embodied and gendered mass culture. For Bürger, the introduction of everyday life objects and practices into the artwork—Heartfield's photomontages, Duchamp's readymades—reconciles the historic split between art and life and explicitly challenges the artisanal aura of the unique artwork. Bürger notes that when Duchamp signs a mass produced, randomly chosen object and enters it into an exhibit, he performs a double act: recognizing the category of art "work" while recognizing the institutional frame—the museum or gallery—in which the work attains value. The fact that the historic avant-garde was ultimately assimilated into the bourgeois culture it criticized marks, for Bürger, its failure to effect social change.

This influential reading seems too schematic to account for the wide range of cultural production in the early twentieth century that would include the politically progressive designs of Constructivism and Der Stijl, the incorporation of popular genres in high modernist works like T. S. Eliot's *Waste Land*, Malevich's folk inspired early paintings or jazz motifs in Ravel's first piano concerto, blues rhythms in the poetry of Langston Hughes, junk collages of Kurt Schwitters, and the blackface minstrelsy in Vachel Lindsay's "The Congo." Diagnosticians of the avant-garde tend to privilege formal issues leaving the materialities of body, sensorium, and cognition as inert content. It is the task of this chapter to complicate the presumptive opposition between autonomous art and mass culture by insinuating the sensate body into both terms, and by understanding avant-garde production as making the disordered body visible as a component of the aesthetic function. Furthermore, it is by looking at the fragmented body of the avant-garde as disabled that one may complicate Huyssen's "great divide" between high art and mass culture as a question of access and legibility.

The problem with thinking beyond the binary oppositions that usually attend discussions of modernism is that they tend to totalize all knowledge into halves: what is outside of high culture must be mass culture. The crisis that the avant-garde announces is largely epistemological: how to imagine a world that is, to paraphrase Wittgenstein, *not "all that is the case?"* The totalizing structures we identify with modernity—Fordist modes of production, eugenicist models of racial purity, positivist science, Saussurian linguistic models, a book about nothing—all leave a residue in the social identities and linguistic or economic practices that refuse to "fit" a total system. James Berger sees this "mis-fit" within modernity as a matter of disarticulation: "[if] a system is presumed to be total and without exterior or remainder, opposition must take the form of a failure of articulation (the disarticulate) or forcible exclusions—dismemberment—from the social-symbolic order (the disarticulate)" (55). Berger understands this disarticulation to be at the heart of much modernist production, the inarticulate or speech-impaired figure (Billy Budd is Berger's test case) as the "bare forked human" who exists outside the social-symbolic order. Berger's thesis is especially important for our concern with avant-garde experiment whose collective activity involves both disarticulation and dismemberment. The linguistic experiments of Gertrude Stein or Vladimir

Khlebnikov and the fragmented bodies of Surrealism cannot be reduced to codes for subterranean narratives; they must be seen as attempts to imagine identities in a process of formation. As I will point out with reference to Marinetti's *Mafarka* the attempt to imagine a new form of reproduction outside of biology veers dangerously close to Fascist ideals of the *Übermensch*. Tzara's *The Gas Heart* with its dramatis personae made of separate facial features draws from the period's awareness of facial disfiguration caused by war but permits new sensory and affective combinations out of that disfiguration.

But is the fragmented body of Surrealism or Dada, in any sense disabled?[7] It may seem that in speaking of Hans Bellmer's recombined and erotically reconfigured dolls as disabled I am engaging in a spurious form of metaphorization that detaches historical bodies from aesthetic products. The fallacy of instrumental form insists that discontinuous, non-linear language in some sense implicates fragmented, non-traditional bodies. Do progressive formal innovations necessarily imply progressive body politics? Tobin Siebers has addressed this issue by studying contemporary visual and performance artists, both disabled and able-bodied, who foreground the abjected, mad, or disabled figure as a site for critical reflections and political reconsideration. He argues that the works of Paul McCarty, Judith Scott, Tyree Guyton, or Damien Hirst "return aesthetics forcefully to its originary subject matter: the body and its affective sphere" (*Disability Aesthetics*, 2). Siebers questions not whether an artist's physical or mental impairment validates a disability aesthetic but whether the aesthetic function is challenged by work that does not presume a specific model of embodiment. Furthermore, he implies that the totality of the object or performance lies not in the product but in the affective interchange between viewer and event. This claim is especially significant in thinking about the historical avant-garde forms that provided important precedents for the artists Siebers studies.

A word about madness. In this chapter I focus largely on physical disability, but I could have profitably devoted a second chapter to a "mad" modernism. Joseph Valente, who has provided the best background for this topic, begins his account by saying that "Modernism must be counted a seminal moment in the cultural representation of cognitive disability" (379), but one could easily reverse the terms and say that cognitive disability fueled a good deal of modernist innovation. Psychological categories that became popular during the early twentieth century—hysteria, anxiety, paranoia, neurasthenia, melancholia, the uncanny—dominate modernist works such as Henry James' ghost stories and Charlotte Perkins Gilman's

---

[7] Janet Lyon addresses this question when speaking of Leonora Carrington whose writing and art, often identified with Surrealism, complicate the humanist division between human and animal. Although several of her works do feature disabled characters (*The Hearing Trumpet* has a deaf protagonist) disability as a specific category is absent in Carrington's work. "Rather," as Lyon says, "normate assumptions about embodiment are dissolved by the possibilities and sheer extensivity of life itself. Thus there are no right or wrong bodies because Carrington's is fundamentally a *zoe*-sphere… animated by the continuum across life and death" ("Carrington's Sensorium," 170). This is an important way to read disability where it is absent or where it haunts the borders of work—as I develop the theme in Chapter 7 concerning *Animal's People*—that refuses the term "human" as a self-evident term for agency and intention.

"The Yellow Wall-Paper" as well as William Faulkner's *The Sound and the Fury*, André Breton's *Nadja*, Schönberg's *Pierrot Lunaire* or *Erwartung*, Joseph Conrad's *Secret Agent*, Edvard Munch's *The Scream*, and Beckett's *Murphy*. But we need to distinguish between the "degenerate" thesis—mental deficiency as a sign of cultural decay—and more utopian versions theorized in the avant-garde. Whereas high modernist literature in T. S. Eliot, Virginia Woolf, or Thomas Mann could use mental disorders as a sign of degeneration (or in the case of Eliot, personal malaise), Surrealists and Dadaists celebrated madness as an alternative to rational, logical cognition. Formal operations to liberate the unconscious such as psychic automatism and aleatory methods of composition attempted to model the logic of dreams or the psychotic speech of mental patients. Surrealism was the most active adherent in an aesthetic of madness and Breton, Bataille, Dali, and others drew directly on psychoanalytical literature and medical research.[8] In a manifesto published in *La Révolution Surréaliste* of 1928 Breton and Aragon celebrate hysteria as "the greatest poetic discovery of the latter part of the century," and as Jean-Michel Rabaté notes, Joyce's *Finnegans Wake* was written for Lucia Joyce, James Joyce's "psychotic daughter" (64, 73).

In this chapter I will look at several writers and artists—F. T. Marinetti, Tristan Tzara, and Frida Kahlo—who represent three of the major aesthetic movements of the historical avant-garde—Futurism, Dada, and Surrealism respectively. Kahlo, as an artist who lived with numerous physical impairments and chronic pain, provides the most explicit correlation of artistic practice and disability, but by including examples of works that do not directly address physical or mental disability I hope to consider "exquisite corporeality" as a prominent feature of modernist experiment. Far from aspiring to the condition of music or sculpture, the work of Marinetti, Tzara, and Kahlo sought to put flesh on the aesthetic, documenting its ardors, pains, and that derangement of the senses Rimbaud saw as necessary for a truly modern poetry.

"AN END-RUN AROUND OEDIPUS": MARINETTI AND *MAFARKA*

According to F. T. Marinetti among the many things that "we" don't want in a futurist paradise are "women, the sedentary, invalids, the sick and all the prudent counselors" (*Selected Writings*, 46). Marinetti's inclusion of "invalids and the sick" along with women and counselors suggests the kind of serial exclusion that was common among eugenicists and criminal pathologists of the period. In the writings of Max Nordau or Otto Weininger, one form of social degeneration infects others and leads, through intercourse, to genetic decay. Against what Marinetti calls "vacillating lives" "we prefer violent death and glorify it as the only thing worthy of man that beast of prey" (46). Anticipating Walter Benjamin's view that Nazism aestheticized politics such that one could witness one's own destruction as spectacle,

[8] On Surrealism's relationship to Freud, see Jean-Michel Rabaté, "Loving Freud Madly."

Marinetti's remarks remind us that the romance of biofuturity contains the seeds of its annihilation. Marinetti uses a collective pronoun to dismiss women and invalids in a document—the manifesto—dedicated to the performative utterance.[9] Such acts of interpellation allowed certain progressive artists to endorse an embodied future against a disabled past. "And like young lions we ran after Death," he says in his first manifesto, racing through urban space in a speeding car (40). The aesthetic of speed is accomplished by youth ("the oldest of us is 30"), male, agile, defiant, and able-bodied (43).

The production of a new collective pronoun announces the birth of a new kind of human, and in his first futurist manifesto Marinetti makes clear that its emergence must exist outside of biological reproduction. He describes setting off with his young friends in automobiles through the city: "Let's break out of the horrible shell of wisdom and throw ourselves like pride-ripened fruit into the wide, contorted mouth of the wind!"[10] Suddenly, his car crashes into a ditch whereupon Marinetti delivers a benediction on his earlier life:

> Oh! Maternal ditch, almost full of muddy water! Fair factory drain! I gulped down your nourishing sludge; and I remembered the blessed black breast of my Sudanese nurse. When I came up—torn, filthy, and stinking—from under the capsized car, I felt the white-hot iron of joy deliciously pass through my heart!   (41)

This baptism into futurism involves replacing the biological with the industrial mother, Sudanese nurse with black sludge. Based to some extent on events in Marinetti's own childhood, this auto-incarnation allows him to be resurrected into a future in which "[w]e will sing of great crowds, excited by work, by pleasure, and by riot; we will sing of the multicolored, polyphonic tides of revolution in the modern capitals" (42). Hal Foster calls this "'autogenetic fantasy...an end-run around Oedipus,' for it positions Marinetti as father, mother, and sacrificial son in one" (*Prosthetic Gods*, 119). Once he has transcended his past (and his passéiste early symbolism), his biological parents, and nurse, he may write his manifesto for the future. Marinetti's Sudanese nurse represents both his childhood past but also a colonial history that "nursed" Italy into modernity and that must now be transcended.

A more elaborate version of this self-creation story occurs in Marinetti's early novel, *Mafarka the Futurist* (1909), a Nietzschean call to arms against feminization, symbolist poetry, and racial others. Its heightened rhetoric, scenes of sexual mayhem, battlefield carnage, and quasi-magical settings situate the novel well outside of the realist tradition and far from the internal monologues of much modernist fiction. Set in Northern Africa, the novel focuses on Mafarka-el-Bar, an Arabian king who seeks to conquer all of Africa. The first half of the novel concerns Mafarka's military victories over his uncle, King Boubassa, and later King Brafane-el-Kibir. The military allegory pits Arab against Negro, white against black, Europe against the Orient. In the second half of the novel Mafarka seeks to extend his

---

[9] On the use of the collective pronoun in manifestos, see Janet Lyon, *Manifestoes* (23–6).
[10] The resemblance to Jack Kerouac's characterization of Neal Cassady driving like a madman in *On the Road* suggests links between Futurist and Beat aesthetics.

legacy by producing a son parthenogenically, "without the help of the vulva" (Barbara Spackman wittily compares Mafarka to a futurist Geppetto [90]). His offspring is Gazourmah, an Icarus-like figure, created out of wood, whose wings allow him to escape the earth. In a semi-erotic moment, Mafarka breathes life into his mechanical son through a kiss that awakens him. Gazourmah subsequently kills his father and flies off to conquer the sun.[11]

Marinetti's biofuturist fantasy of self-reproduction is accompanied by (perhaps produced through) descriptions of rape, carnage, and revenge as Mafarka lays waste to his enemies in bloody battle. Like Odysseus, however, he is also a clever rhetorician who uses his verbal skills in a multi-layered story at the center of the novel. Seeking to defeat his enemy, Brafane-el-Kibir, Mafarka disguises himself as a filthy, "hobbling…crippled beggar" in order to gain entrance to the king's inner sanctum (37). He offers a story to Brafane designed to secure him greater power while insidiously rendering his armies vulnerable. The story within the story is based on Mafarka's earlier career as a horse trader who sells a "superb stallion" to the Devil (44). The horse's vast size and fiery mane mark its magical qualities, and his vast *zeb* or penis "encrusted with sapphires" excites all of the mares he encounters (44). The Devil is unable to control the horse due to its huge size and speed, and he is cast onto the ground. In revenge, he castrates the horse, serving the *zeb* to Mafarka in a dish disguised as a fish. By eating the *zeb* Marfaka obtains the same sexual potency as the horse, growing his penis so long that it achieves the length of eleven meters. With his enlarged cock he satisfies many servant girls and ultimately uses it to conquer his uncle, Boubassa, who upon adopting a passive sexual posture becomes vulnerable to the extensively tumescent Mafarka who seizes his crown and lands.

Brafane is so entranced with this story of power-through-sexual potency that he asks Mafarka the whereabouts of this miraculous horse. Mafarka convinces Brafane that the fiery stallion can be seen in the distance beyond the king's castle. The king gathers his armies together and sets off in hot pursuit. He gives Mafarka his favorite horse, Nebid, to accompany him, but once Mafarka mounts Nebid, he shoots off like an arrow with the armies following. Mafarka speeds ahead and cuts wounds into the horse's flank, allowing Brafane's men to see Nebid as the same as the castrated, red-marked horse of his story. After a wild chase, Mafarka manages to have all of the armies clash together in an ocean of destruction, "like a great lacustrine structure, into a lake of pitch" (60). Needless to say, Marinetti's "plot" and narrative style are in excess of any plausible mimetic rationale but, like Mafarka's tale within the tale, seek to incite affective response that leads to action.

There are familiar elements in this story that resemble Odysseus' masquerading as a beggar upon his return to Ithaca or Scheherazade's life-extending tales. The story allows Mafarka to exhibit his military craft through rhetorical skills that excite his listeners to destruction without his having to wield a lance. Alice Kaplan refers to Marinetti's rhetoric as performative since its function is not merely to represent military might but to *effect* a military outcome by leading Mafarka's enemy to destruction. The phallic focal point—the horse's *zeb*—is the occasion for

---

[11] On the "homophobic economics" of Marinetti's novel, see Barbara Spackman, "Mafarka and Son."

male bonding and the coalescence of power. The story as Kaplan says "becomes true merely because it is believed, although it is 'about' nontruth" (80). Kaplan notes that the story's various forms of disguise—the phallus as fish, Mafarka as beggar—"are so many codes for fiction and for fiction's own phallic power" (80). As Andrew Hewitt says, "Marinetti's texts are not just about machines, they *are* machines" (33).

Mafarka's fabrication of his son, Gazourmah, like the construction of his story, brings the two elements of futurist aesthetics together: biofuturity built on a new performative language and a phallic imperative that transcends the phallus. In producing a son parthenogenically Mafarka becomes a mother, fulfilling Marinetti's futurist desire for a world beyond women. In his preface to the novel Marinetti indicates his own self-generating prophecy: "I tell you that the mind of man is an unpracticed ovary...It is we who are the first to impregnate it!" (3). Gazourmah must not be born through heterosexual conception but constructed out of wood and metal and "fertilized" by the mother/father's kiss. He is born as a futurist through the erasure of women and reproductive sexuality. The "maternal ditch" Marinetti escapes in his manifesto is now the female body itself, rendered inert by the male artificer. The result is a therapeutic cleansing of all "blemishes that come from the inefficient vulva and bias us to old age and death!" Marinetti's misogynist and homophobic conflation of female biology and disability produces a metalized human uncontaminated by procreation and free from collectivist productive labor.

Marinetti situates his futurist allegory in an unidentified region of Africa, merging Arab and African cultures, names, and racial identities. Marinetti was himself born in Alexandria and had a Sudanese nurse, so that the fantastic tale of self-transformation is also the futurist author's self-fabrication. Furthermore he served in the Italian army during the Italy–Turkey conflict in Libya in 1911, and although his novel was written prior to this political conflict, he was certainly thinking of Italy's colonial adventures in Northern Africa in placing his conflict between an Arab king and black Africans. His incorporation of his own history through a fantasy of parthenogenesis is accomplished through the metaphor of an animated, metal-lined aircraft that rises above earthly conflict to conquer the heavens. Subsequent futurist artists such as Giacomo Balla, Filippo Masoero, Gerardo Dottori, and Tullio Crali devoted their futurist art to representing the airplane and particularly the unique perspective it offered on the landscape far below.[12] In *Mafarka* the male body as machine represents several layers of transcendence—release from the earth, rejection of the Oedipal family romance, transcendence of feminine and somatic features. Having avoided "the inefficient vulva" in producing Gazourmah parthenogenically, Mafarka is vanquished by his son who throws him into the sea—a reversal of the Icaran story in which the father, Daedalus, escapes the Cretan labyrinth while his son drowns after flying too close to the sun. Kaplan summarizes the story's denouement by noting that "Gazouramah is an Icarus whose daring is rewarded, and who kills his father *because* he is not a father (a master), but a

---

[12] On futurist interest in aviation, see essays by Emily Braun and Matteo Fochessati in Vivien Greene, *Italian Futurism, 1909–1944.*

mother" (83). Rather than see Gazourmah as a triumph of the male will over the feminine Kaplan rightly understands him as a fusion of the two elements in a new form of the human.

Whereas other modernists of the era looked to archaic civilizations and classic myth, futurists looked to the future through the lens of the present. They did so by imagining a body outside of the *bios*, a fusion of human and machine. Recent cultural theory has returned to this theme in a postmodern context, whether in Donna Haraway's cyborgs, Katherine Hayles' post-humanism, or Stacy Alaimo's theory of trans-corporeality.[13] Where contemporary theory imagines a different body and mind through computers and robotics Marinetti drew from the scripture of Darwin and pasted it onto a new industrial economy. Nature and the sentimental tradition that valorized domestic and rural life had to go, replaced by automobile and airplane but also by words set free from their generic and rhetorical past.

DETACHABLE SENSATIONS: TRISTAN TZARA

Marinetti's manifestos are designed, as Janet Lyon says, to interpellate a constituency that does not yet exist. The plural pronoun of the manifesto is an imagined community joined by the sheer performative force of rhetoric. Eschewing logical proof and syllogistic development, the manifesto challenges, cajoles, hectors in order to incite affective response. Assisted by the use of large font, capitals, exclamation marks, and numbered lists, the manifesto offers a sensual alternative to more reasoned argumentative prose. This quality is reinforced in Marinetti's "Tactilism" manifesto that emphasizes touch as an alternative to the philosophical privileging of sight and sound. In order to develop this haptic sensibility, he suggests that the reader should enlarge the senses by the following exercises:

1. to wear gloves for several days, during which time the brain will force the condensation into your hands of a desire for different tactile sensations;
2. to swim underwater in the sea, trying to distinguish interwoven currents and different temperatures tactilistically;
3. every night, in complete darkness, to recognize and enumerate every object in your bedroom. (*Selected Writings*, 110)

Developing the "art of touch," as he calls it, may remind one of the sensory deprivation exercises used to educate able-bodied students into the experience of disability.[14] By using a wheelchair or wearing a blindfold during the day the student may

---

[13] "Imagining human corporeality as trans-corporeality, in which the human is always intermeshed with the more-than-human world, underlines the extent to which the substance of the human is ultimately inseparable from 'the environment'" (Stacy Alaimo, *Bodily Natures*, 2).

[14] Disability advocates, critical of such simulation exercises, claim they limit the experience of bodily or sensory impairment to only one area—moving through public spaces without adequate signage, ramps, electronic doors, etc.—and thus present a false picture of daily life with a disability. Others complain that these exercises are designed to foster pity among able-bodied persons rather than develop solidarity around the political issues raised by disability.

experience what it would be like to be paralyzed or blind. These pedagogical exercises are designed to stimulate new forms of awareness and cognition, but Marinetti's purpose is primarily aesthetic, "toward the perfection of spiritual communication between human beings, through the epidermis" (111). He explains that the "distinction between the five senses is arbitrary" and that tactilism may promote new forms of aesthetic appreciation.

David Serlin notes that explorations of tactile encounters form an important feature of modernism, one that dethrones the imperial eye and distributes sensation among the various senses. Experimentation with tactility was not limited to aesthetics, however. As Serlin points out, a display at the 1932 Third International Congress of Eugenics taught young women to develop consumerist skills by differentiating qualities of fur by touch. Through an interactive display of multiple pelt samples, the display provided a "specialized test for sense of elegance: quality in Fur" that would confirm that the "ability to distinguish 'quality' fur through tactile means was scientifically verifiable as an inherited trait" ("At your Fingertips," 2). Serlin then discusses works by surrealist artists like Méret Oppenheim's fur-lined teacup or Marinetti's "Sudan-Paris" tactile construction (a panel made of various textured materials—sponge, sandpaper, wool brush, wire brush) to show how avant-garde artists used the tactile qualities of materials to confuse and complicate what the eye takes for granted: "Tactile modernity might best be described as a meta-phenomenon that began to take shape in the first decades of the twentieth century as a result of competing forces seeking either to transform the modality of touch into a distal experience that separates subject and object or to exploit the modality for its proximal relations that deepen the breakdown between subject and object" (10).

Serlin's comparison of eugenicist and artistic uses of tactility reinforces the close connection between forces that sought to regularize the body through categorization and measurement and those aesthetic gestures that denaturalized the body. The use of touch to affirm one's genetic superiority, guided by science's presumed objectivity, is challenged by the Surrealists' attempt to "force the viewer to encounter an ordinary domestic object...in order to lay bare the uncanny and erotic qualities hidden in its recesses or else in the recesses of the viewer's brain" (3). The fusion of political, cultural, and physiological realms has implications for disability; it allows us to think beyond discrete sensory categories to the interplay of, say, sight and touch. For a person who is blind, obviously olfactory, tactile, and auditory senses contribute to what can be known just as for a person who is deaf the eye takes certain precedence. Artists who disaggregated the senses and redistributed their functions may have wanted to unseat the traditional hierarchies accorded to each sense, but they also revealed intersections between sensation and the social body.

René Magritte's 1937 painting, *La Race Blanche* (*The White Race*, Fig. 3.2) complicates this aspect further by linking sensation and race. One of several works created under the same title during this period and apparently indebted to Picasso's 1931 *Figures on a Sea Shore*, *The White Race* reduces the face in a portrait to four of the five sensory organs, arranged to form a dolmen-like structure with sight at the top and olfaction at the bottom. Although the sense of tactility is not immediately apparent in the painting, it is implicit in the surfaces and skin of each sensory

Fig. 3.2. René Magritte, *La Race Blanche.*
© 2018 C. Herscovici / Artists Rights Society (ARS), New York.

organ. The contingent relationship between image and tactility was reinforced in a bronze sculpture cast posthumously in 1967 that would allow viewers (at least in certain museum environments) to touch and feel the organs of sensation, now arranged in the shape of a female nude. Aristotle in *De anima* ranked the senses hierarchically with sight at the top and touch at the bottom, a fact given architectural emphasis in Magritte's witty painting.

The work's title indicates that sensory organs are constitutive for racial identity, the white race defined by its presumed phenotypic difference from people with darker skins. Magritte's deconstruction of Aristotle's hierarchies by seeing them as validating a "white race" suggests the degree to which the senses have been used to rationalize racial as well as sensory divisions. The painting's oval frame reinforces the rhetoric of pictorialism embodied in portrait or bust. Here the face has been reduced to its sensory orifices, disconnected from their spatial arrangement on the face. The dismemberment of sensory organs allows us to "see" sensations as isolated objects, divorced from the body and reinterpreted as sculptural elements. It also allows us to revisit racial characteristics not as "innate" features of character but as products of the regimentation of sensory regimes. It is worth noting that in another painting of the same title, the sculptural collection of sense organs replaces the face of a female nude, her body a collection of separated body parts—as if to suggest the constructed and sexualized nature of racial hierarchies.

Raoul Hausmann's *Holzkopf* (1918) or *Mechanical Head* (Fig. 3.3) offers a variation on Magritte's theme, albeit from a rather different aesthetic vantage. The Dada artist features a wooden mannequin head wearing a tin cup for a hat, a tape measure running down his forehead. Instead of his right ear, Hausmann substitutes

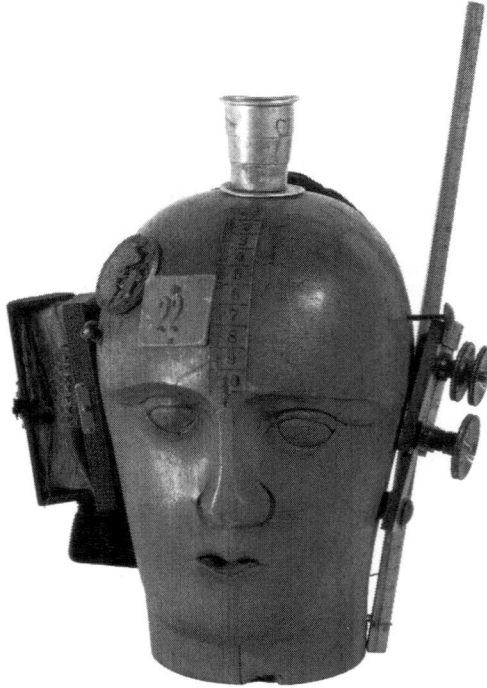

Fig. 3.3. Raoul Hausmann, *Mechanical Head.*
© 2018 Artists Rights Society (ARS), New York / ADAGP, Paris.

an open jewel box and for his left a ruler attached to a tripod. A wallet is glued to the back of the head. The implication according to Hausmann is that "human consciousness [is] nothing but negligible accessories, pasted on the surface, nothing but a hairdresser's mannequin with a pretty wig."[15] Hausmann speaks of the head as prosthetic, attached to objects that measure, catalogue, adorn, or support it. The separation of body from mind is now revealed as a product of a consumerist mentality; the head instead of being the seat of knowledge is a mannequin, its features the contents of a jewel box. The objects attached to the head are not arbitrary insofar as rulers and tape measures were often used to measure craniums in anthropometric experiments. Hausmann's *Mechanical Head*, and Masson's design for *Acéphale* discussed earlier in this chapter, represent two versions of the avant-garde's attack on Cartesian rationality by focusing on the body divorced from intellect and the mind as social prosthesis.

Dada's liberation of the word is accompanied by an explosion of the sensations, nowhere more vividly represented than in Tristan Tzara's farcical theater piece, *The Gas Heart* (1921) where the human head is represented through isolated sensory organs

---

[15] Quoted in Jed Rasula, *Destruction Was my Beatrice* (84).

and body parts. Its characters include Eye, Mouth, Nose, Ear, Neck, and Eyebrow. The titular figure, the Gas Heart, is a non-speaking character who wanders distractedly about the stage, a silent chorus to the sensory derangement that provides the play's *mise-en-scène*. The name "gas heart" fuses two seemingly incompatible realms of the chemical and biological that were becoming increasingly united in an industrial world. Although our current use of the term "gas" suggests petroleum products and automobile culture, in the context of the Great War and the devastating use of sulfur gas, the oxymoronic title has a different register. In John Singer Sargent's 1918 painting, *Gassed*, a line of soldiers wearing blindfolds walk in single file amidst a pile of corpses. Each blind soldier walks with his hand on the person in front—a reference perhaps to Pieter Bruegel the Elder's allegorical painting, *Parable of the Blind*. Although the painting is made in the realist pictorial rhetoric of Courbet, its historical referent points toward the world transformed by chemical warfare. A work like *Gassed* helps to contextualize Tzara's sense that the seat of the emotions in classical literature had been invaded by the grim realities of the present. Whatever verbal hijinks may be present in the play, its title hints at the oxymoronic collisions wrought by chemical weapons.

The play consists of disjointed dialogues among the various characters, their conversations consisting mainly of canned social speech ("how true how true how true...") and non sequiturs (249). Repetition is the dominant rhetorical feature, similar to that in Gertrude Stein's plays, and speeches seldom bear any relationship to a character's action or, indeed, identity. Stanton Garner offers an important disability reading of the play by focusing on its dramatization of the disfiguration, defacement, and disability caused by the recently completed war. Without implying a direct correlation between the play's characters and battlefield trauma, Garner situates Tzara's drama in a world (Zurich–Paris) where the impact of wartime violence was evident in soldiers returning from the front. Whereas most treatments of *The Gas Heart* focus on its theatrical innovations and formal discontinuities, Garner rightly observes that "the act of fragmenting the body onstage and in language, like the radical disfigurements of war-time combat, calls into question such notions as identity, the body-mind continuum, and the human itself" (510). Tzara in his preface attempts to dispel the idea that his Dada play has any real-life significance by calling it a "hoax" that "will satisfy only industrialized imbeciles who believe in the existence of men of genius" (246). But the fragmentation of the body into parts and the violent disconnection between language and action suggest a more accurate representation of the period's trauma. Despite Tzara's claim in his preface that the script "brings no technical innovation to the theater" *The Gas Heart* inaugurates a long tradition of theatrical deconstruction that would lead to Ionesco, Brecht, and Beckett.

Whereas Marinetti and his fellow Futurists celebrated war, Dadaists opposed it, fleeing to Zurich and often satirizing militarism in their plays. In *The Gas Heart* this satire seems focused on the moneyed interests that support war: "Statues jewels roasts / statues jewels roasts" (246). Eye's opening speech marks the upper-class world of commercial value whereas his second speech, "cigar pimple nose / cigar pimple nose" indicates a more proletarian perspective (247). The following dialogue between Mouth and Eye is symptomatic of the enervated conversation in bourgeois theater:

> MOUTH: The conversation is lagging isn't it?
> EYE: Yes, isn't it.
> MOUTH: Very lagging, isn't it?
> EYE: Yes, isn't it?
> MOUTH: Naturally, isn't it?
> EYE: Obviously, isn't it? (247)

Since this interchange occurs at the beginning of the play, before any "conversation" has occurred, it enacts what it indicts.

Despite Tzara's claim to his play's being an intentional "hoax" there are passages that hint of a more critical intent. Perhaps the most referential passage in the play is delivered by Ear who, speaking of no one in particular, observes:

> His neck is narrow but his foot is quite large. He can easily drum with his fingers or toes on his oval belly which has already served as a ball several times during rugby. *He is not a being because he consists of pieces.* Simple men manifest their existences by houses, important men by monuments. (249)

Here Tzara describes a body divided into "pieces" that as a consequence cannot be considered a "being." His enumeration of neck, foot, fingers, toes, and belly seems congruent with his subsequent remark about the differences between "simple" and "important" men. Just as the body is a congeries of separate body parts, so identity is manifested by material possessions—simple men by houses, and important men by monuments. A social critique is embedded in a biological reality that belies Tzara's satiric intent. Where the Futurists imagined a new being manifest in a body transformed into an airplane, Dadaists deconstructed any such totality into its parts. Nose's affirmative response to Ear's remark ("How true how true how true…") is followed by Eyebrow's seeming self-reflexive comment on his own language: "'Where,' 'how much,' 'why' are monuments. Like, for example, Justice. What beautifully regular functioning, practically a nervous tic or a religion" (249). The Eyebrow, one of the face's most expressive features, argues for the monumentality of prepositions that underlie abstract concepts like "Justice" that may serve either as a "nervous tic or a religion." Far from being arbitrary, such speeches redirect the categorical imperatives of truth, justice, power, and religion by pointing to the hierarchies inherent in each.

It would be interesting to think of Tzara's fragmentation of the face as an early anticipation of problems raised by philosophical attempts such as that of Levinas or Buber to render the face as that which confers identity. The face of the other in Levinas implies an obligation toward another person. Unlike more humanist versions that regard the other is a variant of the Self, the Other for Levinas is radically other, resisting any attempt to subsume it into oneself. It is across this unbridgeable gap that language proceeds, as Levinas says, "from absolute difference" (194). But when the face is not present or when the face has been fragmented into parts, speech—as Tzara says—may no longer confer "being." Judith Butler summarizes the ethical barrier that the face in Levinas faces:

> The face, if we are to put words to its meaning, will be that for which no words really work; the face seems to be a kind of sound, the sound of language evacuating its sense, the sonorous substratum of vocalization that precedes and limits the delivery of any semantic sense. (*Precarious Life*, 134)

Butler is not thinking of avant-garde literature here, but she does anticipate the relationship between the precarious sense of being that the other's face confers and our inability to express that sense. By detaching speech from actor and sensory organs from body, Tzara turns the face into "a kind of sound" or "that or which no words really work." At one point Mouth speaks of its solitude in the face of the absent face: "Everybody does not know me. I am alone here in my wardrobe and the mirror is blank when I look at myself" (254). In my discussion of Zemlinsky's opera, *Der Zwerg* in Chapter 2 I note that the dwarf encounters his otherness by looking at himself in a mirror and thus perishes, but here Mouth describes a solitude that stems from the *absence* of a reflection. Instead of a self that is constituted by the other, Mouth—divorced from its function as a communicational vehicle—stresses an affinity with animal and vegetable life: "Also I love the birds at the ends of lit cigarettes. Cat's all animals and all vegetables. I love cats, birds, animals, and vegetables which are the projection of Clytemnestra in the courtyard, bedding, vases and meadows" (254). Mouth may not have its existence conferred by the other's face, but it is not denied access to a larger animate world of "cats, birds, animals, and vegetables."

Levinas' emphasis on the face is dominated by sight. He opens his chapter on "Ethics and the Face" by saying that "access to beings concerns vision, it dominates those beings, exercises a power over them" (194). In order to encounter the Other we must be able to see the Other's face, and while this may be obvious it poses a problem for those persons who are unable to see or who, like slaves, are often invisible. Rosemarie Garland-Thomson connects this fact to the larger phenomenon of staring in which the appearance of disability "makes demands on the viewer" in a manner similar to that which Levinas theorizes. Tzara's play undercuts the ocularcentric emphasis by presenting discourse, however discontinuous, between all sensory organs—as if the incomprehensible face could speak on its own terms without the necessity of responding to a specific address. A person with sight-impairment or a person who is deaf is no less a "being," in Levinas' terms by communicating with others, through speech, Braille, or sign language. "Language is a relation between separated terms," Levinas says, and in Tzara's play this relationality is embodied in the faces reduced to its sensory organs (195).

Taking Levinas' idea that the face confers an ethical imperative not to kill, we could return to the idea that *The Gas Heart* is an anti-war play. It does not attack power directly but stages power as a body without organs, a face without features. In the non-recognition of characters to each other, the "truth" of their temperament is revealed:

EYE ... Are you perhaps awaiting further sensational revelations regarding my
   temperament?
Exit Mouth.
Eye falls to the stage.
NOSE: Huge.
NECK: Fixed.
NOSE: Cruel.
NECK: Broad.
NOSE: Small.
NECK: Short.
NOSE: Shrill ... etc. (254–5)

This sequence of adjectival speeches goes on for a full page, illustrating perhaps the
importance of sensation in what Eye calls "revelations" of temperament. Responses
to Eye's question about revelations include adjectives without complements, parts
of speech without a syntax, held together by the fiction of dialogue.

The performative features of Tzara's play were realized in its initial reception. In the
final performance in Paris in July of 1923 with characters wearing costumes designed
by Sonia Delaunay, Paul Éluard leaped on stage, protesting against an earlier performance in which André Breton was ejected from the audience. Éluard erupted
from the audience, hit Tzara in the face (appropriately enough) and was ejected by
stagehands.[16] It was the end of Dada and, perhaps, the beginning of Surrealism.

FRIDA KAHLO: DETESTING SURREALISM

In Frida Kahlo's late *Self-Portrait with the Portrait of Doctor Farill* (1951) (Fig. 3.4)
the artist sits in a wheelchair next to a portrait of her doctor that stands on an easel.
The painting was used effectively for the cover of Rosemarie Garland-Thomson's
foundational book, *Extraordinary Bodies*, in which she notes "that disability is a
representation, a cultural interpretation of physical transformation or configura-
tion, and a comparison of bodies that structures social relations and institutions" (6).
Kahlo's portrait of her doctor is a representation of this representation, a reversal of
the medical model by which disability is narrated by the doctor's diagnosis, in this
case that of Dr. Juan Farill who treated her for many years. By representing her
doctor rather than being the subject of *his* representation Kahlo provides a critical
perspective on the patient–doctor relationship. And while it testifies to her
affection for Dr. Farill (she gave the painting to him as a gift) it also marks her own
authority as another kind of body artist. It also complicates the self-portrait genre
by recognizing that just as her doctor is the subject of her painting, so she is the
subject of her own self-invention.

---

[16] On the Éluard incident, see Rasula, *Destruction Was my Beatrice* (196).

Fig. 3.4. Frida Kahlo, *Self Portrait with the Portrait of Dr. Farril.*
© 2018 Banco de México Diego Rivera Frida Kahlo Museums Trust, Mexico, D.F. / Artists Rights Society (ARS), New York.

I see this painting as a somewhat anomalous work in the Surrealist tradition with which Kahlo was associated.[17] In contrast to the work of Salvador Dali, Hans Bellmer, André Masson, Man Ray, and other male Surrealists who represented the female body by violent disruptions or fetishized sexual organs, Kahlo uses her disability as both the subject and means of her painting, as suggested by her conflation of bleeding heart and artist's palette. Amanda Cachia notes that male Surrealists often transformed women's bodies into grotesque shapes or collections of body parts, reflecting a misogynist fear of the sexual and reproductive female body ("Disabling Surrealism," 132). Kahlo uses her own "abnormal" body to gain a degree of agency over how her body is represented. Moreover, she used her body in a variety of poses and costumes to complicate the act of self-portraiture, here with cropped hair, there posing as *la Malinche*, elsewhere a plant growing roots.

---

[17] In 1938 André Breton saw Kahlo's painting *What the Water Gave Me* and declared it an example of "pure surrealism." He subsequently published reproductions of the painting in *Minotaure* and his book *Surrealism and Painting*. Being anointed by Breton was significant, but Kahlo's relation to aspects of Surrealist practice such as psychic automatism make her somewhat of an outlier in the movement. Her iconography and stylistic choices are equally dedicated to Latin American religious traditions and to the devotional *retablo*.

Cachia develops this theme in the work of contemporary disabled artists such as Luis Bufano, Chun Shan (Sandie) Yi, and Artur Zmijewski who foreground their non-traditional bodies by drawing on motifs explored in the earlier Surrealist movement.

As is well known, Kahlo lived with a variety of impairments. She contracted polio at the age of six that resulted in one leg being shorter than the other (some have speculated that she was born with spina bifida). When she was eighteen, a collision between the bus in which she was riding and a trolley resulted in a broken spinal column, numerous fractures, and internal injuries that left her unable to bear children. She lived with pain throughout her life, and in 1952 her right lower leg was amputated, due to gangrene. She candidly represented her physical condition in numerous self-portraits, drawing from indigenous Latin American traditions and incorporating, later in life, aspects of her political activism. She often appears with a brace, occasionally bearing bleeding stigmata, pierced by arrows, or prone on a hospital gurney.[18] While disability is prominent in her iconography, what is more significant is the degree to which her depiction of pain and hospitalization intersect with her struggles with gender identification, cultural heritage, and political history.

Perhaps the most vivid representation of pain occurs in her 1944 portrait, *The Broken Column*, in which she appears bare breasted, wearing a brace, the lower part of her body covered in a white drape. The spinal column that caused her excruciating pain throughout her life is visible through her skin, resembling an Ionic column. She stands, tears streaming down her face, with a loose white robe around her waist against a desert landscape, the earth cracked and dry. Parallels to classical paintings of Christ on the cross or St. Anthony are suggested by the nails that pierce her body. The "column" that is literally at the center of her painting and body, with its Ionic capital at the top, suggests that just as the spinal column supports the bodily frame, so it supports classical architectural forms in Western culture. The painting is a summary of Kahlo's various themes: her infertility, signaled by the barren landscape that appears in numerous paintings; the "broken" column of Western civilization in the last years of World War II. Its references to Renaissance portraits of suffering saints and to classical architecture rearticulate authoritative systems of cultural power as the experience of disability, figured through a woman wearing a brace.

The barren landscape of *The Broken Column* appears again in *Tree of Hope* (1946) (Fig. 3.5), painted during the same period. Kahlo represents herself in a double-portrait, following a painful and ultimately unsuccessful operation. On the left she is depicted facing away from the viewer, lying prone on a hospital

---

[18] In *Las Dos Fridas* (1939) two versions of the artist are joined by their hands but also by an artery connected to exposed hearts. Although the painting does not invoke her disabilities, it foregrounds the body in the production of cultural gender roles. The painting is often seen as a response to her recent divorce from Diego Rivera. In the painting the figure on the left is dressed in a traditional white wedding garment while the figure on the right wears traditional Tehuana dress. The artery connecting the two figures is severed in the left-hand figure which she stanches with a pair of forceps, signaling perhaps the open wound of the marriage through the metaphor of hymeneal blood.

Fig. 3.5.   Frida Kahlo, *Tree of Hope*.
© 2018 Banco de México Diego Rivera Frida Kahlo Museums Trust, Mexico, D.F. / Artists Rights Society (ARS), New York.

gurney, her back bearing bloody scars of the operation. On the right, she appears upright in a ceremonial Tehuana costume with a colorful red bow in her hair. In her right hand across her waist she holds a sign, *Arbol de la Esperanza Mantente Firme* while in the left she holds her orthopedic corset. The sign, "Tree of Hope, keep firm," from the Mexican folk song, "Cielito Lindo" signals a post-operation attitude of confidence and recovery. The convalescent figure is painted in the full light of the sun whereas the dressed figure on the right is painted as if through a grey filter, light emanating from the moon. In Aztec mythology the sun is a symbol of human sacrifice whereas the moon, which illuminates the seated figure, may represent the feminine and creative life. As an artist who lived most of her adult life in extreme pain, the painting—one of several double self-portraits—shows the two "states" in which Kahlo lived, but it also hints at her cultural double life as a Mexican woman with a disability, represented by her colorful costume but also by her prosthetic brace. It is as though her naked, bleeding body carries both the stigmata of disability and the cultural stigmata of Catholicism.

Frida Kahlo's painting offers a significant illustration of that collision of disability and modernity that I describe in my introduction. It also offers a way to understand the complexity of Latin American cultural identity through the political movements of social justice with which Kahlo was involved throughout her life. Her work revisits the original political source of the term "avant-garde" that morphed into a term for aesthetics. She was a reluctant Surrealist, saying at one point, "I detest Surrealism. To me it seems a manifestation of bourgeois art" (qtd. in Tibol and Kahlo, 365). Announced into the movement by Breton, she chafed against definitional categories, even as she exploited many of the iconographic and stylistic features of her vanguard friends among the Mexican muralists. In a late photograph of her studio at Casa Azul, her empty wheelchair is shown facing her incomplete portrait of Joseph Stalin, illustrating yet another collision of disability and modernism. This photograph of an incomplete painting of the Soviet leader gives an uncanny account of Frida Kahlo's belief that, as she titled a late painting, "Marxism Will Give Health to the Sick." In this 1954 work painted close to the time of her death, Frida throws off her crutches while wearing her leather corset, flanked by a portrait of Marx. Like her Stalin portrait the painting was never finished, and it may be that the incomplete status of these late works, although certainly related to her growing bodily weakness also testifies to the difficulty of reconciling disability outside of a redemptive social narrative.

CONCLUSION: BECOMING COMPLETELY DIFFERENT

My title alludes to the "exquisite corpse" parlor game whereby Surrealist poets and artists created collaborative works based on aleatory methods. In the former case, a poet writes a line, folds over the page so that it is invisible to the next poet who then adds another line, folds it over, and passes it along. It represents one of numerous attempts on the part of artists to circumvent artisanal authority by interrupting the creative process and allowing discontinuous associations to generate the text. While we may focus on the "exquisite" qualities of surprise and novelty, we may miss the "corporeality" that underpins the phrase, the "different" body produced by disabling certain aesthetic protocols. My three examples suggest that in the pursuit of becoming, as Bataille said, "completely different," the uncanny, fragmented, scarred, and augmented body would provide the necessary surface. The headless body in André Masson's drawing was more than a metaphor for Surrealism's attack on rationality; it was a recognition of the body's variability once freed from its vassalage to the mind.

4

"Every Man his Specialty"
Beckett and the Dialectics of Dependency

"TO DECOMPOSE IS TO LIVE, TOO"

In *Bending over Backwards* Lennard Davis coins the term "dismodernism" to describe the ways that disability challenges ideas of liberal autonomy and able-bodied normalcy that underwrite contemporary identity politics. As a social model, dismodernism shares with theories of postmodernism a skepticism toward grand narratives of subjecthood and historical teleology, but Davis faults much post-modern theory for maintaining a social constructionist view of identity on the one hand while retaining a politics of multiculturalism and core group identity on the other. Reprising recent scientific discoveries in the field of genetics that dis-prove the biological basis of race, sexuality, or ethnicity, Davis, paraphrasing Walter Benn Michaels, asks, "how does it make sense to say there is a social construction of it?" (18). Discourses of race, gender, and sexuality are products of late nineteenth-century medical science—as is disability—but unlike these other areas, disability crosses all such categories and is the one identity position destined, as we age, to include most people. Its pervasiveness and instability permit Davis to see disability as a kind of *ur*-identity constructed within the technologies of biopower yet one not bound by specific genetic, economic, or racial markers. The dismodernist ideal "aims to create a new category based on the partial, incomplete subject whose realization is not autonomy and independence but dependency and interdependence" (30).

Although Davis conflates a postmodern philosophical stance toward performa-tivity with a historical, post-civil rights cultural politics, he points to a key limitation of rights claims that presume a healthy, independent (probably white, probably heterosexual, male) ideal to the exclusion of those deemed "defective" or unable to make "rational choices." In this respect he joins a number of recent theorists—Albert Memmi, Nancy Fraser, Martha Nussbaum, Michael Berubé, Eva Feder Kittay, and Alasdair MacIntyre—for whom a consideration of dependency challenges the social contract as it has been conceived from Rousseau and Hume to Rawls and asks whether contractarian ideals can stand the test of differently abled bodies? Stated succinctly by Eva Feder Kittay, dependency critique asserts that the idea of society as an association of equals "masks inequitable dependen-cies, those of infancy and childhood, old age, illness and disability. While we are dependent, we are not well positioned to enter a competition for the goods of social cooperation on equal terms" (xi). Although liberal theories of social justice stress equal access to the public sphere, they do not account for individuals who, because of cognitive impairment or physical disability, cannot cooperate on "equal" and independent terms. Nor are dependent relations validated in the common weal. Citizens who need special accommodations are often stigmatized as narcissists, whiners, and a drain on public funds. Their requests for "reasonable accommodations" under the Americans with Disabilities Act (ADA) have led to a series of court cases that have been, for the most part, decided against the plaintiffs. The need for interpreters, care-givers, therapists, and social services places persons with disabilities in conflict with liberal ideals of independence and self-reliance.[1] Can a model of independent living—the basis of the disability rights movement—coincide with what Alasdair MacIntyre calls the "virtues of acknowledged dependence" (8) that implicate all of us?

Martha Nussbaum's *Frontiers of Justice* answers these questions with a resounding *not yet* and in particular charges John Rawls' *Theory of Justice* with bracketing the rights of persons with disabilities, poor persons, and non-human animals as constituencies that cannot be included in Rawls' "original position"—those "normal conditions under which human cooperation is both possible and necessary" (27). Against contract models of human rights that stress cooperation for mutual benefit, Nussbaum argues for a rights discourse from the standpoint of what she calls, adapting Amartya Sen, "capabilities"—"what people are actually able to do and to be in a way informed by an intuitive idea of a life that is worthy of the dignity of the human being" (70). The contractarian model presumes a utilitarian theory of justice based on the nation-state and a self-sufficient society of relative equals.[2] Nussbaum's critique of Rawls challenges the equality thesis that underwrites liberal ideals of social justice by pointing to a global economy dominated by unequal relationships of interdependence that benefit dominant nations and consign matters of social justice to charity and debt relief. By deferring social justice to those who either cannot afford access to the public sphere or who find it physically inaccessible, Rawls creates a social contract that is incomplete and partial. It becomes what Walter Lippmann, in another context, calls a "phantom public," an ideal of participatory democracy that cannot be realized in practice under current conditions.[3] As Nussbaum says, "all the major social contract thinkers choose to imagine their

[1] Not all persons with a disability are dependent or share an equal relationship to care-giving. A person in a wheelchair is only dependent when she encounters a building without ramps or elevators; a deaf person is not dependent when signing ASL among deaf family members but becomes so when encountering a classroom without a sign-language interpreter or captioner. Disability rights advocates have been critical of seeing themselves as dependent, based on their long and troubled history with the medical and rehabilitation model. Yet the absence of any discourse about dependency has reinforced a triumphalist mentality that disregards the various forms dependence takes within disability.

[2] From a disability standpoint, we could see the grimmer application of this model in global development where resources are distributed based on the productivity of able-bodied persons or when healthcare is restricted to clinics that only preach abstinence and do not mention abortion.

[3] Walter Lippmann used the phrase "phantom public" in 1925 to describe (and decry) the large number of citizens who choose not to participate in political life. Bruce Robbins has appropriated the phrase to describe debates within the Left about the loss of the public intellectual or the decline of participatory democracy. Robbins' anthology, *The Phantom Public Sphere*, attempts to define those "counter publics" left out of much public sphere discourse, from Lippmann to Habermas. Not surprisingly, the essays in the book do not mention persons with disabilities or the disability rights movement.

parties as rationally competent adults who, as Locke says, are, in the state of nature, 'free, equal, and independent'" (104). Not everyone who enters the state of nature is "free, equal, and independent," and although Rawls acknowledges the needs of such persons he withholds consideration of their "special needs" for some future just state. Nussbaum counters by saying that if a theory of justice is to be adequate it cannot be more adequate for some or deferred until the ethical infrastructure is in place.

I want to explore the dialectics of dependency—the interplay between a social contract based on free, equal agents and one that recognizes contingent interrelationships—by looking at one modernist writer, Samuel Beckett, whose work dismodernizes liberal theories of autonomy and independent agency by creating scenes of what we might call "abject dependency." Beckett's characters often exist in tragi-comic relations of co-dependence that seem to mock communitarian ideals of charity and mutual aid while laying bare the edifice of liberal individualism as a flawed document. Hamm and Clov, Mercier and Camier, Pozzo and Lucky, Winnie and Willie, Vladimir and Estragon—and if we extend co-dependence more broadly—Molloy and Moran, Malone and his reader, old Krapp versus younger Krapp—all rely on each other to "go on." Their formulaic routines and dialogues often seem parodic versions of a rational discourse whose content has been evacuated, leaving interlocutors to exchange empty signs. It is less often observed that many of these characters are disabled and form tenuous alliances for mutual aid. In *Endgame*, to take the obvious example, Hamm is blind and lacks the use of his legs; Clov has a stiff leg and is losing his sight; Nagg and Nell have lost their limbs in a bicycling accident and have been relegated to trashcans.

It is important to recognize that for Beckett disability is not a metaphor. It is something he experienced personally as someone who lived with chronic pain, cataracts, heart palpitations, pleurisy, cysts, and bouts of anxiety and depression throughout his life.[4] We might expand Beckett's personal experience of disability to include his witness of Irish national trauma following the separation from Great Britain. The pervasiveness of disability in all of Beckett's work—from the mental patients in *Murphy* and *Malone Dies* to the disintegrating bodies of Molloy, Krapp, Moran, and Winnie, to the logorrheic mouth of *Not I*—may be seen as a symptom of social and institutional deterioration in the newly formed Irish free state when Beckett was growing up. At that time, care-giving facilities, welfare protection, hospitalization, and adequate medicalization were scare, despite attempts to reform the 1838 Poor Laws during the period of the Irish revolution (1919–21).[5] Nancy Scheper-Hughes describes the pervasiveness of mental illness—particularly schizophrenia—in rural communities as an excrescence of the retreat of rural youth to cities and the continent. Beckett witnessed some of these conditions when working in mental wards at the Bethlem Royal Hospital in London in the mid-1930s and following the war at the hospital at St.-Lô in Normandy. Perhaps the most

---

[4] James Knowlson's biography of Beckett (*Damned to Fame*) chronicles the author's various physical ailments on pp. 55–7, 210, 225, 229, 473, 495.

[5] On Poor Law reform see Donnacha Seán Lucey, "'These Schemes Will Win for Themselves the Confidence of the People': Irish Independence, Poor Law Reform and Hospital Provision."

important way we could understand disability as a symptom of national disintegration would be, simply, to contrast Beckett's dependent and disabled characters against the cult of masculine fitness and autonomy that characterized cultural nationalism in the new Irish free state. Like Leopold Bloom in *Ulysses*, Beckett's characters do not participate in manly Irish rituals of toasting, round-drinking, tale telling, physical exercise, and other homosocial activities. One might say that Molloy or Krapp in their isolation and decrepitude instantiate the actual as opposed to mythic character of masculinity in a nationalist context.

Most critics, as Ato Quayson observes, see Beckett's disabled characters as metaphors for alienation and solitude in the modern world, but do so "in a way as to obliterate the specificity of the body and to render it as a marker of something else" (*Aesthetic*, 56). Quayson notes that the presence of disability produces a certain anxiety or nervousness around the issue of bodily contingency. Stated succinctly in his introduction, he asks "what happens to our interpretation when we examine the status of disability within a representational system in which the discomfort of disability is not accounted for?" (54). Such an interpretive encounter represents a "hermeneutical impasse" in which the presence of pain and disability cannot be interpreted through strictly textual matters. This impasse is the aesthetic version of the nervousness that able-bodied persons experience when confronted by a person with a disability, but in his Beckett chapter Quayson speaks more directly about how characters negotiate such anxieties within a text that provides no simple origin for such nervousness. His chapter coincides with my own in his observation that in the case of *Endgame* Hamm and Clov's co-dependence is a sign of "radical contingency that governs the entire play" (76). Where Quayson locates this anxiety over contingency in pain as "a mode of intersubjective recognition and identity" I locate it in relations of dependency that challenge liberal ideals of individualism (79).

Quayson recognizes the foundational importance of disability in Beckett against the critical tendency to see it as a sign of existential alienation in the modern world. We might understand such alienation, however, as the condition of disability in a world of compulsory able-bodiedness. When disability is the norm—as it is in Beckett's work—the human condition must be revised in terms of non-traditional bodies and sensoria. We might also see characters' co-dependence as a means of survival, the social contract reduced to its most naked form. Beckett's choice of representing his human comedy by disabled figures whose bodies have ceased to be "productive" according to modern imperatives of progress and improvement offers a parable about the limits of agency and community in a post-ableist era.

Beckett offers little in the way of Christian solace, preferring a darker wager that he identifies with the early church fathers: "Do not despair, one of the thieves was saved; do not presume; one of the thieves was damned."[6] Beckett's often-quoted

---

[6] According to many Beckett scholars, this parable does not appear in this exact form anywhere in Augustine, although it seems to resemble a remark from his letters. Beckett quotes it in a statement to Harold Hobson in 1956: "I take no sides. I am interested in the shape of ideas even if I do not believe them. There is a wonderful sentence in Augustine . . . 'Do not despair; one of the thieves was saved.

version of Augustine serves as a caution to those who read *Waiting for Godot* as a modern parable about the existence of belief in a Godless world. Vladimir (Didi) and Estragon (Gogo) themselves seem aware of the odds ("One of the thieves was saved," Didi says; "It's a reasonable percentage") and occasionally entertain the thought that, as Gogo says, "We always find something, eh Didi, to give us the impression we exist?" (44). The form that this "something" takes is a series of verbal pratfalls and vaudeville routines that, in Godot's absence, fill time and keep them together:

ESTRAGON: That's the idea, let's abuse each other
They turn, move apart, turn again and face each other.
VLADIMIR: Moron!
ESTRAGON: Vermin!
VLADIMIR: Abortion!
ESTRAGON: Morpion!
VLADIMIR: Sewer-rat!
ESTRAGON: Curate!
VLADIMIR: Cretin!
ESTRAGON: [*with finality*] Crritic!
VLADIMIR: Oh!
He wilts, vanquished and turns away. (49)

Although such rituals offer a hilarious riposte to the idea of reasonable discourse they expose the pragmatics of communication as a contract among participants to further the language game. They also cement relationships around interdependency that, exemplified by current vernacular performances (dozens, rap, standup) create community and forge alliances. The "Crritic!" whom Gogo invokes to trump Didi, needs to see such routines as socially significant speech acts that "create the illusion that we exist."

Persons with disabilities depend on others in ways that challenge post-Enlightenment ideals of autonomy and independence, and it is here that Beckett's work offers an important challenge to the idea of an embodied norm.[7] His novels and plays depict characters that are thrown into a state of nature without ontological supports or metaphysical assurances. They depend on objects (stones, sticks, bicycles) as prostheses for limited mobility and agency, and their personal interrelationships seem based less on love and affection than on contingency and survival. Although their bodies are in states of increasing decay with limbs becoming unusable and memories unreliable, they acknowledge the fact that, as Molloy ruefully says, "To decompose is to live, too" (25). Although we often think of Beckett's characters as solitary Bartlebies, they are more often locked in complicated

---

Do not presume: one of the thieves was damned.' That sentence has a wonderful shape. It is the shape that matters." Quoted in Michael Worton, "*Waiting for Godot* and *Endgame*: Theatre as Text" (75).

[7] As Nussbaum and Eva Feder Kittay point out, dependency is often gendered. Those who deliver care or who are presumed to be responsible for dependent children and the aged and infirm are invariably women who are either not compensated, because part of the family structure, or poorly compensated, because components of the care-giving industry.

interrelationships, bound by ties whose necessity has long since turned into routine. Even when characters are alone, they are haunted by specters from the past with whom they commune in paranoid, guilt-ridden monologues. *Eh Joe*, *Ghost Trio*, *Krapp's Last Tape*, *Not*, and *Ohio Impromptu* utilize monologue and mime to converse with an absent interlocutor from whom the character is unable to separate himself. Krapp's futile endeavor to control the tape on which an earlier version of his life is recorded represents an attempt to revise a narrative whose present failures are all too apparent. In *Ohio Impromptu*, the silent Listener knocks on a table to indicate when his virtually identical Reader may read aloud what appears to be the former's story of lost love and growing isolation. In such plays, the Subject is split in two, permitted to visit himself (or herself in *Not I*) as Other through a dialogic encounter.

Dependent relationships in Beckett are never symmetrical, and power imbalances between characters are often mediated through parodies of Christian charity, on the one hand, or the master–slave dialectic on the other. Neither scenario—charity or force—is tenable, and characters are left to act out rituals of deference and leadership, support and authority, without knowing why. In Part I of *Waiting for Godot*, Pozzo and Lucky perform a theatrical parody of master and slave with Pozzo as the pompous landowner/impresario who expects dog-like fidelity from his servant and lackey, Lucky. When the two characters return in Part II, Pozzo's authority is diminished, his eyesight lost, his impresario status reduced to helpless appeals for aid. Didi and Gogo, who in Part I, deferred to Pozzo's authority, now imitate it by refusing help while subjecting Lucky to cruel punishment. Not only are dependent relations between master and slave reversed, a reciprocal inversion occurs between disabled and able-bodied characters in the play. Far from reversing the polarities of the master–slave dialectic, Beckett shows its tenacity and adaptability, even when the master's authority has been lost.

The basic formula for Beckett's treatment of abject dependence can be stated thus: individuals cannot realize themselves as independent agents without first recognizing their dependent and contingent relations with others and with their own animal bodies. In a world that valorizes independence and able-bodied normalcy, dependent relations are regarded as signs of weakness, usually gendered as "women's work" or that of ill-paid menials. When individuals find themselves in situations of dependence they act out their ambivalent relations to others and to their frangible bodies through narratives of beset embodiment that mimic conventional social attitudes. As their bodies decline, they become dependent on certain objects as extensions of their atrophied limbs, sight, and hearing. These objects replicate materially the stories they tell that extend their lives through narrative. Sucking stones and music hall routines stave off cosmic boredom, filling the space while waiting for Godot. Mobility, rather than a descriptor of agency, becomes a curse. As Malone says, "If I had the use of my body I would throw it out of the window. But perhaps it is the knowledge of impotence that emboldens me to that thought. All hangs together, I am in chains."[8]

---

[8] *Malone Dies. Three Novels of Samuel Beckett* (218).

The formula I have outlined can be seen in *Rough for Theater I* (*Fragment pour théâtre*), a lesser-known work written in French in the 1950s that could serve as a prologue for *Endgame*.[9] Two old men, A and B, inhabit a deserted corner of a post-apocalypse urban ruin. A is blind and sits on a folding stool, occasionally playing a violin "scratching an old jangle to the four winds" (68). B has lost one of his legs and wheels himself around in a wheelchair that he propels by means of a pole. When B first encounters A, he retreats until he realizes they might "join together, and live together, till death ensue" (67). This recognition scene marks the moment in which dependency is acknowledged as mutually beneficial to both parties rather than being seen as a tragic loss of autonomy. As in other Beckett plays, a character's acquiescence to dependence is figured as a marriage contract, a bond "till death ensue." As B observes, prior to their joining forces, he would "sit there, in my lair, in my chair, in the dark, twenty-three hours out of the twenty-four" (69). Now there seems the possibility for a kind of communion. B performs certain functions for A such as describing the scenery and the quality of light while A pushes B's wheelchair. Soon, however, A fails to accede to B's wishes, and B strikes him with his pole. Feeling guilty over his action, B despairs:

> Now I've lost him. He was beginning to like me and I struck him. He'll leave me and I'll never see him again. I'll never see anyone again. We'll never hear the human voice again. (70)

The blind A threatens to leave the crippled B, but finds himself unable to depart without his "things"—the few material objects: his violin and alms bowl—that represent his tentative hold on reality. Such objects, as we know from the rest of Beckett's *oeuvre*, are both prosthetic and aesthetic, extending and articulating an existence whose ontological supports have been withdrawn. B plays upon A's ambivalence by reinstating him into regimes of pity and obligation. B pleads with A to:

> Straighten my rug, I feel the cold air on my foot. [*A halts.*] I'd do it myself, but it would take too long. [*Pause.*] Do that for me, Billy. Then I may go back, settle in the old nook again and say, I have seen man for the last time, I struck him and he succored me. [*Pause.*] Find a few rags of love in my heart and die reconciled, with my species. (71)

In this passage, expressions of forgiveness and pity are revealed as speech acts whose exchange allows characters to live in the illusion of a moral universe. At different points in the play, each character calls the other "poor wretch," not to express pity but to reinforce the value of expressing it. *Rough for Theatre I* is less a parable about the virtues of mutual aid than a comedic display of human intercourse when relations are founded not on independent agency but on dependence. Beckett's post-lapsarian world of itinerant tramps, clowns, and cripples may simply be the bourgeois order's camera obscura on itself and on bodies it can't imagine or contain.

---

[9] All of the plays discussed here are now available on a DVD set, *Beckett on Film*, produced by Blue Angel Films for Radio Telefís Eireann and Channel 4.

"WHAT A CURSE, MOBILITY!"

A and B's interdependence defines a post-human, prosthetic body in which acts and intentions in one individual are completed by the other. In this sense, the prosthetic body differs from Yoshiki Tajiri's use of the phrase to describe Beckett's characters and "the body that harbours the inorganic other within it" (5). Tajiri is interested in those aspects of Beckett's characters in which parts of the body are felt to be alien or whose body and organs are experienced as a "broken machine." Dependency theory, at least in my understanding of it, treats the other's body as a prosthesis for one's own. In Beckett's work, disability is not a metaphor for something else (blindness as a sign of weakness, immobility as a sign of castration) but an enabling feature of the social contract. In an ableist, goal-driven world that treats dependency as hated subservience, non-contingent acts are deemed wasteful or expendable. At one point A extends his hand to B who exclaims, "Wait, you're not going to do me a service for nothing? [*Pause.*] I mean unconditionally? [*Pause.*] Good God!" (71). Here the non-contingent act, performed out of empathy or generosity, becomes the anomaly. Beckett's favorite philosophical conundrums usually involve aporias of contingency, his favorite being Bishop Berkeley's *esse est percipi* (to be is to be perceived). Critics observe that many of Beckett's works could be summarized by this proposition, from Belacqua's solipsism to *What Where*'s dark vision of state surveillance. In Beckett's 1963 *Film* (for which Berkeley's phrase serves as epigraph) the solitary actor, played by Buster Keaton, spends the entire film evading the camera's scopic gaze. The camera (called "E" for "eye" in Beckett's notes) relentlessly pursues Keaton ("O" for object) through a ruined street, into a vestibule, up a flight of stairs and into a bare room, but he manages to avoid being seen frontally until the very end of the film. People who encounter him on the street inexplicably turn away in horror, but we are never told why. Not only does O evade the camera's gaze, he attempts to efface anything remotely resembling a pair of eyes. He conceals all optical images (a fish in a fishbowl, the eyes of a parrot, two decorative holes in a rocking chair, two circular fasteners on an envelope) that threaten, however obliquely, to hold him in their gaze. When he finally turns toward the camera, Keaton's famous deadpan face is shown with a patch over one eye, as though to indicate that just as the cyclopean eye of the camera reifies its subject, so the Subject is sight impaired. O refuses to be constituted by the Eye, seeking an autonomy that the camera refuses to grant. And while the film focuses on one individual, its entire production illustrates the dualism of all perceptual acts, or as Winnie says in *Happy Days*, "because one sees the other the other sees the one" (28).

Disabled people have long recognized the power (and violence) of such scopic regimes and are now seeking to rearticulate their object status through activism and performance. The social model of disability asserts that a physical impairment becomes a disability when one encounters physical obstacles and environmental barriers, and the same holds true for negotiating the stares and gawking of an able-bodied public. One is not born disabled; one becomes disabled through the objectifying gaze of compulsory able-bodiedness. In Beckett's world, however, all characters are disabled, and their acts of looking and being seen tend to fore-ground the performative features—the theatricality—of such constitutive acts of sight. Their attempts to negotiate a landscape that is inaccessible (whether because of limited mobility or because of an absent God) frame "bare forked man" at his most vulnerable.

Or "bare forked" woman. The drama of *Happy Days* reinforces this constitutive aspect of sight as Winnie, buried up to her waist in act one and her neck in act two, seeks to maintain the illusion that she is still being seen—and thus that she still exists: "Strange feeling that someone is looking at me. I am clear, then dim, then gone, then dim again, then clear again, and so on, back and forth, in and out of someone's eye" (40). Her chipper response to each "happy day" belies her restricted condition, and she alleviates her tedium by pattern and routine. She is awakened by a bell; says a brief prayer; unloads objects from her "capacious black bag, shopping variety"; muses upon each item before returning it to its place in the bag; repeats formulaic phrases to her husband Willie who is half hidden behind her; sings a song at twilight. Willie's terse responses to her questions satirize domestic bliss, but they sustain Winnie's view that the two of them are maintaining some fiction of conjugal relations. Despite the absurdity of her situation, her reduced mobility is never an issue, and a good deal of the play's humor is linked to her buoyant refusal of what would seem to be an intolerable situation. The more Winnie seeks verifi-cation that someone is watching, the more we realize that we, as audience, are sustaining the illusion that she takes for reality.

Winnie is a virtuoso performer in her ability to fill time with an endlessly impro-vised script (and reticent interlocutor). She *performs* normalcy, insofar as her lines are often based on clichéd phrases that are the staples of social parlance (Patrick Bixby refers to Beckett's parody of such language as "intertextual mimicry").[10] On another level, and despite her bourgeois trappings, Winnie is surprisingly well read, quoting fragments from Shakespeare, Milton, Gray, Yeats, Keats, and Browning, often prefaced by the query, "what is that wonderful [or immortal] line?" These "classic" lines establish continuity with tradition—what she calls the "old style"—that like the objects in her reticule keep her afloat. They signal her commitment to affirmative culture, yet their decontextualized usage often effaces the darker themes—madness, chaos, and suicide—that these passages often signal (at one point, in looking for her glasses, she quotes Ophelia's lines from *Hamlet*, "woe woe is me—to see what I see" [10]).

As Beckett's fullest treatment of a female character, Winnie's performance of gender must also be acknowledged as an intersectional link to disability. She performs a specifically feminine version of embodied normalcy that Bishop Berkeley could hardly have anticipated. The objects in her purse—mirror, comb, toothbrush—reinforce her performance as a woman—a performance that she must maintain despite her restricted movement. Stephen Connor notes that "Winnie allows the

---

[10] Patrick Bixby, *Samuel Beckett and the Postcolonial Novel* (119).

dramatization of the gaze as both violation and necessity...Here, the female spectacle looks at itself, and watches the audience look at it" (184). Like Clov in *Endgame*, who, at several points, gestures toward the audience, Winnie is acutely aware of being watched, and when, in act two, she is no longer able to turn around and see Willie, her monologue expresses her desperation at being cut off from this last vestige of human contact. Not only is she being sucked down into that "great extinguisher" the earth, she is facing the horror that she might ultimately have to do it alone. That Winnie's anxiety relates to her disability can be seen by a moment, late in the play when she recounts a memory of an encounter with a "Mr. and Mrs. 'Shower' or 'Cooker'" who look at her in her hill of sand and ask, "What does it mean?...what's it meant to mean?" (56). Curiosity leads to prurience:

> Does she feel her legs? he says. [*Pause.*] Is there any life in her legs? he says [*Pause.*] Has she anything on underneath? he says. [*Pause.*] Ask her, he says, I'm shy. [*Pause.*] Ask her what? she says. [*Pause.*] Is there any life in her legs? (58)

Instead of helping her out of her predicament, the couple speculates on her disabled condition and in doing so participates in a common form of able-bodied voyeurism that sees the impairment for the whole person. Gendered and embodied otherness come together in Mr. Cooker's sexualized gaze.

It might be possible to see *Happy Days* as a comedy of modern solipsism, focused on woman as consumer, "buried" in the world and forced to recreate herself as spectacle. But if we were to see her immobile condition as an allegory of disability we might see the play as being more about dependence and vulnerability and the rhetorical strategies with which we negotiate between the two. There are two levels on which dependence is figured. The first involves Winnie's deictic construction of herself vis-à-vis an absent interlocutor, and the second includes her frustrated conversations with Willie. Both cases rely on Winnie's presumption that someone is hearing her speak, that she is "not merely talking to [her]self." In the absence of any confirmed listener, Winnie has recourse to a rhetorical surrogate, an imagined interlocutor who replaces Willie. In the following monologue, Winnie muses on the meaning of an advertising phrase on her toothbrush:

> Hog's setae. [*Puzzled expression.*] What exactly is a hog? [*Pause. Do.*] A sow of course I know, but a hog... [*Puzzled expression off.*] Oh well what does it matter, that is what I always say, it will come back, that is what I find so wonderful, all comes back. [*Pause.*] All? [*Pause.*] No, not all. [*Smile.*] No no. [*Smile off.*] Not quite. [*Pause.*] A part. [*Pause.*] Floats up, one fine day, out of the blue. [*Pause.*] That is what I find so wonderful. (20)

Monologues such as this imagine an other whose response is anticipated but never fulfilled. In one sense her phrases are empty of content, their function to keep the dialogue moving. Her constant question, "What is that unforgettable line?" mocks its own answer, yet its pragmatic function in securing and sustaining her intersubjective fantasy gives form to an unimaginable situation.

As for Willie he is an inadequate care-giver by any standard, spending most of his time reading his newspaper or else napping in his burrow behind Winnie's hill of sand. Throughout the play, he serves as a foil for Winnie's musings and a parody of husbandly detachment. Winnie strives to get him to respond, and her labors of thwarted communication produce much of the play's grim humor:

> WINNIE: What would you say, Willie? [*Pause. Turning a little further.*] What would you say, Willie, speaking of the hair on your head, them or it?
> *Long pause.*
> WILLIE: It.
> WINNIE: [*turning back front, joyful.*] Ooh you are going to talk to me today, this is going to be a happy day! (23)

Willie's parsimonious response nevertheless excites Winnie to further conversation, just as his vulnerability under the blazing sun occasions her solicitous regard for his exposed skin. At times, Willie's perfunctory remarks seem to allude to his own restricted condition as Winnie's helpmate. Despite the inadequacy of Willie's conversation, at the end of the play he quite literally "comes around," leaving his perch behind her hill of sand and moving, stage front, to climb the hill—with great physical exertion—and stare into Winnie's eyes and pronounce the first syllable of her name, "Win." Since she is now buried up to her neck, she is obviously not "win-ning" the battle against decline. Nor is she able to turn her head, and Willie's act permits her to verify that not only does *he* exist but she also exists in his mirror. It is an ambiguous gesture. We are not sure whether he has come to court Winnie one last time (he is dressed in formal wear) or to pick up the gun that lies at her side and facilitate the suicide she is no longer able to perform. Winnie interprets his gesture as a romantic one, but her remark contains the darker possibility that without his look, nothing of her remains:

> That's right, Willie, look at me. [*Pause.*] Feast your old eyes, Willie. [*Pause.*] Does anything remain? (62)

At one point in *Malone Dies* the titular narrator cries, "I wonder why I speak of all this. Ah yes, to relieve the tedium" (195). Later in the novel he ruminates, "the search for myself is ended. I am buried in the world" (199). This would seem to summarize Winnie's situation as well. She relieves the tedium of being-toward-death by talking-toward-being; she has stopped searching for a self beyond the world and acknowledges her immersion in it. Her most radical acknowledgment of this fact occurs toward the end of act one as she tries to instruct Willie on how to enter his burrow:

> The hands and knees, love, try the hands and knees. [*Pause.*] The knees! The Knees! [*Pause.*] What a curse, mobility! (46)

Far from despairing of her disabled condition, Winnie disparages the limits of mobility if its primary goal is, as in Willie's case, to return to a womb-like solitude. Willie may be more mobile, but his intellectual range is limited to making monosyllabic grunts and quoting "titbits from Reynolds News." Winnie depends on Willie's presence but is not defined by it. Their shared twin initials hint at their interdependent natures, as though one is the complement of the other. If Willie is

Winnie's on-stage audience, we become Willie, to some extent, by our triangulated relationship to Winnie's need to be seen. Hence the curse of Willie's mobility becomes our own; the cure of Winnie's solitude is the presence, imagined or literal, of the other.

"NO MORE NATURE"

The 2006 St. Andrews power sharing agreement in Northern Ireland between the Protestant Democratic Unionists and Sinn Fein caps a century of struggle over Irish governance and national autonomy. Whatever success the new agreement may bring, the legacy of the Troubles will continue to haunt future relations between Britain and Northern Ireland. The endurance of residual social and historical conditions in emergent formations makes it difficult to impose a binary, master–slave model on works of Irish literature with characters like Pozzo or Hamm serving as thinly disguised representatives of Great Britain against their subaltern Irish vassals, Lucky and Clov. Speaking of *Endgame* Nels Pearson points out that the play dramatizes

> the lingering co-dependency between two leftover participants from an imperial/colonial (or at the very least ruler/subject) historical situation that no longer exists. The important thing is that Hamm and Clov maintain the respective roles of ruler and ruled as well as the assumption that there is no alternative to these roles, long after the external causes of specific historical circumstances of those roles have deteriorated.
>
> (215–16)

One might argue that the imperial/colonial situation has by no means gone away in Northern Ireland, but Pearson is right to observe that a strictly top-down model of colonial authority does not account for forms of reciprocal dependence. The co-dependency of Hamm and Clov marks *Endgame*'s reprise of *The Tempest* with Clov playing Caliban to Hamm's Prospero, but as Albert Memmi argues, with regard to postcolonial societies, it would be wrong to assume that this form of dependency is the same as subjection. There are reciprocal dependencies between colony and colonizer in which each sees itself through the mirror of the other. In *Endgame* Hamm holds the combination to the cupboard that feeds Clov while the latter can still walk and see, thus serving as Hamm's legs and eyes. Each resents the other's advantage, yet each recognizes the other's role in constituting himself.

Having introduced the postcolonial context of Beckett's work, it might be useful to test the model of reciprocal dependence that one finds in postwar works like *Godot* or *Endgame* against another version produced at the same time—that of Frantz Fanon's *Black Skin, White Masks* (1952). This comparison allows us to see how disability and race, ableism and colonialism converge in relations of co-dependency, albeit to very different ends.[11] My example in Chapter 3 of Wilde's

---

[11] One should be wary of conflating disability and coloniality through metaphor. To say, as Harlan Lane does, that people who are deaf and use ASL live in a colonial relationship to hearing society or to suggest that people with physical disabilities live under colonial domination by the medical

fairy tale combines the two issues by showing how the dwarf in "The Birthday of the Infanta" mirrors the court's projection of him as both orientalized and disabled subject. His identity as noble knight is confirmed by seeing himself reflected in the mirror of society whereas his death results from seeing his physical difference in a literal mirror. Fanon describes this form of mimetic social death by applying psychoanalytic theory to explain how colonialism imposes its authority through the colonial subject's mirroring of the white colonizer's authority. Feelings of inferiority for black subjects are inculcated through a process of cultural and linguistic erasure; identity is less an individual than a relational category:

> Ontology—once it is finally admitted as leaving existence by the wayside—does not permit us to understand the being of the black man. For not only must the black man be black; he must be black in relation to the white man.   (110)

In his chapter, "The So-Called Dependency Complex of Colonized Peoples," Fanon debates the psychoanalyst Octave Mannoni whose book *Prospero and Caliban* also uses psychoanalysis to explain dependent relations between colonizer and colonized. Mannoni develops the idea of a "dependency complex" to explain the psychological and subjective forces that produce and maintain colonial subordination. Colonial resentment is treated as an Oedipal reaction against the father, for which Shakespeare's *Tempest* provides an exemplary narrative, with Prospero as the father/colonizer and Caliban/Miranda as colonized subjects. Fanon faults Mannoni for suggesting that feelings of racial and cultural inferiority antedate colonialism and for ignoring the importance of economic forces in producing those feelings. Mannoni exculpates Western society from responsibility for racism and locates it in specific classes of disenfranchised whites. The "dependency complex" then is one lodged in the psyche of individuals not necessarily in power relations reinforced by material conditions of colonization.

Against Mannoni, Fanon situates dependency within the structural conditions of a racist society in which differentiating among phenotypes, linguistic usages, and cultural capital preserves authority for some while disempowering others. He uses his own experience in francophone Martinique to show how knowledge of French pronunciation and culture allows the educated class of natives a degree of authority over those who speak in a patois. The tables are turned when that same figure goes to Paris and becomes identified as "native" and who must strive to adopt French socio-cultural norms. The colonizer who becomes dependent for his superior position on racializing others and the colonized subject who structures his identity on white cultural values are co-dependent within a structure of racism. Fanon's several references to black acquiescence as a kind of psychosis or disability suggests an important parallel with Beckett's theater.

In his early work, Fanon describes the interdependent relationship of whites and colonized blacks as a form of mimicry in which the colonial power structure is maintained by blacks who wear a white mask. By the time he writes *Wretched of the*

institution—such metaphoric usages diminish the specific histories of each disability and ignore solidarities established within those conditions.

Earth (1961), however, Fanon sees the world in much starker terms of conflict—"a world divided in two"—in which there is no rapprochement between colonizer and colonized. The Manichaean division of the races ultimately requires resistance, as he recognized during his active participation in the Algerian conflict. What Fanon had seen as a form of Hegelian recognition in *Black Face, White Masks* now is played out as a form of species differentiation. The erasure of blackness that he describes in the earlier work now becomes an irreducible gulf between different biological types. Alvaro Reyes points out that Fanon's "species" rhetoric is "chosen from the vocabulary of the colonists themselves, whose dehumanization of the colonized subject leads them to speak in 'zoological' terms when referring, for instance, to the 'yellow multitudes'" (14). By imagining whites and blacks as inhabiting distinct species, Fanon closes the door on interdependency as a structuring principle and allows for the possibility of "a new subject of political action" (Reyes, 13).

Where Fanon becomes increasingly invested in the fact of colonial conflict in Northern Africa, Beckett seems to move away from any specific reference to postcolonial Ireland in his postwar work—the emphasis here on "seems." Specifically Irish elements of early novels like *Murphy* and *Watt* give way to the blasted, deterritorialized landscapes of *Endgame* and *Godot* and the space-filling dialogues of Vladimir and Estragon. Patrick Bixby notes that the absence of specific references to Irish scenes and culture does not mean that the residue of British imperial authority is gone. Reading a postcolonial narrative in Beckett's later work must

> transform the terms of cultural engagement in a manner that does not lock artistic production into the oppositional dynamics of colonialism and nationalism, but rather marks the possibility of new forms of meaning and alternative strategies of identification—a manner that, however, cannot entirely exorcize the specters of Irish history.   (164)

These "alternative strategies of identification" are lived through Beckett's co-dependent bodies, their deterioration and alienation marking their inability to be represented within a coherent national narrative. If the specific reference to Irish colonialism is missing, his later work nevertheless reproduces the structure of colonial relations in ways that bear a striking resemblance to Fanon's study of colonial psychopathology. Where Fanon sees blacks disavowing their cultural heritage by imitating colonial power, Beckett's characters observe the protocols of deference and authority that bind their otherwise vulnerable and failing bodies together.

Although Beckett's postwar theater—*Not I, All That Fall*, or *Happy Days*—also deals with the interplay of disability and dependence, *Endgame* is the most operatic elaboration of the theme. At its center is a post-apocalypse world in which all life has been destroyed—or perhaps more accurately, in which biological reproduction no longer organizes futurity. At the play's center is a relationship between two disabled characters, one who imitates a fallen king and one who imitates his son and servant. Hamm and Clov ritually interrogate the reasons for their interdependence. "What is there to keep me here?" asks Clov; "The dialogue," replies Hamm (58). Elsewhere Clov asks, "There's one thing I'll never understand. Why I always obey you. Can you explain that to me?" to which Hamm responds,

"No … perhaps it's compassion. [*Pause.*] A kind of great compassion" (76). Hamm knows how to manipulate his subaltern by providing moral justifications for living under oppression. At one point Hamm curses Clov's lack of compassion and compares it to his disability:

> One day you'll be blind, like me. You'll be sitting there, a speck in the void, in the dark, forever, like me … Infinite emptiness will be all around you, all the resurrected dead of all the ages wouldn't fill it, and there you'll be like a little bit of grit in the middle of the steppe. [*Pause.*] Yes, one day you'll know what it is, you'll be like me, except that you won't have anyone with you, because you won't have had pity on anyone and because there won't be anyone left to have pity on.   (36)

Such maudlin rhetoric offers a variation on an all-too-familiar version of charity that maintains Hamm's control and validates Clov's continued subservience. It is also a warped variation on filial piety that visits the disability of the father on the vulnerability of the son. As Nagg heaps abuse on his disrespectful son, so Hamm complains about Clov's inattentiveness. Stanley Cavell observes, "Like his father, powerless to walk, needing to tell stories, [Hamm] masks his dependence with bullying …" (61).

Although Hamm postures and pontificates, he and Clov often acknowledge their impairments as a kind of reciprocity. Having pushed his legless father back into the ashbin, Hamm urges Clov to "Sit on him!" to which Clov responds, "I can't sit."

HAMM: True. And I can't stand.
CLOV: So it is.
HAMM: Every man his specialty. (10)

This brief interchange summarizes what Albert Memmi calls "reciprocal dependency" where "each partner counts on the other for survival or comfort, in which each is simultaneously the dependent of and provider for the other" (24). Although Hamm wields control over Clov's actions, his overblown rhetoric and grandiose theatrics show him to be less a tragic figure than, as his name implies, a ham actor with little power over his realm. The question why Clov stays with Hamm—the subject of many of their dialogues—can be explained as the colonial acquiescence before subjection in the absence of alternative possibilities. Clov has become comfortable in his subjecthood, and because he knows the roles and rules, performs them faithfully, despite his underlying *ressentiment*.

Reading *Endgame* in postcolonial terms has helped to historicize the play's theatricalization of power; however, it does not specify the function of disability in maintaining those relations of power. Within a postcolonial reading, Hamm is a parody of imperial authority, barking commands and feigning sympathy for his colonial subject. Clov must throw off his false consciousness and expose Hamm's autocratic role. Read through a disability optic, however, Hamm and Clov function within an ableist ideology that views dependent relations as weakness. In a world where the blind man in a wheelchair is interpellated as doubly handicapped, his dependence on an assistant is regarded as tragically emasculating. Within the chess metaphor that organizes the play, Hamm is vulnerable to his opponent's pawns. The play's title suggests that the world is coming to an end, but the game must continue to its conclusion. And in a world where the care-giver becomes socially and culturally disabled in the act of serving, reliance on the "patient" is no less disparaged. "We're not beginning to … to … mean something?" Hamm queries, to which Clov laughs: "Mean something! You and I, mean something! [Brief laugh.] Ah that's a good one!" (32–3). The great fear is that the formulaic routines and rituals that maintain their relations of interdependence might be evaporating is almost more than they can imagine. Hamm asks, "Imagine if a rational being came back to earth, wouldn't he be liable to get ideas into his head if he observed us long enough. [*Voice of rational being.*] Ah, good, now I see what it is, yes, now I understand what they're at!" (33). Adorno paraphrases these lines as saying, "Not meaning anything becomes the only meaning," but this imposes a kind of negative dialectics on these lines, seemingly in violation of Adorno's critique of existentialist readings of the play ("Trying," 27). I see these lines as showing Hamm's comedic response to the absurdity of his dependent relationship with Clov by ventriloquizing the voice of rationality and exposing it as a voice of power.

As in *Happy Days*, *Endgame* deploys a theatrical metaphor to reinforce the idea that dependent relations between patient and care-giver follow the pattern of dramatic role-playing. *Endgame* is full of theatrical references to audiences and performances, stage actions and memorized lines. As a ham actor, Hamm veers from pathos to music hall comedy and seems perpetually caught in a vaudeville routine. Hamm and Clov often allude to their empty rituals as performances. At one point, Clov is looking out the window with a telescope. He turns it toward the audience, and Hamm asks him what he sees: "I see … a multitude … in transports … of joy" to which he adds, "That's what I call a magnifier" (29). Hamm repeats Prospero's lines from *The Tempest*, "Our revels now are ended" as a marker of his kinglike status but also as the creator of the play in which he is both author and actor. Hamm, like Prospero, has given Clov language, which his Caliban-like subordinate now uses to challenge parental authority: "I use the words you taught me. If they don't mean anything any more, teach me others. Or let me be silent" (44). Hamm and Clov may resent their interdependence, but they construct their "revels" within recognizable theatrical roles.

Although in *Endgame* Beckett shows the abject character of dependency, he understands its function as a condition underwritten by attitudes about gender and class. Care-givers, as Feder Kittay and Nussbaum demonstrate, are invariably women, responsible both for child-rearing and care for the aged and infirm. Moreover, care-giving is unrewarded, if within the family, and when a component of work, ill remunerated. Beckett builds Hamm and Clov's relationship upon such unequal, gendered divisions of labor with Hamm as a pitiful version of the breadwinner who sparingly doles out biscuits to his small fiefdom while Clov is relegated to the domestic kitchen to stare at the walls. We tend to think of Clov as Hamm's surrogate son, but we forget that he also occupies the position of wife and helpmate. If, as Feder Kittay says, dependency work is "labor that enhances the power and activity of another" (38), then Clov is certainly a dependency worker, dispensing painkillers and moving wheelchairs but never given credit for his labors. The seeming symmetry of his dependency upon Hamm for survival reinforces the grim reality of unremunerated domestic service. Clov is not female, but by participating in dependency work, he occupies the subject position often occupied by women as nurses, mothers, midwives, and care-givers.

Finally, there is the question of life after Hamm. The play's ending hinges on whether one believes that Clov will leave Hamm and eke out an independent life or remain perpetually bound to his master's service. This is a version of the more philosophical question of whether the play "means" anything beyond its own meaninglessness—whether it dramatizes a universal human essence or, as Georg Lukács complained, mirrors the chaos of modern life without taking a position on it.[12] The play leaves the question unanswered, not because Beckett wants to question Clov's willpower or Hamm's authority (or art's pedagogical potential) but because there is no post-diluvian life beyond dependence. The endgame is not resolved by perpetuating another variant of Oedipal transgression, the son triumphing over the father by becoming independent of his reason. Rather the condition involves recognizing that independence and equality are bound to others, that, as Feder Kittay says, "interdependence begins with dependence" (xii). The boy that Clov spies through his telescope offers a glimmer of hope for life outside the box, yet there is the equal possibility that Clov will reestablish on this newcomer the regime of dominance he has learned from Hamm. Their final dialogue reinforces this promise of repetition, now figured through the theatrical mise-en-scène:

> CLOV: This is what we call making an exit.
> HAMM: I'm obliged to you, Clov. For your services.
> CLOV: [*turning sharply*] Ah, pardon, it's I am obliged to you.
> HAMM: It's we are obliged to each other. (81)

Whether this is simply a set of empty remarks made upon parting or a redemptive summary of their relationship in general, Beckett leaves the door (quite literally) open without showing Clov leaving the stage. The mutual obligation—what I have been calling reciprocal dependency—is the social contract viewed not as an alliance of separate individuals for a common good but a recognition of the labor such alliances entail. If Beckett presents a dystopic version of dependency, it is because the labor of love has yet to find an adequate narrative.

---

[12] Lukács sees Beckett's *Molloy* is the "*ne plus ultra*" of modernism's treatment of social neurosis by reducing man to an animal state: "In Beckett's novel we have the same vision twice over. He presents us with an image of the utmost human degradation—an idiot's vegetative existence. Then, as help is imminent from a mysterious unspecified source, the rescuer himself sinks into idiocy." By focusing entirely on subjective states, Beckett, in Lukács' mind, lacks historical perspective by which value can be ascertained. However, by regarding Beckett's work through theories of dependence and care, rather than existential interiority, we may understand the deeply social nature of his work. *Realism in our Time* (31).

DEPENDENT RATIONAL ANIMALS

"There is no more nature"—whose corollary, as Adorno has observed, is that there is nothing left that is not made by man. The catastrophe that *Endgame* survives could be an atomic holocaust with the play's characters depicting "the bombed-out consciousness [that] no longer has any position from which it could reflect on that fact" (Adorno, "Trying," 13). Although it is always dangerous to pin a specific historical allegory on Beckett's works, it is worth thinking of how plays like *Endgame* try to imagine a future when the grand narratives of Self, Soul, and Nation no longer seem to hold. Rather than being a form of "writing after Auschwitz" which implies that something positive *could* survive, *Endgame* might better be seen as articulating what conditions still remain, what elements of the Enlightenment narrative of improvement and Darwinian survival still organize the way we understand biofuturity. Nagg and Nell in their trashcans are the sad evidence of social attitudes about the aged and infirm that treat human life, once past its prime, as disposable. That, as Adorno says, "is the true gerontology" ("Trying," 32). Expanded to my concern with disability, we might say that in Beckett's plays, the old, the animal, the infirm, and the poor coincide, not as signs of what nature cannot contain but of what society cannot afford to exclude.

And this returns me to Martha Nussbaum's critique of John Rawls' original position. A theory of social justice forged on equal access to "resources" rather than "capabilities" provides a constricted definition of participation in the social contract and limits human potential largely to economic considerations: "The main idea," Rawls claims, "is that when a number of persons engage in a mutually advantageous cooperative venture according to rules, and thus restrict their liberty in ways necessary to yield advantages for all, those who have submitted to these restrictions have a right to a similar acquiescence on the part of those who have benefitted from their submission."[13] This sounds good, Nussbaum says, if all individuals are independent actors, but when one of those persons is in a wheelchair or is engaged in dependent care for a child who is mentally ill, that "mutually advantageous" cooperation no longer applies. What does it mean for someone to "submit to restrictions" in a society that refuses to recognize her as fully human? Nussbaum argues for treating individuals not in terms of abstract personhood but in terms of what they are capable of, what anyone needs to live with dignity. And this includes taking into consideration physical and cognitive variability. Thinking about differently abled persons also means taking into account their varying levels of care, whether this is delivered by a family member or by a paid employee. Finally, it means incorporating the care-giver into the dependent relationship as a full participant.

Beckett was obviously not thinking specifically of the claims of disability on social justice, but by making his characters disabled and co-dependent, he counters the tendency to think of such conditions as belonging to "them" and not to "us." The human condition in Beckett's plays *is* living with disability and dependence, however abject their portrayal may be. In a liberal society, committed to liberating

---

[13] Quoted in Nussbaum, *Frontiers of Justice* (59).

the healthy, independent individual, dependency must be bracketed (as it is in Rawls) or else subjected to various forms of paternalism. "Pity would be no more / If we did not make somebody poor," Beckett's favorite poet, William Blake, observes in "The Human Abstract" (216). The disability rights movement in its challenge to celebrity telethon versions of pathetic impairment has gone a long way toward retrieving the disabled person from such patronizing myths but in doing so has often had recourse to the same individualist ethos that it deplores. Beckett's writings display the limits of liberal individualism as the *telos*, the endgame, of civilization. At the end of *Endgame*, Clov halts at the threshold of the room. He and Hamm stage their last dialogue, one that they have been repeating since the beginning of time: "It's we who are obliged to each other." We never know whether Clov can extricate himself from this play—or this room—but we do see the drama of their dependent relations as the "game" that keeps them alive. A society that brackets such relations from the social contract fatally ignores, as Alasdair MacIntyre says, the "virtues that we need, if we are to confront and respond to vulnerability and disability both in ourselves and in others" (5).

5

Pregnant Men
Biofuturity in Djuna Barnes and Virginia Woolf

"What you get married for if you don't want children?"
(T. S. Eliot, *The Waste Land*)

QUEER FUTURES AND THE REPRODUCTIVE HORIZON

When the heat died down from the 2008 US presidential election and the question of whether the candidates—including Hillary Clinton—were *man* enough for the job, it became appropriate to acknowledge another political figure whose gendered authority came under scrutiny. From his election in 2003 until his final term in 2011, California's governor, Arnold Schwarzenegger, rocked the Republican cradle by supporting stem cell research, domestic partner legislation, and depending on the month, abortion rights. In the process he morphed from body builder to terminator to governator. Perhaps as foreplay to his run for the governorship nomination, Schwarzenegger's 1994 movie *Junior* shows him, as Alex Hesse, morphing from terminator into progenitor. Hesse and Larry Arbogast, played by Danny DeVito, are genetic scientists who experiment with in vitro fertilization by implanting a fertilized egg in Arnold's hunky body. The plan is to bring the fetus into the first trimester, market a hormone that facilitates growth, and then terminate the pregnancy while cashing in on the new patent. The experiment works, and soon the terminator is coming to terms with the inconveniences of morning sickness, hormone imbalance, and the pursuit of a full figure wardrobe. Despite these discomforts the formerly dour Hesse likes the kinder, gentler person he becomes through pregnancy and refuses to follow-through on the plan to abort. The joke involves seeing Mr. America become Mrs. America, and although Hesse becomes a mom, cross-dressing at one point as a steroid-enhanced ex-East German female athlete at a maternity hospital, the film makes sure to reinforce the idea that he is not a girlie man by introducing a love interest between him and Diana Reddin (Emma Thompson), a fellow genetic scientist. Their relationship is complicated by the fact that the "anonymous donor" egg Hesse has fertilized, unbeknownst to Reddin, is one of her own that she is using in her research. Thus in the end, Hesse has the baby that the two of them would have had anyway, and in the last scene, a visibly pregnant Reddin shows that the governator still has the right stuff.

Junior poses a question that may become more common in the genomic future: if a pregnant woman is the most natural thing in the world, what is a pregnant man? The movie's answer is that he's simply a more sensitive male, but perhaps another answer is that he is disabled. As Arbogast tells Hesse, "if this gets out, you're a freak!" It turns out that the proximity of non-heterosexual reproduction and "freakish" disability is a common concern in a number of recent films and novels beginning with *Blade Runner* and continuing through *Coma*, *Never Let Me Go*, *Oryx and Crake*, *The Island*, *Gattaca*, the *X-Men* trilogy, and *The Children of Men* that raise bioethical questions about genetic research, surrogacy, and transplant surgery gone awry.[1] The fantastic—or comic—narrative of a pregnant man becomes one among multiple futuristic scenarios for the biologically modified natural order. Such works are usually classified as speculative or science fiction, but one could see them as disability narratives insofar as they unseat the presumed normalcy of embodied life and display the nightmares of genetic futurity as the lived reality of disabled and dependent people.

If the scenario of a pregnant male has provided a freakish lens for the representation of disability, it has offered a normalizing lens on queer identity in an age of same-sex marriages, gay domesticity, and transgender parenting. Nowhere is this phenomenon more evident than in the case of Thomas Beatie, a transgender, legally male individual who is married to a biological female, Nancy. The couple had wanted a child, but when Nancy had to undergo a hysterectomy, due to endometriosis, they decided that Beatie would stop taking his testosterone injections that had prevented his menstrual cycles and attempt, with the aid of a sperm donor, to become pregnant. After one unsuccessful pregnancy, Beatie became pregnant again and delivered a baby girl successfully in 2008. In an article in *The Advocate*, Beatie remarked on his then pregnant state, "How does it feel to be a pregnant man? Incredible. Despite the fact that my belly is growing with a new life inside me, I am stable and confident being the man that I am. In a technical sense I see myself as my own surrogate, though my gender identity as male is constant." Beatie's pregnancy and his interviews with Barbara Walters, Oprah, and others sparked an outcry in tabloids and among late-night hosts, many echoing Arbogast's concern about the freakish nature of the condition. Yet in all of his interviews, Beatie stresses the ordinariness of his desire to give birth and his confidence in his masculine identity.

Although he does not address Beatie's pregnancy, Lee Edelman sees such events as a symptom of a new pronatalist scenario of compulsory reproduction that challenges queer identity's historically subversive character. Edelman argues that futurity is increasingly being written around the Child, capital "C," which remains "the perpetual horizon of every acknowledged politics, the fantasmatic beneficiary of every political intervention" (3). This family values scenario has, of course, been

---

[1] In an ad for Absolut Vodka, an obviously pregnant male stands next to a svelte, blonde woman in a black dress who holds a martini glass in her hand. The incomplete phrase that accompanies the image, "In an Absolut World…" is completed by the image, suggesting that among those sophisticates who drink Absolut Vodka, nothing is absolute and gender becomes porous.

operative within the religious Right for some time, but it now applies to activism on behalf of gay marriage, domestic partner legislation, and child-raising that threatens to transform queer politics into something a good deal more mainstream and heteronormative. Edelman notes the peculiar logic of this syndrome that says if the Child represents the positive future for gays and lesbians, then queer must mean negative futurity: "*[Q]ueerness* names the side of those *not* 'fighting for the children,' the side outside the consensus...outside and beyond its political symptoms, the place of the social order's death drive..." (3). Why death drive? Because within the all-consuming logic of biological futurity, not accepting the *telos* of the child involves naming "what the queer, in the order of the social, is called forth to figure: the negativity opposed to every form of social viability" (9). It is here that queer and crip identities merge since "social viability" usually means "compulsory able-bodiedness" as well as heteronormativity.[2] In the legal rhetoric of euthanasia proponents, to be "invalid" as a subject means having a life "not worth living." Hence, by a similar logic, crip futurity might be seen as the negation of those forms of embodiment and reproduction that medicine, psychoanalysis, and genetics must reinforce and affirm. As the 2005 Theresa Schiavo case and the controversy over the Clint Eastwood film *Million Dollar Baby* demonstrate, the non-productive body that medical science would consign to the dustbin is always, potentially, the body we wouldn't want our daughter to bear, the body we wouldn't want to keep on life support, the body that, could it speak, would want not to be born.

Edelman's argument raises the question of what embodied futures can be envisioned when reproduction is no longer the province of the heteronormative family, when the child no longer authorizes the narrative of biofuturity. Debates about surrogacy and in vitro fertilization invariably circle around whether such reproductive technologies simply update eugenic practices that historically isolated and in some cases euthanized the deviant, disabled, or feeble-minded. If social reproduction mirrors biological reproduction, the Child, as Edelman says, performs important cultural labor in securing the Holy Family against contamination (19). When reproduction occurs outside of the female womb, the child that results—like Dionysus, born from the thigh of Zeus—may lead to social chaos and Bacchic excess. As I will argue with respect to Doctor Mathew O'Connor in Djuna Barnes' *Nightwood* the figure of the pregnant male is the site of such uncanny futurity—a figure feminized in his ability to bear children, queer in challenging traditional gender roles, disabled because pregnant and thus subject to medical and therapeutic care.

My reference to Dionysus reminds us that the theme of male pregnancy is hardly new. It is the foundation of many Western narratives—from Greek myth (the birth of Athena from the head of Zeus) to the Old Testament (Eve born from Adam's rib) to rituals of male *couvade* and sympathetic birthing to early modern literature. Plato in *Theaetetus* speaks of "philosophical pregnancy" in which the corporeal

---

[2] On "compulsory able-bodiedness," see Robert McRuer, *Crip Theory* (1–32).

pregnancy of women is contrasted to the philosophical travail enabled by Socrates.[3] Eighteenth-century molly houses or gay taverns included yearly "Festival Nights" in which men participated in acts of cross-dressing, birthing, and lying-in as a form of gay parturition camp.[4] Shirley Velasco points out that the image of male pregnancy appears in numerous medieval and early modern works by Cervantes, Boccaccio, Shakespeare, and Dryden. In such early narratives the figure of male pregnancy rearticulates biological reproduction by positing epistemological or aesthetic creativity against female conception, gestation, and birth (in his prologue to *Don Quixote* Cervantes describes his book as "the child of my brain").[5] In the modernist era, however, what had been a trope for aesthetic fecundity—the male author's ability to transmit his literary legacy parthenogenically—becomes a biofuturist potentiality. At a moment when racial science and eugenics presented brave new worlds purged of defective, degenerate bodies and where sexological discourse made visible (and pathological) a new set of practices and subjects, the spectacle of male pregnancy was enlisted to imagine futures written in biopolitical terms. As F. T. Marinetti says in *Mafarka*, speaking of a futurist revolution, "the mind of man is an unpractised ovary...It is we who are the first to impregnate it" (3).

Modernist cultural representations of the pregnant male foreground the spectacle of reproduction loosed from its putative organic site in the female body and displace it elsewhere—the test tube, the surrogate womb, the male body, and, not insignificantly, the novel. I see this displacement as both a queering and cripping of normative attitudes toward reproductive health and the futures that such embodiment implies. It also warps traditional *narrative* attitudes toward biological futurity when the family romance no longer reproduces the heterosexual family. It is in this context that I read Djuna Barnes' novel *Nightwood* and Virginia Woolf's *Orlando* not as baroque anomalies among stream-of-consciousness narratives of Joyce, Stein, or Faulkner, but as perhaps *the* representative modernist novels insofar as they offer inside narratives of individuals interpellated within biological science and legal personhood. Rather than seeing the cultural logic of male pregnancy as a simple reversal of gestation from female to male body, I see it as a diaspora of sexual and gendered identities among differently abled bodies and cognitive registers.

As I have suggested in earlier chapters, modern progressive movements, both in the USA and Europe, encouraged practical applications of eugenic theories in asylums, hospitals, and prisons where "inverts" and mental "defectives" were sterilized,

---

[3] Socrates says to Theaetetus, "My art of midwifery is in general like [female midwives]; the only difference is that my patients are men, not women, and my concern is not with the body but with the soul that is in travail of birth. And the highest point of my art is the power to prove by every test whether the offspring of a young man's thought is a false phantom or instinct with life and truth" (*Theaetetus* 150b). I am grateful to Page DuBois for pointing out this reference.

[4] As Ned Ward, an eighteenth-century journalist, writes, on Festival Nights men would "cusheon up the Belly of one of the *Sodomitical* Brethren, or rather Sisters as they commonly call'd themselves, disguising him in a Womans Night-gown, Sarsnet-Hod, and Nightrale, who, when the Company were met, was to mimick the wry Faces of a groaning Woman, to be deliver'd of a joynted Babie they had provided for that Purpose, and to undergo all the Formalities of a Lying in" (Norton, "Of the Mollies Club").

[5] For a thorough catalogue of male pregnancy figures, see Sherry Velasco, *Male Delivery* (1–27).

incarcerated, or euthanized in the name of racial and psychological purity—not to mention national consolidation. If eugenics imagined a future of better babies and healthy families, it also constructed a past to which those deformed and disabled bodies could now be consigned. Thus the "Old World" could be used to describe both the backwardness of immigrants who refused to relinquish their cultural traditions and those deemed lower (and earlier) on some Darwinian evolutionary scale. Modernist writers often annexed their futurisms—including their linguistic innovations—to such biopolitical reforms, prompted by the writings of Francis Galton, Magnus Hirschfeld, Otto Weininger, and Richard von Krafft-Ebing. These fatal alignments have made it impossible to dissever Ezra Pound's historical poetics or Gertrude Stein's theories of the bottom nature or F. T. Marinetti's post-human futurism or T. S. Eliot's anthropological interests from their intellectual pursuits of racial science and eugenics. Nor were their investments strictly theoretical:

> If I had my way, I would build a lethal chamber as big as the Crystal Palace, with a military band playing softly, and a Cinematograph working brightly. Then I'd go out in the back streets and main streets and bring them in, all the sick, the halt, and the maimed; I would lead them gently, and they would smile me a weary thanks.
>
> (D. H. Lawrence, qtd. Childs 10)

D. H. Lawrence's fusion of commercial exhibition and gas chamber suggests that within the cultural advance guard two futures were envisioned: one for racial others, persons with disabilities, and sexual "inverts," and another for northern European, heterosexual able-bodied persons.[6] The latter were provided with utopian solutions, Socialist and Fascist, for a future free of what was politely called "amalgamation." For the former, however, there was to be no future. They represented the past, the ill formed, the animal, that needed to be expunged for the "right" future to be possible. As we will see with respect to *Nightwood* this negative future also produced a carnivalesque modernism that contests Lawrence's draconian version.

In these examples, male maternity becomes a metaphor for the ways that modernism figured negative futures around the threat of non-traditional forms of reproduction. The figure of the pregnant male could be seen as an inverted mirror on modernity's anxieties over violated biology and traduced nature.[7] Freud's analysis of Daniel Paul Schreber is the exemplar case. In Freud's 1911 case study,

---

[6] Lawrence's remark says a good deal about why Clifford Chatterley is in a wheelchair. His crippled condition makes possible—and necessary—his wife's infidelity with the gamekeeper, Mellors. As Jan Gordon observes, the fact that Clifford's paralysis was caused by World War I (thereby a potentially heroic wound) is effaced by another kind of disability—his intellectualism—for which the game-keeper's "natural" sexuality is therapeutic (203).

[7] Lee Edelman, although certainly not speaking of male pregnancy, suggests that such negative futures, based around non-reproductive sexuality, lie outside of meaning altogether: "Which is, of course, to say no more than that sexual practice will continue to allegorize the vicissitudes of meaning so long as the specifically heterosexual alibi of reproductive necessity obscures the drive *beyond* meaning driving the machinery of sexual meaningfulness: so long, that is, as the biological fact of heterosexual procreation bestows the imprimatur of meaning-production on heterogenital relations" (13).

Schreber's paranoid psychosis, as described in his *Memoirs of a Neurotic*, takes the form of a messianic feeling that he must redeem the world by producing a superior race of men. In order to fulfill his destiny he must first be transformed into a woman and then become impregnated by God. Freud reads this fantasy as a diversion of Schreber's conflicted homosexual desires onto a transgendered scenario, but he (Freud) does not confront the maternity that is at the heart of Schreber's fantasy. In order to diagnose the *vehicle* of Schreber's fantasy—homosexuality as pathology—Freud must avoid the fantasy of parthenogenesis—his "womb envy"—that is the troubling *tenor*. This form of desire (and Freud's attempt to contain it within a diagnosis of "perverse" sexuality) becomes particularly salient at a moment when medical science is intervening in reproduction by attempting to stabilize gender and racial differences and by monitoring reproductive processes and potential sexual partners. Within eugenic futurity, such engineering would force women to cede control of reproduction to males and thus become ancillary to the biological order. As Freud's diagnosis illustrates, Schreber's desire to redeem the world through pregnancy is the "outburst of homosexual libido" that must be returned to heterosexual conformity (145). The specter of male maternity would be those forms of reproductive life that cannot be figured through the narratives of health and improvement nor modernist aesthetics' formalism of the spatial or organic text.

Schreber is one among a small but significant modernist gallery of male characters who in various ways assume reproductive roles. One might say that Surrealism was born out of just such a character in Apollinaire's 1917 satirical play, *The Breasts of Tiresias* (*Les Mamelles de Tiresias*).[8] As the work in which the term "surrealist" first appears, Apollinaire's play is situated amidst two important historical crises: the liberation of women and Malthusian concerns over the threat of depopulation in the wake of World War I. Apollinaire's witty send-up of both takes the form of a vaudeville-like drama set in a mythic Zanzibar. The play's heroine, Thérèse, has grown tired of her domestic role and wants to be a soldier: "to make war . . . and not make children" (68). As Thérèse/Tiresias, she/he grows a beard, and her breasts fly off like balloons. Meanwhile her husband (known only by his title) observes, "Since my wife is a man / It's right for me to be a woman" and promptly produces "40,049 children in one day alone" (80). Apollinaire says in his preface that he has written his surrealist drama to "warn [the French] of the grave danger, recognized by everybody, that not making children holds for a nation that wishes to be prosperous and powerful, and to remedy the evil I have shown them what must be done" (58). What must be done, as the play demonstrates, is for men to assume childbearing and raising duties, not predictably out of displaced maternal desire but in pursuit of economic gain. As the resigned husband says:

> The more children I have
> The richer I'll be and the better able to live
> It's said that the cod produces enough eggs in a day

---

[8] In his Preface, Apollinaire says of his play, "I have used a neologism which as I rarely use them, I hope will be excused: I have invented the adjective *surrealist*, which does not at all mean *symbolic* . . . but defines fairly well a tendency in art which, if it is not the newest thing under the sun, at least has never been formulated as a credo, an artistic and literary faith" (56).

To supply the whole world for a whole year
With cod paste and garlic
Isn't it wonderful to have a numerous family
Then who are those idiotic economists
Who've made us believe that the child
Means poverty   (84)

A second and more familiar example of male maternity is Leopold Bloom in Joyce's Nighttown chapter of *Ulysses* who relives his daytime cultural and racial ostracism at night through a sado-masochistic nightmare of abjection in Bella Cohen's brothel. Wearing a corset and forced onto his knees by the "whoremistresses," Bella, Bloom endures the slings and arrows of female domination and authority. Stately plump Buck Mulligan, in his capacity as medical student, appears on this phantasmagoric scene to pronounce Bloom, who is about to have a baby, "bisexually abnormal." "O I so want to be a mother," Bloom declares, whereupon he promptly produces "eight male yellow and white children...wellmade, respectably dressed and wellconducted, speaking five modern languages fluently and interested in various arts and sciences" (403).[9] Throughout his peregrinations in Dublin, Bloom has mourned the loss of his son, Rudy, and repressed his sexual alienation from his wife, Molly. Now, in his nightmare confrontation with his own femininity he becomes, as Mulligan says, "a finished example of the new womanly man" (403). Sandra Gilbert and Susan Gubar read such fantasies of "sexual inversion" as signs of "the excesses of female misrule associated with women's liberation during the war years" that Bloom casts off in the novel's final scenes by taking control of his domestic situation (334). But as with Freud's analysis of Daniel Schreber, critics like Gilbert and Gubar tend to read such scenes of feminized masculinity as signs of historical gender trouble that patriarchy strives to monitor. They do not account for the womb envy and erotic pleasure identified with female sexuality that Bloom has experienced throughout the day and that appear in their more carnivalized forms in the Nighttown chapter.[10]

My third example of male pregnancy appears in Ezra Pound's "Canto XII" in which the poet repeats a story that the lawyer and arts patron John Quinn told a group of bankers about a sailor who, while in hospital following a bout of drinking, appears to have delivered a child. When the sailor wakes up from his ordeal, the hospital staff present him with a child just delivered by a poor prostitute and then declare "Here! this is what we took out of you" (56). The sailor recovers, saves and

---

⁹ Joyce was aware of Apollinaire's play and may have drawn on the Husband's prodigious delivery of 40,049 children "in a single day" when he was writing the "Circe" chapter of *Ulysses*. On Joyce and surrealism see Catherine Flynn, "'Circe' and Surrealism: Joyce and the Avant-Garde."
¹⁰ In a 1912 letter to Nora Barnacle Joyce, Joyce figures his novel as a kind of birth. He thinks "of the book I have written, the child which I have carried for years and years in the womb of the imagination as you carried in your womb the children you love, and of how I had fed it day after day out of my brain and my memory" (*Selected Letters*, 202–3). Joyce's description is, of course, a more direct statement of Stephen Dedalus' aesthetics as described in *Portrait of the Artist* and in the "Scylla and Charybdis" chapter of *Ulysses*.

invests his money, and having prospered, sends his child to college. On his deathbed, the honest sailor responds to his son's solicitude:

> *Don't, don't talk about me, I'm all right,*
> *"It's you, father."*
>   *"That's it, boy, you said it.*
>   *"You called me your father, and I ain't.*
>   *"I ain't your dad, no,*
>   *"I am not your fader but your moder," quod he,*
>   *"Your fader was a rich merchant in Stambouli"*   (56–7)

Pound draws upon the Dantean condemnation of usurers and sodomites as those who pervert nature through economic and sexual practices that prevent natural increase. Quinn's story mocks the bankers he addresses (*"Alias* usurers in excelsis") by suggesting that the sailor's belief in having produced a child due to a homosexual encounter is a bawdy version of what the bankers themselves practice by charging interest (55). Like Eliot's Mr. Eugenides in *The Waste Land* who solicits a homosexual tryst with the poem's narrator, the honest sailor of "Canto XII" is identified with the merchant class whose mobility and cosmopolitanism are a threat to both heterosexual and national stability. In each of my examples, male pregnancy is linked to the conflation of material wealth and biological dystopia, whether through the Husband's belief that his ability to reproduce will result in economic advantage, Bloom's absorption of anti-Semitic slurs about thrift and money lending, or the honest sailor's merging of childbirth with the increase of wealth. And although it might seem a stretch to link these scenes of male pregnancy with disability, they expose the artifice of bodily normalcy by imagining biological reproduction as an unnatural act performed through an unnatural body.

My three male authors figure pregnancy through the lens of an era haunted by eugenically tinged fears of "degeneration," marked by a weakened gene pool due to feminization and miscegenation. Male authors who represent scenes of masculine reproduction, however fantastical or aestheticized, offer a defense against the period's pursuit of female suffrage, economic empowerment, and independence. When Virginia Woolf figures pregnancy in *Orlando* (1928) it is not through a scene of male fecundity but through cross-gender transformations that complicate the specificity of gender categories altogether. What links *Orlando* to my previous examples is a certain continuity between fears of economic powerlessness and sexual potency in a world of mobile gender roles. Apollinaire spins his fantasy of extravagant male maternity through a national allegory about postwar depopulation and Pound links usury to perversions of "natural" increase. Woolf's variation on this theme offers a subtle analysis of precisely this connection between fears of male economic powerlessness and female emancipation.

In *Orlando* the titular protagonist begins in the sixteenth century as an aristocratic male youth who frequents the court of Queen Elizabeth and through her advocacy achieves fame, property, and "the jeweled order of the Garter." While engaged in diplomatic service in Turkey (fleeing the lure of Lust inspired by the Archduchess Harriet Griseldas) he falls into a week-long slumber, only to awake as a woman.[11] The eccentric premise is extended by the fact that "she" continues to live through the next three hundred years, frequenting salons and ateliers of eighteenth-century England (she debates with Pope, Swift, and Addison), composing an endless poem, "The Oak Tree," moving through the aesthetic movements of Victorian England and ending up in 1928 (the year in which *Orlando* was written), driving a car and witnessing the descent of an airplane. The novel is actually a satirical biography of Woolf's friend and lover, Vita Sackville West, whose life provides many of the details of the story. The novel has often been read as an important contribution to gay and lesbian literature (and a tribute to Sackville West's own public lesbian identity) and, more recently, transgender studies. But its treatment of fluid gender roles also calls into question the integrity of embodiment as the marker of gendered normalcy.

Although it occupies only a few lines, pregnancy does make a brief and important appearance. In the second half of the novel Orlando, impregnated by her husband Shel, gives birth to a child. "It's a very fine boy, M'Lady," says the midwife, Mrs. Bantling. The naming of the child's gender turns out to be significant in many ways. It echoes the opening lines of the novel which affirm Orlando's sexual status: "He—for there could be no doubt of his sex, though the fashion of the time did something to disguise it..." (11). The emphasis placed on the naming and certainty of masculine gender is relevant since the novel goes to elaborate lengths to discredit the social and legal meanings attached to such assurances. Once the child is named as male, he disappears from view, and the novel proceeds without any further reference to what would ordinarily be an epochal moment in the narrative of a woman's life. But Woolf slyly suggests that the child is not born from a woman's womb so much as from a set of legal prescriptions that determine masculine economic authority. As a male, Orlando was able to inherit his vast family fortune and estate, but now as a woman, following his/her sex change, "she" is no longer eligible. Only when her gender is confirmed through reproduction of a male heir can succession proceed. Far from confirming that "there could be no doubt of his sex," as Woolf's narrator insists, Orlando's gender specificity is fluid and unstable. Her reproductive abilities may appear to confirm her gender, just as "his" name confirms his.[12]

---

[11] As in Wilde's "The Birthday of the Infanta," Joyce's "Nighttown" chapter of *Ulysses*, Marinetti's *Mafarka* and other texts discussed here, the "Orient"—in this case Turkey—is the site for gender-bending scenarios and homoerotic passions. On orientalism in *Orlando* see Karen R. Lawrence, "Orlando's Voyage Out."

[12] In Sally Potter's 1992 film version of *Orlando* the director transforms the ending by making the child a girl. This rather radical revision of the novel suggests that just as Woolf focuses her attention on the legal and economic productivities of pregnancy, Potter foregrounds the novel's deconstruction of gender binaries. At the end of the movie we see Orlando (played by Tilda Swinton) riding a motorcycle with her daughter in a side-car. Both are dressed in leather riding outfits and racing goggles that efface gender specificity. In the film's final scene, Orlando's daughter is wandering through a brightly lit field, wielding a camera that captures both nature and her mother (we see through the camera's lens). Jane Maree Maher sees Potter's gesture as "rethinking and reworking visual meaning as a strategy to challenge deterministic accounts of pregnancy and the body" (20). In the novel Woolf's narrator provides assurances that, indeed, Orlando is male—and later female, yet Potter's use of visual media allows us to "see" in Tilda Swinton's body and face the difficulty of assigning gendered categories.

Orlando's pregnancy is a necessary corollary to economic realities, defined by a legal system that prohibits women from inheriting property. In order for her to be a woman in the full biological sense of the term she must enter the defiles of a male legal world. Orlando as woman spends a good part of her life pursuing legal remedies to the prohibition against inheritance. When she finally wins her lawsuit, she still must produce a male heir in order to be viable in the order of succession. Woolf elaborates on the relationship between gender and economics in *A Room of One's Own*, but in *Orlando* she creates an entire novel around this relationship. The novel's scant treatment of biological birth belies the social function it serves during the 400-year period that the novel covers. Rather than limit Orlando to a single gender category—female capable of gestation—she/he recognizes that she is multiple: "she has a great variety of selves to call upon." It is as though the confirmation of her biological gender liberates her, as a former male, to occupy many subject positions—including that of a pregnant male.[13] If she produces a child as a biological woman, she reproduces a child through patriarchy. Hence, my (admittedly tenuous) inclusion of *Orlando* in a gallery of modernist representations of male pregnancy.

What is queer about *Orlando* is its playful mixing of gender roles, narrative conventions, and narrative temporalities. And while it might seem a stretch to think of such fluidity as characteristic of disability, the novel's deconstruction of embodied identity has implications for what it means to "signify" as human. Woolf's focus on the long history of patriarchy and its suppression of women's rights and agency is conducted through a carnivalesque version of biography—as if Vita Sackville West's life as a lesbian and author could stand in for all of those moments—from Shakespeare's plays to Wilde's dwarf to Whitman's expansive self to Joyce's feminized Bloom—in which the integrity of the male body meets the social expectations of its functions. When those expectations include gestation and parturition, male writers have produced an aesthetic justification that situates the creative act as a form of insemination. When the female author takes on the social meaning of pregnancy she recognizes its inscription in roles that have historically denied her a room—and body—of her own.

"IMPERMISSIBLE BLOOD": *NIGHTWOOD* AND THE GENEALOGICAL IMPERATIVE

A more complex case of this fusing of sexuality, disability, and reproduction is Dr. O'Connor in Djuna Barnes' *Nightwood* (1936). Although his qualifications as a pregnant male are not quite as overt as in my previous examples, O'Connor's queer identity is specifically organized around his reproductive desires: "[F]or no

---

[13] Orlando is not the only transgendered character in the novel. The father of Orlando's child, portentously named Marmaduke Bonthrop Shelmerdine Esquire, is variously described as a woman. Upon meeting "him" Orlando cries, "You're a woman, Shel!" to which he responds, "You're a man, Orlando!" (184). Just as Orlando is reincarnated as a woman, so the Archduchess Harriet, whose heterosexual desire inspires Orlando's flight to Turkey, appears later in the novel as a man.

matter what I may be doing, in my heart is the wish for children and knitting. God, I never asked better than to boil some good man's potatoes and toss up a child for him every nine months by the calendar" (91). As a sham gynecologist-cum-psychoanalyst, Matthew O'Connor is the carnivalesque version of those late nineteenth-century professions within which the minds and bodies of women, disabled persons, and homosexuals were monitored. O'Connor violates the terms of clinical practice, from his filthy room and brimming "swill pail" to his decaying obstetric equipment ("a rusty pair of forceps, a broken scalpel") and his reversal of the psychoanalytic protocols (he *asks* rather than *answers* the questions; he lies on the couch while the patient occupies the analyst's position in the chair [79, 78]).[14] But as self-acknowledged outsider, "the old woman in the closet," O'Connor is uniquely positioned to advise one of the main characters, Nora Flood, about the vagaries of interstitial identity (78). In the novel's central scene, Nora encounters him late at night at home, cross-dressed in a woman's nightgown and wig, heavily made-up, and surrounded by cosmetics ("perfume bottles, almost empty, pomades, creams, rouges, powder boxes and puffs" [79]). She has sought his counsel on the matter of her abortive lesbian relationship with Robin Vote, but his elliptical answers are as much informed by his own abject status as they are by his psycho-analytic understanding. As someone whose "only fireside is the outhouse" and who haunts the "pissoirs as naturally as Highland Mary her cows," he domesticates the underworld of Paris and regards his circulation within the queer demimonde as a bucolic *dérive* that if it includes casual sex in public may as easily include a stop at the Catholic church—not, as it turns out, to hear Mass but to masturbate (91). In short, his queerness occupies narratives of both sexual abjection and domestic or institutional normalcy.[15]

As a cross-dressing male with maternal desires, as the doctor who "helped to bring [Nora] into the world," Dr. O'Connor combines the roles of father and mother, obstetrician and pregnant woman, analyst and analysand that medical science seeks to keep separate. By blending these roles he functions much as Tiresias in *The Waste Land* as a prophet of dystopic futurity, albeit in a more Rabelaisian version. If he is *un*-reproductive as mother or doctor, he is *pro*-ductive as raconteur and storyteller, his bawdy anecdotes and salacious gossip providing much of the "matter" of the novel. O'Connor's rambling speeches refuse a linear narrative that ends with familial resolution and restoration of order. Rather, the novel's non sequiturs, baroque rhetoric, and elaborate hyperbole force attention onto the surface of language rather than elucidating some interior psychological state. Barnes' novel is the antithesis of the modernist interior monologue that attempts to render some subterranean, unchanging bottom nature or core personality. O'Connor's monologues shatter stable identities, merging scatological and theological rhetoric, vernacular and dynastic culture, ornate metaphors and performative denunciations.

---

[14] Jane Marcus provides a lucid summary of the ways that O'Connor inverts the Freudian analytic session (231–50).

[15] On *Nightwood* as a tale of urban slumming, see Scott Herring, *Queering the Underworld* (150–92).

Such linguistic mixing is a textual version of that racial and sexual ambiguity that threatened the interwar European bourgeoisie. And as I will point out with respect to Barnes' portrayal of disabled characters, O'Connor's verbal grotesquerie is a textual equivalent of the non-traditional body, the circus freak and mentally ill patient that cannot be assimilated into normative models of health, growth, and the statistical average. In this respect Dr. O'Connor's "child" is the text his *logorrhea* continually produces.

O'Connor expresses his reproductive desires within a novel with a child at its center, but the child, rather than redeeming history often serves as a reminder of its loss. The novel's opening lines suggest that in *Nightwood* (much like *Orlando*) childbirth is not a matter of biology but of discourses about race and the body:

> Early in 1880, in spite of a well-founded suspicion as to the advisability of perpetuating that race which has the sanction of the Lord and the disapproval of the people, Hedvig Volkbein—a Viennese woman of great strength and military beauty, lying upon a canopied bed of a rich spectacular crimson, the valance stamped with the bifurcated wings of the House of Hapsburg, the feathered coverlet an envelope of satin on which, in massive and tarnished gold threads, stood the Volkbein arms—gave birth, at the age of forty-five, to an only child, a son, seven days after her physician predicted that she would be taken. (1)

As Joseph Boone has observed, this opening passage establishes a theme of "estrangement and permanent wandering" that characterizes this marginal society and that finds its primal form in the birth trauma (238). The child, Felix Volkbein, is born not into the *heimlich* family but into perpetual alienation and dislocation, a product of his parents' aspirations for national and cultural authority. To some extent he is the prototype for all other characters in their deterritorialized relationship to family, nation, and heteronormalcy. Barnes' baroque prose with its multiple subordinate elements and qualifiers imitates the ornate features of the Volkbein coat of arms, a design whose elegance contains both the schematic memory of Habsburg greatness and the anti-Semitism at its secret heart. It turns out that the heraldic design is utterly fabricated, a pastiche invented by the father, Guido Volkbein, in an attempt to fashion a noble lineage as a bulwark against racial memory. Everything about Guido and Hedwig's life is fragmentary or fake. The family portraits that Guido displays on his walls were found "in some forgotten and dusty corner and had purchased them when he had been sure that he would need an alibi for the blood" (7). The originals for the portraits turn out not to be a royal couple at all but a couple of actors. Guido's coat of arms is "a bit of heraldry long since in decline beneath the papal frown" (6). The couple live in a vast home overlooking the Prater which is decorated with Roman fragments, "white and disassociated; a runner's leg, the chilly half-turned head of a matron stricken at the bosom, the blind bold sockets of the eyes given a pupil by every shifting shadow" (5).

Like so much else in the novel, surface design belies uncertain origins. Hedvig Volkbein's dedication to Austro-Christian militarism is qualified by her fear that the son she is about to bear contains the "impermissible blood" of the Jew. Her husband, although steeped in Christian and aristocratic trappings, is Jewish and lives with the memory of his historic racial oppression. For early critics of the novel like Philip Rahv who felt that Barnes simply "exploited perversion to create an atmosphere of general mystification and psychic disorder," such passages suggest that the "psychic disorder" has a historical referent in the anti-Semitism that haunted fin de siècle Europe and would lead, ultimately, to the death camps (qtd. Parsons, 60).

Felix Volkbein, as the child with whom the novel opens, embodies the dying embers of European empire, epitomized by his mother's Habsburg origins and father's diasporic (Italian/Jewish) lineage. His father wears a handkerchief commemorating a fifteenth-century Roman ordinance that forced Jews to race in the public square with a rope about their necks "for the amusement of the Christian populace" (2). By flaunting this bit of sartorial display, Guido Volkbein signals a tragic awareness of his racial ostracism yet at the same time distances himself from the "impermissible blood" that is his heritage. His son Felix inherits his father's "remorseless homage to nobility" and his Viennese mother's militarism and hopes to pass them on to his own son (2). Lacking any contact with his biological parents and obsessed with history, he creates a mythical past based on "Old Europe," Old Masters paintings, excellent manners, royal titles, and the Catholic Church. Because he has no authentic link to royalty he creates a *soi disant* aristocracy out of the circus and the theater, "sham salons in which he aped his heart" (11). Caught between fake aristocrat and wandering Jew, Felix is the epitome of the "rootless cosmopolitan" despised equally by Hitler and Stalin, whose home is the café, the salon, the hotel foyer and whose origins lie in the racially assimilated culture of Habsburg middle Europe.

If Felix expresses a nostalgia for the blood of aristocratic privilege and the hierarchical authority of the sovereign, his son, Guido, is a stereotype of eugenicist degeneration theory through in-breeding:[16]

> ...as time passed it became increasingly evident that his child, if born to anything, had been born to holy decay. Mentally deficient and emotionally excessive, an addict to death; at ten, barely as tall as a child of six, wearing spectacles, stumbling when he tried to run, with cold hands and anxious face, he followed his father, trembling with an excitement that was a precocious ecstasy.   (107)

The fact that the son of Felix Volkbein and Robin Vote, Jew and lesbian, is mentally ill is no small feature of the novel's representation of the ostracized other, a fact as important to its modernist diagnosis of decay as Benjy Compson's cognitive disability is to *The Sound and the Fury* or the Czar's son, Alexis Romanov's hemophilia is to the narrative of the Bolshevik Revolution. The disabled child becomes the specter of tainted blood that eugenics sought to control.

---

[16] Michel Foucault speaks of modernity as marking a shift from a culture based on power expressed through "blood" and the sovereign's power over bodies, to a "society of sex," in which "mechanisms of power are addressed to the body, to life, to what causes it to proliferate, to what reinforces the species..." (*History of Sexuality*, 147). *Nightwood* is a somewhat elaborated version of Foucault's formulation.

The child's historically over-determined existence—developmentally disabled, Jewish, motherless, physically stunted—marks the novel's thematic treatment of the child as the site of dystopic futures. Unlike the romantic *Bildungsroman* that must return the orphaned child to his familial legacy, Barnes' children—real and imagined—are perpetual outcasts who upset the domestic ideal of the stable, heterosexual family and the continuity of biologically reproductive futurity that is the centerpiece of much narrative fiction. And he is not the only child in the novel. The novel's discrete object of desire in the novel, Robin Vote is often called a child, her bisexuality, sexual adventurousness, and somnambulism suggesting Freud's pre-conscious, infant state that exists outside of or prior to socialization. If O'Connor is logorrheic, Robin is virtually mute, uttering only a few phrases in the novel as a sign, perhaps, of her pre-Oedipal, pre-linguistic status. The lesbian relationship she shares with Nora is defined as one between an overly protective mother and a way-ward child. Figured as a child, she is also a mother of a child—Guido—although her maternal abilities are non-existent, leaving the child-raising aspects of her married life to her husband, Felix. Robin bears some similarity in her passiveness and blankness to a doll, which becomes an important metonym for the lesbian relationship itself and an object toward which charged emotional energies are focused. Nora and Robin share a doll that they call their "child," and when she becomes angered at Nora's possessiveness, Robin smashes the doll to the floor. Later, when Robin leaves Nora for a new lover, Jenny Petherbridge, the latter gives her a doll as a sign of their new relationship (147).[17] O'Connor, ever wise in the meaning of partial objects, links dolls specifically to queer identity:

> The last doll, given to age, is the girl who should have been a boy, and the boy who should have been a girl! The love of that last doll was foreshadowed in the love of the first. The doll and the immature have something right about them, the doll because it resembles but does not contain life, and the third sex because it contains life but resembles the doll. (148)

This comparison of lesbian and doll summarizes the period's sexological character-izations of homosexuality as a stage of arrested (bisexual) development, but it hints at the performative character of queer identity in which the doll becomes a theat-rical surface upon which "normal" sexual relations are embossed. Where Krafft-Ebing or Havelock Ellis pathologized the "third sex," Barnes treats it as a form of innocence that escapes both Felix's genealogical imperative and Nora's parental restrictions. O'Connor, in his late-night analytic session with Nora encourages her to "bow down" to that innocence, for which the doll is a partial object, and accept difference as a mode of being.

[17] There are many dolls in *Nightwood*, representing to some extent the liminal realm between childhood and adult, human and non-human. The doll, as a replicant figure, parallels the circus fig-ures whose costumes, fake titles, and showmanship ape the audiences before which they perform. The trapeze artist, Frau Mann, is sewn into her costume such that she ceases to obey human form: "The stuff of the tights was no longer a covering, it was herself; the span of the tightly stitched crotch was so much her own flesh that she was as unsexed as a doll. The needle that had made one the property of the child made the other the property of no man" (13).

Nightwood was written at a transition point in eugenicist and sexological discourses. Although the date of its origin is in dispute, begun possibly as early as 1927 and published, with the help of T. S. Eliot, in 1936, it clearly chronicles Barnes' passionate love affair with Thelma Wood which began in 1921 and ended in 1929.[18] Despite the fact that many of her contemporaries and friends (Mina Loy, Natalie Barney, Gertrude Stein, T. S. Eliot) absorbed eugenics theories Barnes is not known to have been interested in movements for racial purity, but her novel's cast of queers, cross-dressers, disabled persons, and racialized outsiders seems drawn from one of Bertillon's or Lambroso's catalogues of defectives. The period during which *Nightwood* was composed saw a shift from theoretical to more negative applications of eugenics through the increased use of incarceration, euthanasia, and sterilization that would lead to the Nazi Final Solution.[19] Felix Volkbein's sham aristocracy and nobility ape the racialized and sexualized characters' perverse relationship to eugenics taxonomies. Against the imperative to categorize and monitor bodies, Barnes creates a world, as Jane Marcus says, of "merging, dissolution, and above all, hybridization—mixed metaphors, mixed genres, mixed levels of discourse from the lofty to the low" (223). Barnes' characters, far from being a side show to the main event, are the primary agents of the novel who accept their alien status and form what Joseph Boone characterizes as "demimonde of the 'inappropriate'" (234).

The centerpiece of this demimonde is the circus. Most of the characters are, in some way, connected to carnival and theater as a sign of their marginal relationship to the dominant society. Significant events occur in dressing rooms and backstage areas where the division between reality and fantasy, body and costume, human and animal become confused. The false Baron, Felix Volkbein, frequents the circus because its denizens defy his acquisitive temperament: "The circus was a loved thing that he could never touch, therefore never know... The people of the theatre and the ring were for him as dramatic and as monstrous as a consignment on which he could never bid" (12). Through Dr. O'Connor, we meet Nikka, the black, tattooed bear wrestler and the trapeze artist, Frau Mann, "the Duchess of Broadback" and others, "gaudy, cheap cuts from the beast life, immensely capable of that great disquiet called entertainment" (11). In an arena where characters are already marked racially or sexually, the circus provides a richly embroidered backdrop for that inversion of roles that Bakhtin characterizes as the carnivalesque. Felix's obsession with royal titles is mimicked in the circus performers' adoption of titles: Princess Nadja, Principessa Stasera y Stasero, and King Buffo. Nora Flood is

[18] Robert McAlmon reports that Barnes and Thelma Wood, the prototypes for Nora Flood and Robin Vote, spent time in Berlin along with Berenice Abbott, Marsden Hartley, and McAlmon, and lived near Magnus Hirschfeld's Institute for the Study of Sexual Sciences. According to McAlmon, they encountered a number of transgender individuals in the streets of Berlin, but Barnes did not accompany the group on its late-night forays into what Deborah Parsons calls "the fluid space of an itinerant and liminal subculture" (70).

[19] The precise date that Barnes began to write *Nightwood* is unclear. According to Cheryl Plumb and based on entries in Emily Coleman's diary, the origins of the novel could have begun as early as 1927. It is clear that the novel was well under way in 1932, when she was living at Hayford Hall, Peggy Guggenheim's summer residence in England.

a publicist for the Denckeman Circus in New York who meets her love interest, Robin Vote, in front of the lion cage. Robin leaves Nora for Jenny Petherbridge whom she meets at a performance of *Rigoletto*, an opera with a court jester and hunchback in its title role. On another occasion Robin meets Nora at an evening at Count Altamonte's in which the attendees are described as "living statues." O'Connor's speeches themselves always seem to be dramatic monologues, full of quotations from plays (in his preface Eliot compared the novel to Elizabethan tragedy). Felix provides the best gloss on the value of carnival performativity when he says "[one's] life is peculiarly one's own when one has invented it" (118). Readers may hear vestiges of Wildean aestheticism in this remark—and, indeed, Felix does seem to be a kind of deterritorialized dandy—but it achieves particular historical valence in the context of Weimar era disruptions.

Perhaps most important in reinforcing the carnivalesque are the many references to animals. Robin is described as a "beast becoming human" and elsewhere, Dr. O'Connor describes her as "an eland coming down an aisle of trees…a hoof raised in the economy of fear" (37). Like the animal trainers and side show characters in Todd Browning's movie *Freaks*, circus performers often resemble the animals they tend ("the men smelling weaker and the women stronger than their beasts" [11]). In the novel's last scene Robin demonstrates her abject status to Nora by getting down on all fours in front of Nora's dog, barking and crawling after him in a "fit of laughter, obscene and touching" (170). The obvious inversion of the word "God" in "dog," the fact that Robin performs this act while in a chapel, suggests the ultimate reversal of theological and sexual values implied in the eugenicist term, *degeneration*. With respect to our concern with biological futurity, such moments call into question species identity and blur the boundaries between human and animal, animate and inanimate, sacred and profane. Robin's much analyzed imitation of a dog seems less a sign of her lesbian abjection, as critics have said, than a fulfillment of O'Connor's injunction to Nora to "bow down" to an animal nature her rational human nature repudiates.

NAMING SICKNESS

Critics have devoted extensive attention to the novel's feminist, lesbian, and anti-racist features, but they have not attended to its representation of disability, either as a set of characters within the novel or as a diagnostic tool for testing attitudes about bodily normalcy. On the one hand, Barnes trades in rather typical stereotypes of impairment as character flaw, Guido's mental illness and his father's monocular vision being the most obvious.[20] On the other hand, disability underlies many of the characterizations of marginality in the novel, making it a kind of marker for the stigmatized body—from Nikka's tattooed body to Robin's dementia. Despite his fake credentials as a doctor, Matthew O'Connor

---

[20] Felix not only wears a monocle, he has sight only in one eye ("his blind eye had kept him out of the army" [9]).

offers an excellent diagnosis of the social model of disability. Speaking of Guido's mental illness, he notes that:

> His sanity is an unknown room: a known room is always smaller than an unknown. If I were you, the doctor continued, I would carry that boy's mind like a bowl picked up in the dark: you do not know what's in it. He feeds on odd remnants that we have not priced. He eats a sleep that is not our sleep. There is more in sickness than the name of that sickness. In the average person is the peculiar that has been scuttled, and in the peculiar the ordinary that has been sunk; people always fear what requires watching.
>
> (120)

Instead of regarding Guido as a "defect" or "retarded child," O'Connor treats him as a field of potential, a reminder of the "peculiar" that the rational mind must repress. O'Connor anticipates current theoretical accounts that regard disability not as the name that medicine gives to impairment but as those limits that the so-called average person imposes on the non-traditional body and cognition. As O'Connor concludes, in a remark that could apply to many of the marginal figures in *Nightwood*, "people always fear what requires watching." Since all of the characters in the novel are the objects of a scopic regime, whether as theatrical actors or as cross-dressing freaks, they "require watching." O'Connor's play of words on "require" suggests that persons with disabilities "require" policing and monitoring, yet their difference fascinates and amazes—*requires*—that we watch.

A second modality of disability in the novel is as a metaphor for excessive or liminal existence. Barnes describes Nora's desire for Robin during the latter's late-night perambulations as that of an amputation:

> As an amputated hand cannot be disowned because it is experiencing a futurity, of which the victim is its forebear, so Robin was an amputation that Nora could not renounce. As the wrist longs, so her heart longed, and dressing she would go out into the night that she might be 'beside herself.' (59)

Robin has begun to "wander," both literally into the city but sexually into other relationships, and Nora stays awake at night like an anxious parent, experiencing her lover's absence as a phantom limb. In Barnes' complicated figure, disability is a marker of absence, but it is also a marker of lesbian desire insofar as the body from which Nora feels alienated is like her own. At one point Nora acknowledges "Robin has been both my lover and my child. For Robin is incest, too; that is one of her powers" (156). Hence, when she goes out at night, she is "beside herself" with anxiety for the beloved but also one with the beloved as an aspect of herself. Barnes explicitly repudiates Freudian treatment of homosexuality as arrested sexual development, saying in a letter to Emily Coleman, "[well] of course those two women would never have been in love with each other if they had been *normal*, if any man had slept with them, if they had been well f—and had born [sic] a child." To the heterosexist logic that equates fulfillment with male intervention, Barnes responds that this is "ignorance and utterly false. I married Robin to prove this point, she had married, had a child yet was still 'incurable'" (qtd. Plumb, xviii). Barnes' mocking use of queerness as disease ("incurable"), heterosexuality and ableism as cure, undercuts the way that biologistic theories of normative sexuality and embodiment reinforced a heteronormal ideal whose default is reproduction. As one of Eliot's cockney pub denizens says to Lil in *The Waste Land*, "What you get married for if you don't want children?" (42).

Eliot's speaker's question states in demotic terms the poet's elegiac theme of unproductive nature, but whereas the author of *The Waste Land* bemoans the aridity of sexual relationships, Barnes sees pronatalism's compulsory character as a ruse to isolate and marginalize. Despite these differences in evaluation, Eliot's admiration of *Nightwood* stems from the way Barnes figures the crisis of post-Habsburg Europe through images of debased or mad bodies that bear the full weight of historical loss. In one crucial passage Dr. O'Connor is trying to describe Felix Volkbein:

> There's something missing and whole about the Baron Felix—damned from the waist up, which reminds me of Mademoiselle Basquette, who was damned from the waist down, a girl without legs, built like a medieval abuse. She used to wheel herself through the Pyrenees on a board. (26)

O'Connor sees Felix (whose false baronial title mimics the doctor's own fake medical credentials) as the inverted reflection of Mademoiselle Basquette whose missing legs damn her from the waist down, the more so because they render her vulnerable to abuse:

> a sailor saw her one day and fell in love with her... So he snatched her up, board and all, and took her away and had his will; when he got good and tired of her, just for gallantry, he put her down on her board about five miles out of town, so she had to roll herself back again, weeping something fearful to see, because one is accustomed to see tears falling down to the feet. (26)

Mademoiselle Basquette's vulnerability as a disabled woman is the other half of Felix's disability as a Jew in pre-Nazi Austria. O'Connor's response to this story is to see her pathos as the way that disability unsettles the usual image of suffering: "Ah, truly, a pin board may come up to the chin of a woman and still she will find reason to weep. I tell you, Madame, if one gave birth to a heart on a plate, it would say 'Love' and twitch like the lopped leg of a frog" (26–7). In his elaborate metaphor O'Connor reduces love to an involuntary muscle, one that, like Nora's phantom limb relationship to Robin, is both separate from the body yet able to live an independent life. On the one hand it is a figure of the endurance of affect—the idea that even in the most reduced circumstance, the heart has its reasons of which reason is unaware; on the other hand, it is a figure of abjection that we see everywhere in the novel—the body without organs, the body violated, and most importantly, the disabled body subject to the able-bodied sailor.

By reading *Nightwood* against the backdrop of Fascism, Marcus and others have usefully shown how the novel's subversive treatment of an alternate society of Jews, queers, and disabled persons must be read within the context of Hitler and Mussolini's rise to power in Europe as well as through the period's use of medical science in the name of racial purity. The child born with a cognitive impairment becomes, in the public mind, the logical outgrowth of aristocratic inbreeding and women's independence. In *Nightwood* there is no redemptive, atavistic survival or folkloric tradition waiting to redeem the shards of fragmented culture. The modernism of *Nightwood* rests in its exposure of the cultural logic whereby bodies and affective states are marshaled into categories of able-ness and heteronormativity. Barnes strikes at the heart of how those categories are normalized within the family by queering the family unit, presenting us with a transgender obstetrician who wants to become pregnant, a lesbian mother who is more a child than her own child, and a heterosexual Jewish male who wants his mentally disabled son to be the next Czar. If these scenarios sound like variations on Freud's case studies of sexual delusion, they also constitute the family values ethos of Barnes' Rabelaisian fiction and pose a different (and more sympathetic) assessment of those emasculated men and neurasthenic women that populate modernist texts.

LEGAL FICTIONS

In her book *Pregnant Men*, the feminist legal theorist Ruth Colker argues that restrictions on reproductive freedom for women are hampered by the fact that the Supreme Court refuses to regard that freedom as gender based. "Put simply, there are no pregnant men to which we could compare women to show gender-based treatment. All pregnant *people* are treated alike; it is irrelevant (to the Supreme Court) that all pregnant people are women" (128). In the early 1990s, when Colker's book was written, this formulation may have seemed unremarkable, but today, with the increased use of genetic engineering, surrogacy, and in vitro fertilization, the question of pregnant personhood is a good deal more complex.[21] In order to deal with gender discrimination around pregnancy and reproductive health, as Colker observes, "We need a way to talk about *pregnant men*" (128). If we could, she observes, we would see that many of the legal claims for equal rights do not take female biology into account, nor do they take into account the misogynist nature of groups that oppose abortion and support violence against women and doctors at abortion clinics. Colker uses a *legal fiction*—a pregnant male—to situate a *legal reality* that ultimately disempowers women by ceding reproduction to males.

My (admittedly) hyperbolic view that male pregnancy is a form of disability is a way of talking about repro-futurity outside of its heteronormative frame. Doing so illustrates what happens when reproduction is removed from female biology and shifted discursively onto other bodies. I am not saying that we should seriously consider male parenting as equivalent to childbearing—as popular self-help books seem to be doing lately—but that in speaking about male pregnancy we are also implicitly describing a close relationship between disability and sexuality. We might say, adapting Stuart Hall and Paul Gilroy, that disability is a modality through

---

[21] Shirley Velasco notes that adding to the de-gendering of pregnancy is the return of various forms of *couvade* in popular parenting literature with titles like *Birthing Fathers: The Transformation of Men in American Rites of Birth* or *Pregnant Fathers: Becoming the Father You Want to Be* (8).

which sex is lived.[22] The castration complex, to take one example, involves aligning a missing limb with an attitude about male sexual potency—and by extension the lack of that potency in women. The fear of losing that limb, in Freudian thought, translates into the fear of becoming a woman. Or as Dr. O'Connor says of Nora, "[she is] one of those deviations by which man thinks to reconstruct himself" (53). Historically the merging of disability and sexuality has occurred through the pathologizing of the "invert" as mentally defective, and by sexualizing the cognitively disabled person as sexual threat to the gene pool. The castrating of mental patients during the eugenic 1920s when *Nightwood* was written is only one version of a more pervasive form of negative eugenics based around the control and monitoring of disability.

What Colker diagnoses as a problem with legal equality theory applied to women's health also applies to queer politics in a moment of reproductive futurism. The new queer family values ethos that Lee Edelman critiques in *No Future*, utilizes the seemingly egalitarian claims for male pregnancy and the integrity of the child to remove control of female biology from women while reinscribing heteronormativity onto queer culture. As I have indicated, cultural producers have been talking about pregnant men for some time, albeit from rather different metaphoric vantages. The figure of the reproductive male in modernism, as Schreber and Dr. O'Connor illustrate, is a sign of the ways that negative futures were being written around homosexual men. But we need to distinguish between the two figures, judge and doctor, by thinking of how their two authors—Freud and Barnes—figured that futurity. For Freud, Schreber's paranoid delusion that he must become a woman and become impregnated by God is a form of homosexual panic, the result of Oedipal anxieties regarding Schreber's father, who was a doctor, and his own doctor, Flechsig (this staging of homosexual panic as "doctor panic" is one of Freud's less acknowledged contributions to disability studies). For Freud, Schreber's gender-bending fantasies of impregnation and pregnancy are pathological signs of mental illness, that necessitate institutionalization and analysis. For Woolf, fluid gender positions allow Orlando to produce a child as a woman who was once a man. For Barnes, Dr. O'Connor is comfortable as "the old woman in the closet" whose "wish for children and knitting" stand in stark contrast to Felix's rigid code of masculine filial piety or Nora's rather bourgeois notion of lesbian monogamy. O'Connor's acceptance of his oxymoronic position as female-male gives him a queer perspective on Nora's bourgeois normalcy—her desire to create Robin as a faithful spouse—and on her need to "bow down" to her own sexuality. Where Freud sees disability, Barnes sees an alternate ability; where Freud sees deviant homosexuality, Barnes sees a spectrum of sexual identities in a world facing a Fascist and eugenically controlled future.

In my introduction to this chapter I posed a question that pertains to the new biopolitical order: if childbirth in women is nature, what is childbirth in men?

---

[22] Hall's remark, paraphrased by Paul Gilroy is that "[race] is the modality in which [class] is lived (qtd. Gilroy, 85). Gilroy, speaking of 2 Live Crew, adapts Hall's comment to say "gender is the modality in which race is lived" (85).

Is it, for example, disability? By framing the question this way, I want to call into question the usual binaries of nature/culture, reproduction/production, that have dominated sex roles for centuries and ask whether in a world in which reproduction is being increasingly divorced from gender the default of nature is not culture but, rather, disability, read as the defamiliarizing condition for the spectacle of bodily normalcy. We could complicate this chiasmic ratio further by asking if the birth of the male child into self-consciousness is the ground of the *Bildungsroman*, what happens when that birth is literalized in and through the male body? Does this alter the ideological course of narrative as a recuperative vehicle for family values and pronatalist futurity? What eugenics attempted to secure within the heteronormative family, novels like *Nightwood* explode into the biofuturistic scenarios of William Burroughs, Octavia Butler, Samuel Delaney, and Margaret Atwood—and ultimately pop culture films like *Junior*.

6

Uncanny Encounters
Dramas of Contingency in Modernism

FACES IN THE CROWD

The street around me roared, deafening.
Tall, slender, in deep mourning—majestic in her grief,
A woman passed—with imposing hand
Gathering up a scalloped hem—
Agile and noble, her leg like a statue's.
And as for me, twitching like one possessed, I drank
From her eyes—livid sky brewing a storm—
The sweetness that fascinates and the pleasure that kills.

A lightning-flash...then night!—Fugitive beauty,
Whose gaze has suddenly given me new life,
Will I see you again before the close of eternity?

Elsewhere, very far from here! Too late! Perhaps *never*?
For where you're off to I'll never know, nor do you know where I'm going—
O you whom I could have loved, O you who knew it too![1]

Walter Benjamin notes that in Baudelaire's sonnet, "To a Woman Passing" ("À une passante") "the crowd is nowhere named in either word or phrase. Yet all the action hinges on it, just as the progress of a sailboat depends on the wind" ("On Some

---

[1] The translation used here is the one printed in Walter Benjamin's *The Writer of Modern Life: Essays on Charles Baudelaire*. The translators include Howard Eiland, Edmund Jephcott, Rodney Livingston, and Harry Zohn, p. 76. The original is as follows:

> La rue assourdissante autour de moi hurlait.
> Longue, mince, en grand deuil, douleur majesteuse,
> Une femme passa, d'une main fastueuse
> Soulevant, balançant le feston et l'ourlet;
>
> Agile et noble, avec sa jambe de statue.
> Moi, je buvais, crispé comme un extravagant,
> Dans son oeil, ciel livide où germe l'ouragan,
> La douceur qui fascine et le plaisir qui tue.
>
> Un éclair...puis la nuit!—Fugitive beauté
> Dont le regard m'a fait soudainement renaître,
> Ne te verrai-je plus que dans l'eternité
> Ailleurs, bien loin d'ici! trop tard! *jamais* peut-être!
> Car j'ignore où tu fuis, tu ne sais où je vais,
> O toi que j'eusse aimée, ô toi qui le savais!

Motifs," 184). A woman, briefly glimpsed, shatters the viewer's composure, inspiring fascination, desire, and loss. "[T]hese verses could only have been written in a big city," Benjamin says, quoting Thibaudet, adding that "they reveal the stigmata which life in a metropolis inflicts upon love" (185). The shock of the crowd is displaced onto a glance, the modern metropole felt not in the surging movement Poe memorialized in "The Man of the Crowd" but in the "stigmata" scored by the city on "a lonely man" (185). Benjamin's comparison of the crowd's absent presence to the wind that powers a sailboat provides a felicitous metaphor for a good deal of modernist representation where the text renders the ghostly presence of what can't be articulated. Whatever "glance" the passing woman conveys produces a "wild eccentricity" and inebriation in excess of what the face actually registers.

Adapting Raymond Williams, we might say that Baudelaire's poem embodies a structure of feeling around modernity, measuring the "ephemeral" and "contingent" qualities that the poet, in "The Painter and Modern Life," identifies with Second Empire Paris ("Painter," 13).[2] Williams uses "structure of feeling" to describe the impact of social conditions "still in process…at the very edge of semantic availability" and as such have not as yet been formed into "formal concepts of 'world-view' or 'ideology'" (132). By adapting Williams' phrase to modernist aesthetics I may be doing some violence to his usage which, as Sianne Ngai argues, is not to describe personal feelings but to "mobilize an entire affective register, *in* its entirety, and *as* a register, in order to enlarge the scope and definition of materialist analysis" (360). But what is an "affective register" without individuals so affected? Thinking of modernism as a structure of feeling allows us to consider the impact of experiences "lived and felt" before being defined and also allows us to locate what Williams sees as "the very edge of semantic availability" beyond matters of formal experiment and linguistic estrangement. Williams recognized that his phrase "has a special relevance to art and literature, where the true social content is in a significant number of cases of this present and affective kind, which cannot without loss be reduced to belief-systems, institutions, or explicit general relationships" (133).[3]

My example from Baudelaire, taken from the beginnings of European modernism, expresses what it might mean to "feel modern" and suggests the extent to which modernism, in addition to being a series of movements, manifestos, and formal innovations is also an affective response to quotidian events in the present: a woman buying flowers for a party, a man carrying a potato through the streets of Dublin, a poet seeing faces emerging from a Metro station.[4] Such ephemeral moments condense much larger historical transformations whose representation is inadequately expressed through more familiar rhetorical terms (metaphor, objective correlative,

[2] Williams' theory of the structure of feeling is anticipated by Marx's remark, "[the] world long possesses the dream of something before the consciousness to be able to truly possess it" (qtd. Lunn, 166).
[3] Jonathan Flatley provides a concise definition of how structures of feeling mediate quotidian experience: "If the function of an ideology is to narrate our relation to a social order so as to make our daily experience of that order meaningful and manageable, then *structure of feeling* would be the term to describe the mediating structure—one just as socially produced as ideology—that facilitates and shapes our affective attachment to different objects in the social order" (26).
[4] Justus Nieland has usefully developed the relationship between feeling and what he calls "modernist publicness" in *Feeling Modern: The Eccentricities of Public Life*.

image).[5] Perhaps "feeling" is itself a product of modernity, forged in biopolitical regimes of medical science and psychoanalysis such that to "feel modern" is to experience novelty through a lens created for that experience.

Modernist aesthetics is built around discourses of feeling and emotion, from Kantian detachment to Eliot's impersonality to New Critical prohibitions against fallacies of intention and affect to Fredric Jameson's worry about their waning. Either art must act as a barrier against the sentimentalized products of mass culture (Pound advocated verse that would avoid "emotional slither") or it must create new feelings in the beholder, a systematic derangement of the senses ("Retrospect," 12). Eliot's impersonal theory is the most famous example of the former tendency, yet his attack is less on emotional excess than on an inadequate frame or "objective correlative" to contain it. According to Eliot, Shakespeare's *Hamlet* fails to explain his protagonist's madness because the playwright was unable to separate his feelings of loss for his son, Hamnet, from his fictional character through an adequate rhetorical frame. Terms that we associate with feeling in modernity—depression, ennui, spleen, shock, *ressentiment*, melancholia—are hardly new to the late nineteenth century, but they mean something different with the rise of diagnostic sciences that renegotiated affect in the body and cognition and not in miasma or humoral theory.

I am influenced in thinking about modernism as a structure of feeling by recent theories of affect that have returned the body to cultural discourse after a long sojourn in textuality and performativity.[6] If in post-structuralism the Subject is dead, there is little reason to speak of its emotion or feeling. This shift in focus should not be seen as a return to biologism or identity politics so much as recognition that post-structural theories of identity often bypass the phenomenological experience of individuals in social environments, the social and political contexts in which feelings are produced. This return to corporeality acknowledges that the pre-discursive body is still a body, despite what meanings accrue to it over time.

Affect theorists often distinguish between affect and emotion, between physical sensations and the meanings that we bring to them. From William James and Henri Bergson to Silvan Tomkins, William Connolly, Eve Sedgwick, and Brian Massumi, affect is regarded as a pre-cognitive, non-intentional response to the environment, whereas emotions or feelings constitute what we make of those responses. As William James summarized this fact, "we feel sorry because we cry, angry because we strike, afraid because we tremble, and not that we cry, strike, or tremble, because we are sorry, angry, or fearful, as the case may be" (450). A woman in mourning passes in a crowd, inspiring a poet to feelings of longing and fascination that he transforms into a sonnet. The discontinuity between poet's gaze and ensuing interpretation suggests that affect is not lodged in the individual—the

---

[5] Laurent Berlant, echoing Raymond Williams, notes that the central claim in her book *Cruel Optimism*, "is that the present is perceived, first affectively: the present is what makes itself present to us before it becomes anything else, such as an orchestrated collective event or an epoch on which we can look back" (4).

[6] On affect theory's response to post-structuralism, see Patricia Clough, "The Affective Turn: Political Economy, Biomedia, and Bodies," and Rei Terada, *Feeling in Theory: Emotion after the "Death of the Subject."*

Subject of emotion—but in its circulation between and among individuals, objects, and incidents, what Lauren Berlant calls the "messy dynamics of attachment" (15).[7] Unlike Freudian drives, whose etiology is in the subconscious, affects, as Sara Ahmed says, are components of what she calls, "'the drama of contingency,' how we are touched by what comes near" (*Promise*, 22). It is this latter feature of affect as a circulation or transmission of emotions that reinforces Benjamin's observation that the crowd, though invisible, is contained in a woman's look.

Theorists of affect have, as I have said in previous chapters, said little about disability even though its very subjects—feelings, sensations, emotions—are at the center of disability experience. In earlier chapters I have discussed "dramas of contingency" as they apply to disability: the dwarf in Zemlinsky's opera whose sight of himself is his ruin; interactions between Beckett's co-dependent characters, Hamm and Clove, Winnie and Willie, whose endlessly protracted conversations cement their relationship; Nora Flood's abject response to Robin Vote's silences. Perhaps the best illustration as it applies to disability is my opening anecdote about Theodor Adorno's meeting with the paraplegic actor, Harold Russell. Adorno's startled response—and Charlie Chaplin's mimicked version—suggests the degree to which disability is produced as an interchange among individuals rather than a condition lodged in a single body. The anecdote also implicates the aesthetic insofar as Chaplin's reenactment of Adorno's reaction is a literal "drama" of bodily contingency among the three actors in this incident.

Within disability studies, one of the clearest statements of the embodied nature of the aesthetic is Tobin Siebers' assertion that "[a]esthetics studies the way that some bodies make other bodies feel" (*Disability Aesthetics*, 25). By "bodies" he includes objects, paintings, artifacts, animals, and natural phenomena. The emphasis here is on the feelings produced "in bodies by other bodies" through involuntary response. "Aesthetics is the domain in which the sensation of otherness is felt at its most powerful, strange, and frightening. Whether the effect is beauty and pleasure, ugliness and pain, or sublimity and terror, the emotional impact of one body on another is experienced as an assault on autonomy and a testament to the power of otherness" (25).

In this chapter I look at this "power of otherness" as an affective response intimately connected to the formation of modernity itself. I explore the implications of modernist affect in several texts that register the impact of dynamic—perhaps traumatic—changes in the late nineteenth and early twentieth centuries in works by Sigmund Freud, Frank Norris, Henry James, Virginia Woolf, and Jean Toomer. I have not chosen more obvious example of modernist affect identified with the revolt from romanticism and sentimentality, embodied in aesthetics of impersonality and detachment. Nor have I chosen the more heated rhetoric of emotion in Futurist manifestos or the expressionist colorations and spatial distortions of Edvard Munch's *The Scream*. Fredric Jameson sees the latter as a "canonical expression of

---

[7] Patricia Clough argues "focusing on affect—without following the circuit from affect to subjectively felt emotional states—makes clear how the turn to affect is a harbinger of and a discursive accompaniment to the forging of a new body, what I am calling the biomediated body" (207).

the great modernist thematics of alienation, anomie, solitude, social fragmentation, and isolation, a virtually programmatic emblem of what used to be called the age of anxiety" (*Postmodernism*, 11). While agreeing with his assessment of Munch's painting, I want to look at equally powerful invocations of modernist affect located not in a dialectic of surface and depth, latent and manifest, authentic and inauthentic that Jameson, drawing from Lukács, sees as defining modernist binaries but in more pedestrian events and interactions that anticipate future disturbances. It is in such moments of sudden apprehension that the materiality of modern life meets the materialities of bodily and psychic life.

AESTHETIC INVESTIGATIONS

Freud's qualification in the opening to his 1919 essay, "The Uncanny," speaks volumes about his ambivalence over the role of aesthetics in psychoanalysis: "Only rarely does the psychoanalyst feel impelled to engage in aesthetic investigations, even when aesthetics is not restricted to the theory of beauty, but described as relating to the qualities of our feeling" (123). This rejection of "aesthetic investigation" contradicts Freud's well-known use of classical drama, early modern art, and folklore that mark many of his key theoretical insights. One might observe that his worries concern the risk that aesthetics and flights of fancy might tarnish scientific objectivity. He pleads guilty to "obtuseness" about uncanny events, even though his essay features numerous personal examples of exactly such experiences. Almost grudgingly he confesses "now and then it happens that he has to take an interest in a particular area of aesthetics, and then it is usually a marginal one that has been neglected in the specialist literature" (123). Such defensiveness is surely one of the weirder openings to one of his essays, perhaps reflecting Freud's own ambivalent relationship to a subject with which he identifies all too closely.

Although the works by Norris and James that I will consider next were written before Freud's essay, "The Uncanny" may serve as a post hoc commentary on their fictional renderings of affective response. Not a fictional work, "The Uncanny" is intensely devoted to aesthetic matters. The long philological excursus on the words *Heimlich* and *Unheimlich*, the lengthy reading of E. T. A. Hoffmann's folktale "The Sand Man," and the use of personal anecdotes situate "The Uncanny" as a mixed-genre work of poetic and biographical criticism. Freud's opening remarks, quoting E. Jentsch, stipulate that uncanny effects can best be produced through story-telling, "leaving the reader wondering whether a particular figure is a real person or an automaton" (135). The essay has not been seen as a key document in affect theory, yet it is perhaps Freud's most direct elaboration of emotional states.

For my purposes "The Uncanny" is also an essay about affective relations to disability insofar as Freud probes whether "a figure is a real person or an automaton." Every attempt to define the uncanny is accompanied by reference to embodied otherness—madness, blindness, amputation, epilepsy—that for Freud unsettles the domestic security and threatens bodily norms. He notes, for example, that "we can speak of a living person as uncanny" or that "the fear of going blind is quite often a substitute for the fear of castration" (149, 139). He compares the confrontation with epilepsy or madness to encountering an individual possessed of "secret forces" (150). "Severed limbs, a severed head, a hand detached from the arm, . . . feet that dance by themselves" all "have something uncanny about them" (150). Such phenomena remind Freud of incidents in which he confronts his own body as other. In an important footnote, he describes being startled by seeing his reflection in the mirror of a darkened railroad car whereupon he experiences "intellectual uncertainty" about his own physical identity. The sudden confrontation with himself as an "an elderly gentleman in a dressing gown" causes Freud to question whether it is "a vestige of the archaic reaction to the 'double' as something uncanny?" (162).

Freud defines uncanny experience as "that class of terrifying which leads back to something long known to us, once familiar" (124). Uncanny experiences occur when a sudden confrontation triggers long suppressed infantile complexes or when "primitive beliefs which have been surmounted seem once more to be confirmed." His lengthy etymological tour through various definitions of the German word *Heimlich* ("homely") leads him to realize that this term for domestic security and homeliness may be used coextensively with its opposite, *unheimlich*, or "unhomely." It is this close conjunction of the familiar and strange that motivates his sense that uncanny encounters return us to something once known but then repressed. The essay was written at a moment when Freud was shifting his focus from the development of childhood sexuality and the formation of the ego to the formation of rationality in cultural matters that he was to explore in *Beyond the Pleasure Principle*, *Civilization and its Discontents*, and *Moses and Monotheism*. The two foci, subjective and social, are contained in his description of two classes of uncanny: the return of infantile complexes (fears of castration and womb anxiety) and the return of primitive beliefs (the animistic theories of universe, return of the dead, omnipotence of thought).

A common thread connects Freud's examples of the uncanny: either they correspond to animistic stages in primitive, archaic civilizations or else they define inanimate objects (dolls, automatons) that seem possessed of life. Freud describes the titular figure in E. T. A. Hoffmann's story "The Sand Man" as a demonic visitor who steals the eyes of misbehaving children by throwing sand into their eyes. The story's protagonist, Nathaniel, associates the Sand Man with a mysterious visitor who comes to visit the boy's father. The fear of the Sand Man, now associated with the paternal figure, is a fear of losing his eyesight. Freud's familiar Oedipal linkage of blindness with castration reappears throughout Nathaniel's life, associated often with the loss of the father and the immanence of love and sexuality. The uncanny elements of the story are embodied in Nathaniel's obsession with Olympia, a life-sized doll with human eyes, a figure both familiar yet inanimate. Freud aligns Nathaniel's fear/ love of Olympia to his (Freud's) own experience of finding himself lost in a street in Italy in a neighborhood of prostitutes. Here it is the gaze of the women that is uncanny; they are like Olympia, painted and doll-like yet human. Once again, it is the fear of castration—the fear of seeing the "unheimlich" female genitalia—the entrance to one's "man's old home," as Freud says—that causes his aversion (151).

Because Freud's theory of castration is always seen as a story about male differentiation of gender and the emergence of the ego separate from the body, it is often forgotten that the tenor of the Oedipal story—blindness—is also a condition of disability. One could say that Nathaniel's fear of losing his sight (and Freud's fear of encountering himself) is not a regression to an undifferentiated childhood state but the anxiety produced by the possibility of sensations outside of an ocularcentric regime. The primary narcissism to which castration is consigned is a story about sightedness—Narcissus' sight of himself—and audition—Narcissus' inability to hear Echo's cries. Narcissism may be "mastered" by repression in the formation of the mature ego, but it may also signal a repression of the body and its vulnerability and volatility. "Nowadays we don't believe in such things," Freud says about the return of animism and superstition, but his essay perhaps proves the contrary (154).

EPIC IDENTIFICATIONS: FRANK NORRIS

Benedict Anderson's view of imagined citizenship produced through technologies of print could be modified for the modern period by reference to other technologies that contribute to national and, as I will indicate, global belonging. Consider the tickertape. The first stock ticker that transmitted stock prices electronically to a keyboard appeared in 1867. By the time Frank Norris wrote *The Octopus* in 1901, Thomas Edison's redesigned ticker was a ubiquitous feature of commercial enterprise. In one scene in Norris' novel, the owners of several large California wheat ranches sit around the tickertape machine, receiving stock quotations from the world's markets:

> The offices of the ranches were thus connected by wire with San Francisco, and through that city with Minneapolis, Duluth, Chicago, New York, and at last and most important of all, with Liverpool. Fluctuations in the price of the world's crop during and after the harvest thrilled straight to the office of Los Muertos to that of the Quien Sabe [ranch], to Osterman's and to Broderson's [ranches]. During a flurry in the Chicago wheat pits in the August of that year, which had affected even the San Francisco market, Harran and Magnus had sat up nearly half of one night watching the strip of white tape jerking unsteadily from the reel. *At such moments they no longer felt their individuality. The ranch became merely the part of an enormous whole, a unit in the vast agglomeration of wheat land the whole world round, feeling the effects of causes thousands of miles distant—a drought on the prairies of Dakota, a rain on the plains of India, a frost on the Russian steppes, a hot wind on the llanos of the Argentine.* (italics added, 54)

This is, among other things, a powerful early description of globalization as experienced on the US western frontier. It is also an invocation of homosocial relations reinforced by male bonds of shared economic concern that extend far beyond the California Central Valley. In such moments and through the tickertape machine, the ranchers "no longer [feel] their individuality"; their ranches become "part of an enormous whole, a unit in the vast agglomeration of wheat lands the whole world round." If this passage chronicles a loss of individualism among wheat farmers it is framed through a social Darwinist ideology that explains their exploitation of natural resources by a metaphor of natural selection. Norris was an adherent of Zola's theory of the scientific novel in which "[terrible] things must happen to the characters of the naturalistic tale. They must be twisted from the ordinary, wrenched out from the quiet, uneventful round of every-day life, and flung into the throes of a vast and terrible drama that works itself out in unleashed passion, in blood and in sudden death" ("Zola," 274). The ranchers are synonymous with the land they cultivate, moved by forces beyond their comprehension. Plowing the soil becomes, in Norris, an elemental sexual assault:

> It was the long stroking caress, vigorous, male, powerful, for which the Earth seemed panting. The heroic embrace of a multitude of iron hands, gripping deep into the brown, warm flesh of the land that quivered responsive and passionate under this rude advance, so robust as to be almost an assault, so violent as to be veritably brutal.   (130)

Norris' over-heated rhetoric embodies a primal struggle to wrest natural power into economic consolidation, a rhetoric whose acquisitive pleasure is masked by sexual violence. Such "unreasoned" passions are brought under control by contingencies made possible by the tickertape machine and, not insignificantly for our theme, the railroad.

The novel's title refers to the railroad's tentacle-like reach into the west that made such exploitation possible. Norris describes the railroad as a satanic monster, and, most importantly, a circulatory system that joins, like telegraphic technologies, vast spaces and temporalities, into a common commodity form. Norris based his novel on a historical confrontation between agents of Southern Pacific Railroad and settlers who had been deeded property rights along the railroad's projected route. When the railroad was completed in the California Central Valley, Southern Pacific raised the price on the now much improved land that the homesteaders could ill afford. Land that had been purchased at $2.50 an acre could now be sold for forty or fifty times that amount. The standoff between the railroad and the settlers led to a confrontation at Muscle Slough, near Hanford, in May 1880 that resulted in the death of five settlers and two railroad agents. Marx used the incident as an example of American class conflict and the speed at which capitalism was expanding in California.[8] And it is precisely the issue of speed and development that requires, in Norris, a countervailing aesthetics of sublime wonder and awe.

The story of capitalist expansion in the rural west contrasts with the novel's other epic theme: the power of Nature as embodied in the vast wheat fields, a power experienced through Presley, the novel's poet and Norris' alter ego. He views the Central Valley not as a site of potential development but as an epic landscape, "the whole gigantic sweep of the San Joaquin" that will inspire his as-yet unwritten epic poem. His failure to write his epic of the wheat becomes his private tragedy and serves as a counterpoint to the entrepreneurial success of emergent agribusiness. Presley's presence in the Central Valley is described as part of a rest cure from

---

[8] On the Muscle Slough incident, see Richard Maxwell Brown, "Violence."

tuberculosis, which in the Nativist rhetoric of the day positions him as a product of cosmopolitan sensitivity and eastern refinement against the masculine ethos of the wheat ranchers and the anonymous railroad barons of the Railroad Trust. Standing on a hilltop, surveying the vast valley, Presley begins to read Homer's *Odyssey*, and inspired by its rhythms, attempts his own poem:

> Ha! there it was, his epic, his inspiration, his West, his thundering progression of hexameters. A sudden uplift, a sense of exhilaration, or physical exaltation appeared abruptly to sweep Presley from his feet. As from a point high above the world, he seemed to dominate a universe, a whole order of things. He was dizzied, stunned, stupefied, his morbid supersensitive mind reeling, drunk with the intoxication of mere immensity. Stupendous ideas for which there were no names drove headlong through his brain. Terrible, formless shapes, vague figures, gigantic, monstrous, distorted, whirled at a gallop through his imagination. (47)

In a way, this passage is a companion-piece to my earlier example of the tickertape. Where the wheat barons sense immensity through the tickertape's invocation of world markets, Presley experiences a Nietzschean identification with forces for which his metaphors of intoxication and stupefaction crumble. If the wheat farmers experience a loss of individualism through global capital, Presley experiences a loss of self through the sublime. In a way both parties experience a kind of desolation, one diverted onto other forms of identification. Rather than see these two moments as antithetical, I see them as the Janus face of territorial expansion, much like Klee's *Angelus Novus* as described by Walter Benjamin, the angel of history being propelled "into the future to which his back is turned, while the pile of debris before him grows skyward. This storm is what we call progress" ("Theses," 258).

Although my example from *The Octopus* does not refer specifically to disability it does express the way encounters with novelty produce, as Presley says, "terrible, formless shapes, vague figures, gigantic, monstrous, distorted," for which there are no names. We might see such reactions as a latter-day version of the sublime or the grotesque, but we could also see such inexpressibility as the work of feeling in an age of increasing mechanization, the intrusion of globalization through a ticker-tape machine. The homosocial bonds formed around entrepreneurial capital among the Central Valley ranchers testify to the power of emotional bonds in the face of unimaginable wealth and expansion.

THE "GHOST OF REASON": HENRY JAMES

Norris' villain in *The Octopus* is Shelgrim, President of the Pacific and Southwestern Railway, a figure "whose power was so vast...whose potency for evil so limitless" yet who is a "sentimentalist and an art critic" (574). He combines the two determinants of progress embodied by my two examples above, vast wealth with aesthetic refinement. Encountering him in his office, Presley acknowledges Shelgrim's inscrutability: "[n]o standards of measurement in his mental equipment would apply to the actual man" (574). Shelgrim's immeasurability, as Nicola Nixon points out, is similar to a remark made by William James about seeing John D. Rockefeller in a restaurant in New York in 1904. Nixon suggests that such figures—the Morgans, Carnegies, and Rockefellers—made a strong impact on William's brother, Henry, who may have had these plutocrats in mind in his various capitalist portraits, from Christopher Newman in *The American* to Daniel Touchett in *Portrait of a Lady*. When he returned to New York in 1905, James had occasion to see the effects of American finance capitalism, which he described as being "like a train covering ground at maximum speed and pushing on, at present, into regions unmeasurable" (*American Scene*, 9). This "unmeasurable" wealth he encounters is described in *The American Scene* "as a power by itself, a power unguided, undirected, practically unapplied, really exerting itself in a void that could make it no response, that had nothing—poor gentle, patient, rueful, but altogether helpless, voice!—to offer in return" (9). James' characteristic indirection ("power unguided," "no response," "nothing," "helpless voice") is a marker of a vacated agency that the cosmopolitan writer attempts to reconstitute through his boyhood memories. This is, to some extent, the theme of his late story, "The Jolly Corner" (1908) written very much in response to his American sojourn.

In this story, Spencer Brydon has come back to New York after thirty-three years living abroad. He renews his friendship with Alice Staverton who becomes, like so many women in James novels and stories, his companion and accomplice. Of the changes he experiences upon his return he says, "Everyone asks what I think..." but he avoids responding to their curiosity, feeling perhaps that *his* experience of modern New York differs from what his interlocutors expect (550). He finds New York to be uncanny; everything upside down; skyscrapers, streetcars, and crowds have transformed the city into a phantasmagoria, a game of "ombres chinoises." New York's street grid becomes, for him, a vast "ledger page" centered only around the cash nexus (552). A good deal of the story's opening concerns Brydon's responses to these changes, which, like his avoidance of public curiosity, he expresses through metaphors of emptiness and vacancy.

The occasion for his return is a chance to view two pieces of property that he owns, one a "tall mass of flats" that he is turning into money-making real estate and another, the "jolly corner," which was his ancestral home. Brydon keeps this latter house empty, wandering its unfurnished halls at night unbeknownst to Alice or anyone else. As his American conscience, Alice muses that he can afford to keep his house empty because he lives on the proceeds (she calls them "ill gotten gains") of the other properties. When confronted with this accusation he responds that in a modern world where there are no values "other...than beastly rent values," keeping his house empty is a kind of aesthetic response (555). His belief that he has not a "ghost of reason" for such indulgence is belied by his nightly hauntings of the house that bespeak an obsession with the property's hold on him. Such an obsession is a form of what Michael Hardt calls "corporeal reason," the degree to which affects unseat the separation of mind and body and give shape to a body that can't be known (x).

What Brydon "feels" about the house—his "corporeal reason"—is that there is some alter ego haunting it, a figure whom most critics agree is the ghost of what he might have been had he stayed in the USA. He might have been a man of business or an engineer, an architect of the very flats being converted out of his own property. By haunting the house of his childhood he seeks to meet and trap that ghostly figure and discover what that lost potential might look like. Late on one such evening, Brydon's wanderings in the upper regions of the house produce an uncanny sense that this figure might be standing behind a closed door:

> He knew—yes, as he had never known anything—that, *should he see* the door open, it would all too abjectly be the end of him. It would mean that the agent of his shame—for his shame was the deep abjection—was once more at large and in general possession; and what glared him thus in the face was the act that this would determine for him.   (569)

This is a richly ambiguous passage in terms of affect. The free indirect style permits us to occupy two positions, subjective and objective, at the same time, mimicking at the level of narrative the psychological position of the protagonist who imagines himself as the other. The narrator "takes on" Brydon's anxiety, facing not the ghost but the shame it inspires. Brydon's anticipated shame at witnessing the ghost seems an odd response to what for most people would be "fear" or "dread." Silvan Tomkins notes that shame, characterized by a loss of face, is a "sickness within the self" in relation to another's face, something that makes one avert one's eyes and lower one's head (136). But in this case, the "other face" would be Brydon's own and thus is a shame at seeing some aspect of himself to and by himself. The interrupted communication between self and other that characterizes shame is turned back onto the experiencing subject who shuts the door against his own abjection.

But all of this is stated in the conditional tense: "*should* he see the door open, it *would* all too abjectly be the end of him." Verbal self-protection prevents his confrontation with an abasement he has striven to keep at bay. Refusing to open the door as a gesture of refusal, he climbs down the stairs, confident he has conquered his fears, but at the bottom of the stairs, he encounters a figure "[rigid] and conscious, spectral yet human" with a "grizzled bent head and white masking hands" the latter of which are missing two fingers (571). The idea that the lived life may be represented by amputated fingers reinforces the historical fact of disability produced by workplace accidents. James' rhetoric in this confrontation scene captures Brydon's surprise that his hunt for himself has revealed a more frightening figure:

> the face, *that* face, Spencer Brydon's?—he searched it still, but looking away from it in dismay and denial, falling straight from his height of sublimity. It was unknown, inconceivable, awful, disconnected from any possibility—! He had been 'sold,' he inwardly moaned, stalking such game as this… the face was the face of a stranger.   (572)

Facing this face, he swoons, and when he is awakened to Alice Staverton's nurturing arms, he describes what he has just seen: "this brute's a black stranger. He's *none of me,* even as I *might* have been" (575).

Criticism of this scene tends to divide along two major lines. One sees the confrontation with this "black stranger" as Brydon's repudiation of his capitalist doppelgänger. The other is that he experiences a moral panic, rejecting a male erotic self (a "quite erect confronting presence") from which he must dissociate himself. James' narrative, by ending with Alice Staverton's redemptive embrace, helps in this dissociation by offering a convenient heterosexual denouement. Brydon *is* as Eric Savoy says, a deeply closeted figure, marked both by his aestheticist trappings and bachelor status. He has lived a "frivolous, scandalous life" in Europe, pursuing, as he says, "strange gods," a covert sign of homosexuality. I see both readings, materialist and queer, as mutually constitutive; money and moral panic vie for affective seats in Brydon's conflicted consciousness. His characterization of the ghost as "black beast" indicates the degree to which his fear of "coming out" as crass materialist or "invert" requires a racial subtext for identities he can't imagine. James' Gothic conventions—a haunted house, a ghost, flickering candles—provide the trappings for a drama of contingent relations between financial and sexual economies, and between past and present. As Savoy says, Brydon "is brought closer and closer to an unthinkable fate that he originally left America to avoid, a fate generated by the interlinearity between his retrospective curiosity and Alice's heterosexual compulsions" (4). The "ghost of reason" that keeps the Jolly Corner empty is the threat, experienced through Brydon's fear, that these compulsions still inhabit the house of Reason if not the House of Fiction.

AFFECTIVE HAUNTING: VIRGINIA WOOLF AND JEAN TOOMER

Janet Lyon describes a passage from Virginia Woolf's journals from 1915 in which, while walking on a towpath, the author encounters "a long line of imbeciles...It was perfectly horrible; they should certainly be killed." As Lyon observes, commentators have not known "quite to do with this violent speech act" ("On the Asylum Road," 552). It seems wildly in excess of the event, an extreme utterance in contrast to the otherwise mundane meeting. Lyon sees it as a particularly modern phenomenon, merging "modernism's investigations of consciousness, the contested political realm of visibility, and the affective conditions for shock" (552). I want to probe the tripartite structure that Lyon brings to this incident in developing what it means to "feel" in modernity. The three areas she mentions—new theories of consciousness, the politics of visibility, and affective conditions for shock—encapsulate the uncanny experiences in my previous examples where the sight of difference triggers affective realms for which there seems no rational explanation. Laws protecting citizens from exposure to deformed or disabled persons, asylums and sanitaria to sequester such persons from view, exhibitions displaying freaks and oddities were historical attempts to either prevent the visibility of otherness or provide a convenient narrative to explain it.

Woolf's most extensive meditation on the urban uncanny is her 1930 essay, "Street Haunting," that describes her encounters with various forms of corporeal and cognitive otherness, discovering ultimately "that one is not tethered to a single mind but can put on briefly for a few minutes the bodies and minds of others" (239). As we will see with my example of Jean Toomer, this sudden assumption of the other's body and mind, however provisional, distributes affect among individuals. At one level "Street Haunting" parallels other modernist works of urban wandering from Poe's "Man of the Crowd" or Baudelaire's flâneur to Bloom's perambulations in Dublin or T. S. Eliot's "Love Song of J. Alfred Prufrock" ["Let us go then you and I..."]. Woolf's "flâneuse" sets out to buy a homely pencil in the Strand, but acknowledges at the outset that it is only a pretext for being out in the world, "rambling the streets of London" (225). Despite her disclaimer about the insignificance of the object of her adventure, the pencil *is* central to her *flâneurie*, enabling contact with strangers, other classes, and bodies.

The essay is fortuitously for my purposes a version of modern *Unheimlich*. Woolf begins by describing the solitude and comfort of her domestic interior. A bowl on the mantelpiece reminds her of a day in Italy, a quarrel between an innkeeper and his wife, and meeting a "melancholy Englishman" (226). The bowl is the focal point for the familiar *Heimlich* realm that she leaves behind: "But when the door shuts on us, all that vanishes" (226). Once among the men and women on the street she joins "that vast republican army of anonymous trampers whose society is so agreeable after the solitude of one's own rooms" (225). London's nighttime beauty is a phantasmagoria of lights and shadows, "points of brilliance burning steady like low stars—lamps" (227). However beautiful the London night, the city betrays an apparitional quality that Woolf attempts to domesticate by comparing the urban landscape to rural spaces ("islands of light," "passage down the smooth stream") or by spying domestic scenes through lit windows.

Woolf uses the present tense throughout to enlist the reader in her wandering. As she stops to look in shop windows or doorways, so the reader accompanies her gaze. Her shifting perceptions and observations apostrophize an unseen interlocutor: "But here we must stop peremptorily" (228). Each stage of her journey toward the elusive pencil is an occasion to comment on perception as it organizes the strange into the familiar: "for the eye has this strange property: it rests only on beauty; like a butterfly it seeks out colour and basks in warmth" (228). This aesthetic reverie is broken suddenly when she halts at the door of a boot shop and asks herself "What, then, is it like to be a dwarf."

This question is at the center of the essay, an incident that Janet Lyon has analyzed brilliantly so that my comments are more of a footnote to her treatment. Woolf observes a short statured woman trying on shoes:

> She came in escorted by two women who, being of normal size, looked like benevolent giants beside her. Smiling at the shop girls, they seemed to be at once disclaiming any lot in her deformity and assuring her of their protection. She wore the peevish yet apologetic expression usual on the faces of the deformed. She needed their kindness, yet she resented it. But when the shop girl has been summoned and the giantesses, smiling indulgently, had asked for shoes for 'this lady' and the girl had pushed the little stand in front of her, the dwarf stuck her foot out with an impetuosity which seemed to claim all our attention. Look at that! Look at that! she seemed to demand of us all, as she thrust her foot out, for behold it was the shapely, perfectly proportioned foot of a well-grown woman. (229)

Woolf concentrates on scale and on the ways that differences in bodies are normalized in relation to the observer, constructing the woman's companions as "giantesses." Woolf's attempt to narrate the scene is reinforced by her repetition of the word "seems" and her interpretation of facial gestures, imagining for instance that "[s]eeing nothing but her feet, she imagined perhaps that the rest of her body was of a piece with those beautiful feet" (229). She interprets the expression on the short woman's face as "apologetic" or "usual on the faces of the deformed." Despite her construction of the dwarf as "deformed" she confesses that the foot of the dwarf is "perfectly proportioned." As the woman tries on shoes, she demands (in Woolf's account) that her feet be seen. After having purchased a pair, the atmosphere changes: "with the parcel swinging from her finger, the ecstasy faced, knowledge returned, the old peevishness, the old apology came back, and by the time she had reached the street again she had become a dwarf" (230). The passage describes the author's attempt to narrate a situation that, as with the encounter with "imbeciles" on the towpath, she cannot understand. Her parting remark, "she had become a dwarf" offers a consoling sense that although the dwarf had become a woman in the store while trying on shoes once she returns to the street she becomes a category.

As she leaves the boot shop, Woolf notes that the dwarf "had changed the mood":

> she had called into being an atmosphere which, as we followed her out into the street, seemed actually to create the humped the twisted, the deformed. Two bearded men, brothers apparently; stone-blind, supporting themselves by resting a hand on the head of a small boy between them, marched down the street. On they came with the unyielding yet tremulous tread of the blind, which seems to lend to their approach something of the terror and inevitability of the fate that has overtaken them. (230)

Here, the "atmosphere" created by a brief glimpse produces the condition for subsequent encounters with the "humped, twisted and deformed." The two blind figures flanked by a sighted boy are a reversal of the short statured woman and her "giantess" companions. Once again, Woolf strives to interpret disability, seeing blindness as "terror and inevitability of the fate that has overtaken them." This encounter is followed by the appearance of "a bearded Jew, wild, hunger-bitten, glaring out of his misery" and "the humped body of an old woman flung abandoned on the step of a public building with a cloak over her like the hasty covering thrown over a dead horse or donkey." Woolf concludes by noting that *At such sights, the nerves of the spine seem to stand erect; a sudden flare is brandished in our eyes; a question is asked which is never answered* (231, emphasis added).

Teresa Brennan has described this productive quality of atmosphere as the "transmission of affect," the way that the mood of an environment is produced by social encounters experienced physiologically. In Brennan's account, affective response does not arise in the individual but occurs through the individual's inter-action with other bodies and environments. Woolf's observation that such scenes cause the "nerves of the spine seem to stand erect" seems an apt description of this socially transmitted atmosphere that seems to demand interpretation. Woolf's ini-tial question upon encountering the different body had been "What, then, is it like to be a dwarf?" and the entire passage attempts to provide an answer by measuring, interpreting, and projecting. But as the passage above reveals, the question remains unanswered since it is less about what it feels like to be a dwarf but what it feels like not to be oneself.

Something of this same sense of self-differentiation occurs in a very different social milieu from Woolf's London in Jean Toomer's Washington DC. In both sites a confrontation with a dwarf provides a brief moment of affective identification that changes the mood of a metropolitan outing. In "Box Seat," one of the urban stories in *Cane*, Toomer represents tensions in the African American community around assimilation and displacement during the Great Migration of African Americans from the south to the north. In the second section of the novel, set in Washington DC and Chicago, black characters struggle to escape the legacy of southern racism yet feel caged in middle-class proprieties that both domesticate and alienate.

Dan Moore, the protagonist of the story, "born in a cane-field," is now displaced in urban Washington DC. He feels his outsider status acutely, constrained by the "box seat" that provides a metaphor for his theatrical view of a white dominated world. He pursues Muriel, a schoolteacher who is anxious to assimilate into middle-class life and proprieties that are threatened by passions that Dan excites in her. She lives in a boarding house run by Mrs. Pribby whose repressiveness and conformism mock aspects of black uplift. Dan experiences visiting Muriel at Mrs. Pribby's as a violent disruption. Waiting to be admitted, he muses:

> Break in. Get an ax and smash in. Smash in their faces. I'll show em. Break into an engine-house, steal a thousand horse-power fire truck...And then the cops come. "No, I aint a baboon. I aint Jack the Ripper. I'm a poor man out of work." (77)

Once admitted to the house by Mrs. Pribby, Dan's rhetoric toward Muriel changes from his internalized stereotype of black male violence to an idealized romantic rhetoric: "Life bends joy and pain, beauty and ugliness, in such a way that no one may isolate them" (81). Muriel's ambivalence over her feelings for Dan reflects her conflicted relationship to upwardly mobile class aspirations:

> Muriel: Shame about Dan. Something awfully good and fine about him. But he don't fit in. In where? Me? Dan, I could love you if I tried. I don't have to try...Mrs. Pribby who reads newspapers all night wont. What has she got to do with me? She is me, somehow. No she's not. Yes she is. She is the town and town wont let me love you, Dan. (80)

The theatrical frame in which "Box Seat" is set is established in the second part of the story that takes place at a variety show at the Lincoln Theater. Muriel has gone with her friend Bernice, and Dan follows them. Dan's presence at the theater upsets not only Muriel but unsettles other members of the audience as well. He talks out loud, steps on people's feet, and at one point challenges one man to a fight. As in his confrontation with Mrs. Pribby's boarding house, he seeks to blast away at the walls of the building and discover roots beneath the floor. At one point he sits next to a "portly Negress": "A soil-soaked fragrance comes from her. Through the cement floor her strong roots sink down. They spread under the asphalt streets" (85). Dan also notices an old man in the audience, "And he was born in slavery.

I did see his eyes...He saw Grant and Lincoln. He saw Walt—old man, did you see Walt Whitman? Did you see Walt Whitman! Strange force that drew me to him" (89). The eruption of the South in the northern theater, the inescapability of regional forces and slavery in migratory patterns, complicates a unitary narrative of class aspirations.

As with my Woolf example, confrontation with a short statured person transforms the mood of the room. One act of the variety show involves dwarfs engaged in a boxing match. The victor of the match is then enlisted to sing a song while holding a white rose on which blood has dripped from his exertions. While singing his sentimental aria, he holds a mirror by which he flashes light onto the person to whom he's singing. The dwarf offers his white rose to Muriel who, revolted by what she sees as a grotesque figure, hesitates to accept it. Dan looks deeply into the dwarf's eyes and rather than seeing grotesquery sees "a thing of wisdom and tenderness, of suffering and beauty. The eyes are calm and luminous. Words come from them..." (90). Those words are a call to which Dan responds:

> Do not shrink. Do not be afraid of me.
> *Jesus*
> See how my eyes look at you.
> *the Son of God*
> I too was made in his image.
> *was once—*
> I give you the rose.   (90)

Completing what he imagines to be the dwarf's remarks, Dan leaps to his feet and shouts "JESUS WAS ONCE A LEPER!" From here, Dan leaves the theater "cool as a green stem that has just shed its flower" (91).

We now see the intersection of race and bodily difference. The dwarf offers a spectacle to the black audience of their own reduced status, one at which they can laugh. But Dan sees a redemptive potential in the dwarf that he connects with Christian values "of wisdom and tenderness, of suffering and beauty." Dan's remark about Christ as leper contributes to this intersection by connecting the suffering savior with a disabled figure. His dramatic response to the audience in the Lincoln Theater shatters the barrier between audience and actors, making himself the abject figure of difference. As an actor, the dwarf is also like Dan, playing a role, using his mirror not to reflect himself but to allow the audience to see themselves in him. It is an elaborate, perhaps overly ornate metaphor yet it is the moment in the novel when the different body helps reveal a common inheritance endlessly repressed in the constraining enclosures of houses, theaters, and box seats. Dan experiences a restorative identification with the different body, one that marks his racial ostracism but also his identity within a larger community of suffering and beauty.

This incident reflects Toomer's well-known ambivalence about race, his refusal to be called a "Negro writer" or to have his work appear in Alain Locke's *The New Negro*. He wrote *Cane* following his own return to Georgia, and "Box Seat," marks a convergence of race and class that can be found in many other writers of the Harlem Renaissance from James Weldon Johnson to Nella Larsen. What is often overlooked in treatments of *Cane* is the importance of the different body in the call and response structure that organizes many chapters in *Cane*.[9] "Box Seat" complicates the reciprocal relationship established by black preacher or singer and audience or chorus by bringing displaced southern black male and theatrical dwarf together in a duet of marginal identities. Dan's ability to empathize with the short statured person differentiates him from Muriel and other members of the Lincoln audience and transforms alienation of the dislocated southern figure into participant in a larger community.

FEELING MODERN

I began by noting the use of affect theory to understand how modernism has been accomplished through what Madeleine Detloff calls a "memorializing impulse" of modernist works (12). This important tendency is usually framed through Freud's writings on mourning and melancholia and the ways that a traumatic loss lives on in the present. My examples, on the contrary, are less about losses than about possible futures and how literary forms imagine those futures through affective encounters in the present. Frank Norris witnesses the rise of global capital produced by agribusiness and transportation through a mechanical device that brings frontier entrepreneurs together. Henry James describes turn-of-the-century gender trouble through a story of building and investment. Jean Toomer imagines a reciprocal relationship between raced and different bodies. Affect theory's emphasis on the return of the repressed must include the mirror of the present in which the uncanny crowd, Baudelaire's contingent and ephemeral, is contained in a sudden glance.

Sara Ahmed notes that the promise of a happy ending organizes our concept of "the good life." Objects become happy if they fulfill "the fantasy that happiness is what would follow if only we could have 'it'" (*Promise*, 32). The qualified or downright unhappy endings of modern novels (*The Great Gatsby, The Waves, The Awakening, Absalom! Absalom!, Native Son*) testify to the unfulfilled promises of modernity. The tickertape machine that brings isolated ranchers together and expedites trade also disempowers indigenous people, divides communities, and exploits nature. Virginia Woolf's momentary identification of a short statured woman quickly turns her into a category. Those who, like Dan, Presley, and James' bachelors who fail to live up to the promise of heterosexual, marital bliss are "affect aliens," in Ahmed's terms, excluded from the promise of happiness that organizes normative affective protocols.

I began with Raymond Williams' definition of structures of feeling as a way of thinking about how modernity is experienced before it becomes modernism. His point, as I understand it, is that once we apply "world view" or "class outlook" to an emergent social formation, we begin the "slide towards a past tense and a fixed

---

[9] On the call-and-response structure of *Cane* see John F. Callahan, *In the African-American Grain* (62–114).

form" and thus remove it from its experiential locus (129). I will end with another of Williams' observations that the social always lives in the past and that "we must find other terms for the undeniable experience of the present...the specificity of present being, the inalienably physical, within which we may indeed discern and acknowledge institutions, formations, positions, but not always as fixed products, defining products" (128). Those other terms, as I've indicated, may be found in the excessive rhetoric of naturalist novels, the wandering sentences of James, and the *flâneurie* of Virginia Woolf. Modernism exists within the paradox, observed some years ago by Paul de Man, that it is a movement based on capturing the ephemeral present that once canonized as a movement historicizes what it claims to escape. By looking at modernism as sites of affect we may better arrive at that "specificity of present being" through the sudden appearance of a face in the crowd, the "deafening street" screaming all around Baudelaire. This is modernism's drama of contingency—what might happen experienced as what is already felt.

7

Missing Bodies
Disappearances in the Aesthetic

Thus far in *Invalid Modernism* I have focused on work produced during a long modernist period to show the various ways in which disability is an absent presence in the theory and practice of cultural production. In this penultimate chapter I want to bring things into the present by looking at how contemporary artists and writers have confronted embodiment, both through the materiality of their work and through an awareness of the historical and material forces that have marginalized or disappeared bodies. The dwarf in Alexander Zemlinsky's *Der Zwerg* may be a tragic hero, but he is nevertheless a pathological category whose death is necessary to social order. When another short statured person appears in Indra Sinha's 2007 novel, *Animal's People*, his species-bending identity as "animal" challenges liberal humanist versions of species integrity and social justice. Such figures occupy what Tobin Siebers calls "complex" and David Mitchell and Sharon Snyder call "peripheral" embodiments to describe bodies and minds that do not register in a social calculus.

In a similar fashion, my examples in this chapter illustrate an awareness of how modernist formal strategies may be enlisted to appropriate the rhetorics and legal justifications that invalidate some and render others invisible. The biopolitics of disability in a neoliberal period, as David Mitchell and Sharon Snyder have written, is no longer written around institutionalization, incarceration, sterilization, or segregation.[1] Rather it is written through seemingly benign economic considerations—the elimination of affordable healthcare to reduce national debt; the closing of clinics in developing countries that discuss birth control; the winnowing of provisions of the ADA to protect small businesses; the outsourcing of labor to avoid toxic contamination on national soil; the elimination of personal assistance services under the terms of "austerity measures." The so-called "linguistic turn" in contemporary art includes not only an emphasis on the materiality of language but also the exculpatory rhetoric that diminishes access under the promise of growth.

By speaking of contemporary artists "appropriating" public rhetorics I mean to account for the ways in which writers foreground the institutional, discursive means by which the "human" is defined. M. NourbeSe Philip's *Zong!* quotes from

---

[1] David T. Mitchell and Sharon L. Snyder, *The Biopolitics of Disability: Neoliberalism, Ablenationalism, and Peripheral Embodiment*.

a legal case concerning the actuarial implications of murdering African slaves during the Middle Passage; Rachel Zolf critiques political rhetoric of "hospitality" by drawing on public records relating to the Palestinian–Israeli conflict. Amanda Baggs' video "In my Language" rearticulates—literally—the idea that persons on the autism spectrum have no language by using a digitized voice that translates her typewritten text. Where modernist writers like Pound or Eliot could quote from classical sources to buttress a monument of elite cultural value, the figures whom I discuss here appropriate public rhetorics that keep and burnish that monument.

*   *   *

In 2007 the British artist and designer Simon Starling began creating a large installation for the Massachusetts Museum of Art based on a haunting photograph.

The image was a stereoscopic picture of Chinese workers who had been brought to a shoe factory in North Adams, Massachusetts in 1870 as strikebreakers (Fig. 7.1).[2] The photograph shows the imported Chinese workers, ranging in age from fourteen to their mid-twenties, standing in their work aprons in front of the factory. They were the first of many waves of Chinese immigrants who came to the East Coast, often brought by companies to crush unions or, as in the case of the recently completed Transcontinental Railroad, conduct labor at wages no white worker would touch. To inaugurate his installation Starling extracted silver particles

Fig. 7.1. *Henry Ward, View of C. T. Sampson's Shoe Manufactory, with the Chinese Shoemakers in Working Costume, North Adams and vicinity, circa 1875.* Stereograph, 7.46 cm × 15.88 cm.

---

[2] According to Anthony Lee, the attempt to crush the union by importing Chinese workers was successful. The photograph was taken five years after their arrival (20).

from a photograph of the stereoview and placed them under an electron microscope where they were magnified twenty-five thousand times in order to produce models for large clay and plaster sculptures that are a million times larger than their original trace particles. In order to create his large biomorphic shapes, Starling hired Chinese workers in Nanjing to cast them and then polish the stainless-steel skin to a brilliant sheen on which visitors to the installation may see their severely distorted reflections (Fig. 7.2).

Installed at MASS MoCA in North Adams, Massachusetts (site of the former shoe factory) Starling's project works across several scales: the transformation of photography into sculpture, the enlargement of the very small to the very large, the traversal of vast geopolitical landscapes, the exchange of labor across varying stages of capital. In the process he raises questions of racialized labor, the emergence of globalization, and the transformative role of photography in modernity. He does so by recreating bodies missing from history through the means by which those bodies were first spectacularized through stereoscopic viewing. Although the original photo did not contain the names of the Chinese workers in North Adams, Starling in his installation provides the identities of the Nanjing workers who cast his sculptures, thereby completing a circuit begun when bodies began to replace bodies in a global economy. It is no small aspect of his project that Starling installed his sculptures in a museum that once housed the shoe factory, thereby linking two forms of production, material and aesthetic, in a common site. Starling's installation is one of many examples of a re-visibilization that restores the body to the

Fig. 7.2. Simon Starling, *The Nanjing Particles* (After *Henry Ward View of C. T. Sampson's Shoe Manufactory with the Chinese Shoemakers in Working Costume, North Adams and Vicinity, circa 1875*) 2008. Installation image at MASS MoCA, Photograph by Arthur Evans.

aesthetic while representing the biopolitical regimes that erase it. His emphasis is less on the finished sculptures as objects than the processes he undergoes in tracing the larger economies of labor and production. In his work, the missing laboring body is returned to history through an aesthetic that links corporeality with the materiality of cultural production.[3]

His procedure complicates a revived ocularcentrism where the body seems to be increasingly visible, whether through digital imaging, video endoscopy, MRI and CAT scans, or the post 9/11 security state. Several specific examples of the visible body come to mind. In 1994 the Visible Human Project created a vast "digital image library of volumetric data representing a complete, normal male and female" that, according to the Center for Human Simulation at the University of Colorado provides "a universally-accessible, national resource for anatomical information for researchers, educators, medical professionals, as well as the general public" (Cartwright, 24). Current arguments by anti-abortion forces for fetal personhood often use sonogram images to make the unborn fetus visible as a "baby." Perhaps the most symptomatic example of the visible body is the *Body Worlds* exhibitions of Gunther von Hagens whose plastination process replaces cadavers with polymerized replicas.[4] And in a broader cultural context, we might add the increased visibility of queer, racialized, and disabled bodies that are now standard features of sit-coms, advertising, and films.

Starling's installation seems to confirm Monica J. Casper and Lisa Jean Moore's observation that for every newly visible body there are alarming numbers of missing bodies—disappeared in internecine conflicts, abducted in sectarian warfare, killed by pilotless drones, rendered stateless by suspension of habeas corpus, denied access to representation through indefinite detention, renamed through actuarial, census, and redistricting protocols. Persons displaced by civil wars in Sudan, Syria, and Mali have led to entire generations of children—such as the "Lost Boys" of Sudan—living in permanent refugee status, stateless, homeless, and invisible.[5] Gunther von Hagens' *Body Worlds* exhibitions may make the body's interior visible for a mass public, but his displays infamously erase the specific gendered and racial backgrounds of the Chinese convicts that often supplied cadavers for his experiments. The "state of exception" described by Giorgio Agamben in his critique of Carl Schmitt, focalizes this "no-man's land between public law and political fact," where the suspension of rights during civil conflict and through edicts such as the USA Patriot Act (2001) produce "a legally unnamable and unclassifiable being" (3). The current period's buoyant claims for increased visibility, crime prevention, and rights must be set beside the darker realities of what those claims occlude.

[3] A good introduction to Starling's project and to his other works can be found in Susan Cross' catalogue essay in *The Nanjing Particles*.

[4] Ari Larissa Heinrich has provided an extensive discussion of the *Body Worlds* exhibitions in his book, *Chinese Surplus*. He also describes an exhibition by the Chinese artist Zhang Dali that extends my remarks about Simon Starling's installation. Zhang's *Chinese Offspring* installation "consists of multiple full-body casts of migrant laborers suspended from exhibition space ceilings, the better to reflect (as the art critic Feng Boyi has pointed out) the migrant laborers' 'extremely low position in society and the plight of their inverted reality' " (130).

[5] On the "lost boys" see Jeffrey Gettleman, "A New Wave of 'Lost Boys' in Sudan War."

Avery Gordon refers to such absent presences as a form of the sociological uncanny, "a seething presence, acting on and often meddling with taken-for-granted realities... The ghost is not simply a dead or a missing person, but a social figure, and investigating it can lead to that dense site where history and subjectivity make social life" (8). Gordon's three case studies—the absent Sabina Spielrein in Freud's psychoanalytic project, the disappeared women during Argentina's "dirty war" described in Luisa Valenzuela's novel *Como en la Guerra*, and the ghostly "Beloved" of Toni Morrison's titular novel—offer powerful studies of how women are erased within masculinist historical discourse yet reemerge in uncanny, unsettling forms. Investigating ghosts can also lead to that contradictory site where the somatic collides with the aesthetic, where sensation and affect meet their (presumed) apotheosis in the formal object. As I have said in earlier chapters, classical aesthetics is, among other things, concerned with the impact of the world on the body, on the sensuous response to objects (and other bodies) beyond any consideration of their functionality or instrumentality. The absent body is the ghost in the machinery of the aesthetic, necessary for its smooth functioning yet hidden in the end product. If this sounds a good deal like Marx's description of the commodity form it suggests the close proximity of material and cultural labor.

Of course by speaking of the "body" here as ghost, it might seem that I could as easily be speaking—as does Avery Gordon—of the "subject" or "person," but I want to insist on corporeality as that element of the human most vulnerable to objectification through the exercise of biopower. Slaves who were thrown overboard in the 1781 Zong massacre, which I will discuss later, were not considered subjects but, rather, lost cargo for which an insurance claim could be filed. To speak of them as individuals or "subjects" is to grant them a level of agency denied by their actuarial status as property. If biopolitics represents the absorption of power into and through the body, we might consider *biopoetics* as the reinscription of the missing body in aesthetics. Biopoetics describes the degree to which art is founded on or derived from representations of the *bios* which Giorgio Agamben describes as the "form of living proper to an individual or group," unlike *zoē*, "the simple fact of living common to all living beings (animals, men, or gods)" (1). Of course a poetics of embodiment is not new. An earlier generation of poets and artists took the doctrine of disinterestedness to task by foregrounding the body as source and agent of aesthetic production. The most obvious examples would be the gestural or projectivist arts of the 1960s (body art, action painting, living theater, "field" composition, happenings, etc.), but in such cases the body is presumed to be the natural, neutral origin for agency and action. In contrast, more recent work regards the body as a site of biopolitical control and monitoring. The ideal of an originary voice, scored by the poetic line, gives way, in recent poetics, to a heteroglossia of appropriated sources from the technoscapes and mediascapes that produce and legitimate bodies.[6] Nor does the work I am considering propose a utopian alternative—cyborg,

---

[6] In *Modernity at Large*, Arjun Appadurai describes "technoscapes" and "mediascapes" as spatial forms that "stress different streams or flows along which cultural material may be seen to be moving across national boundaries" (45–6).

interspecies, queer—to the human. A biopoetics implies not only a thematic treatment of embodiment but also a transformation of formal means—a politics of form—of thinking through the body as a discursive and institutional site.

In developing a poetics of embodiment, we might think of several recent works in which missing bodies are the basis for aesthetic practices, the most operatic version being Roberto Bolaño's *2666* which chronicles the disappearances and murders of hundreds of women in Ciudad Juarez. Helena Viramontes' story "The Cariboo Café" concerns the fate of children disappeared in political conflicts in Latin America and the punitive immigration laws in the USA as viewed through several overlapping first person voices. Palestinian artist Taysir Batniji's installation *To my Brother* (2012) features a series of sixty etchings on white paper that at first appear blank but which, upon closer viewing, show photographs of his brother, Mayssara's wedding several years before being killed by an Israeli sniper. Images are transposed to paper by the artist applying pressure to the photograph, providing a ghostly outline of lost family during the Intifada.[7] Myung Mi Kim's *Commons* (2002) explores the displaced condition of the diasporic individual by exhibiting fragments of Korean language, quotations from medical treatises, and graphic and typographic elements. Alex Rivera's 2008 film *Sleep Dealer* depicts a dystopic future where a fortified wall has prevented migrant workers from crossing the US/Mexico border. Mexican workers conduct virtual labor from factories in Mexico through implanted nodes in their bodies that coordinate physical labor by robots on American construction sites. Such examples explore the ways that bodies are disappeared or rendered voiceless through rational procedures and then reconstituted through the public rhetorics that represent them. Bolaño's novel does not set out to expose possible perpetrators of the Juarez killings so much as link these disappearances to the rise of the Maquiladora zone, cosmopolitan mobility, and global free trade agreements. As Derrida says in *Specters of Marx* "[the] name of the one who disappeared must have gotten inscribed someplace else," perhaps like the Chinese laborers in Starling's sculptures, in new forms unrecognizable to the original (4).

I want to focus briefly on several recent works from very different arenas in which the absent bodies in the socio-political world meet the absent body of the aesthetic. My examples, Indra Sinha's novel *Animal's People*, Amanda Baggs' video "In my Language," Rachel Zolf's *Neighbour Procedure*, and M. NourbeSe Philip's *Zong!* read the missing body first through the perspective of globalization theory, second through disability studies, third through cosmopolitan political theory, and fourth through critical race studies. The first addresses the death and disablement of victims of the Bhopal, India disaster through the voice of a nineteen-year-old survivor who identifies as "animal." The second attacks a neurotypical view of embodied and psychological normalcy by means of a video of an autistic woman's "native language" of repetitions and bodily gestures. Zolf's poem reimagines the Israeli–Palestinian conflict by renaming sites and persons evacuated by military procedures. Philip's documentary poem *Zong!* remembers bodies of African slaves massacred in the Middle Passage recuperated through fragmented quotations from legal documents and actuarial reports. In each work, the uncanny presence/absence

---

[7] I am grateful to Soraya Abuelhiga for introducing me to Batniji's work.

of bodies is reinforced by textual and acoustic practices that foreground the body's inscription in public discourse.

Although my examples are drawn from rather different genres and media, they share a common emphasis on the body as cenotaph for bodies lost, disregarded, or evacuated of agency. Sinha's novel poses as a series of ethnographic tapes, recorded by a narrator who is disabled by an industrial accident and who refuses the descriptor "human" or "victim." Baggs' video treats the body as a signifying system in which seemingly empty repetitive gestures connect the person with autism to inanimate objects and spaces. The artist presents herself as a series of body parts, her voice mediated by software, marking her estrangement from normative models of embodiment and communication. Zolf's text draws almost entirely from printed sources relating to the Israeli–Palestinian conflict. Many of these sources recuperate lost or disappeared names of Palestinian communities displaced by Israeli settlements, bystanders killed in ongoing warfare, and historical events erased from authoritative documents. Philip's account of the Zong massacre, its language appropriated from a court trial, provides names for slaves unnamed in the court case. If the body in each work is a memorial for lost bodies, so the novel, video, or poem becomes, in its own way, an archive containing unread (or unreadable) documents of historical displacement.

BECOMING ANIMAL: INDRA SINHA'S
ANIMAL'S PEOPLE

The protagonist of Indra Sinha's 2007 novel, *Animal's People*, is a nineteen-year-old survivor of an industrial accident based on the 1984 Bhopal disaster in India.[8] He has been disfigured by the poisonous gas leak (methyl isocyanate or MIC), and walks on all fours, his spine curved by scoliosis. At times he goes "mad" and hears voices, including those of unborn fetuses of mothers killed in the disaster. Orphaned at age six by exposure to the poisonous gas he has forgotten his birth name and calls himself "Animal," having concluded that if humans can create disasters like Bhopal, he'd rather throw in his lot with other species. Unlike the millions displaced by the toxic leak, Animal continues to live in the neighborhood—the "Nutcracker"— where the disaster occurred, the "World capital of fucked lungs," as one character says (231). The novel's title, *Animal's People*, refers to the slum-dwellers and poor laborers affected by the chemical company Kampani (in reality, Union Carbide) along with the activists who agitate for justice and reparations. Rob Nixon calls the novel an "environmental picaresque" that combines comic elements of the picaro against the backdrop of profound ecological and social trauma. Animal's wit

---

[8] My subheading references Deleuze and Guattari's discussion of "becoming animal" in *A Thousand Plateaus*. Their discussion of a non-evolutionary perspective on species identity is relevant to *Animal's People*, especially their view that "neoevolution" or the becoming of animal nature depends on "a pack, a band, a population, a peopling, in short, a multiplicity" (239). In the case of Sinha's novel, Animal's invisible ghetto community constitutes his "pack" and his decision to adopt the descriptor "animal" results directly from his awareness of how the dominant society demands "animal characteristics to use for classifying people" (239).

and cynicism provide him with survival skills that protect him from the various lures offered by reparation, rehabilitation, and neoliberal adjustment policies that follow catastrophic disasters.

I begin my discussion of missing bodies with *Animal's People* for several reasons. First and foremost is the novel's focus on a landscape where thousands of people literally disappeared—either through physical displacement, injury, or death. The poor and sick denizens of the "Nutcracker" slum who eke out a subsistence living are invisible, both to the Kampani and to the government whose complicity with the industry has led to years of neglect and indifference. As humans and citizens, the novel's characters do not exist: they represent, as Andrew Mahlstedt says, the "spectacular invisibility that defines third-world poverty under recent globalization" (60). My second reason for including this novel concerns its critique of globalization's impact on disability. Union Carbide India Limited, a subsidiary of Union Carbide in the USA was responsible for the gas leak that instantly killed 3,787 individuals and resulted in 558,000 injuries, many of which led to permanent impairments. Within the next several years, over 8,000 people died from complications arising from the leak. To adapt the title of a recent book on global inequality, many are "dying for growth."[9] A third feature concerns the novel's focus on the ways that biotechnology impacts species identity by linking disabled human and non-human animals together. The novel asks what it means to belong to the "same" species and to what extent one's species identity is based on biological, environmental, ethical, or economic factors. A fourth point of relevance is the way that the novel situates disability as a temporal modality, something that occurs over the life course. Industrial catastrophes like Chernobyl and Bhopal experience what Rob Nixon calls "slow violence" produced by "geographies of concealment" over long periods of time. Union Carbide's deferral of restitution (by merging with Dow Chemical) and suspended cleaning of toxic waste contributed to an impact that was gradual and invisible for many years. By situating his narrative twenty years after the event, Sinha emphasizes the long shadow cast by such disasters.

Animal's People could serve as a companion piece to Mel Chen's recent book, *Animacies*, which questions the fine line separating human from animal and organic nature. Rather than see humans as the opposite of, say, stones, Chen treats humans and stones on what she calls an "animacy continuum" that links the organic and inorganic world. In treating humans as occupying a scalar position on this continuum Chen suggests that not only are we what we eat but also what we ingest, what we share with other animals, and what we become when interpellated as "non-human." By thinking of humans as part of a continuum rather than a hierarchy Chen is able to study kinship formations and affective alliances, which, like the subaltern populations of *Animal's People*, live in the interstices of modern society and on the margins of the human.

Chen's use of the term "animacy" is derived from her training as a cognitive linguist where the "animacy continuum" in language refers to the privilege accorded words associated with humans over those associated with objects in a syntactic

⁹ Jim Yong Kim et al., *Dying for Growth: Global Inequality and the Health of the Poor.*

chain ("the people who wait for the bus" over "the bus for which people wait"). For linguists, as she points out, "animacy is the quality of liveness, sentience, or humanness of a noun or noun phrase that has grammatical, often syntactic, consequences" (24). As we see, the hierarchical nature of the animacy continuum has consequences, beyond linguistic structure, for considerations of race, gender, sexuality, affect, and ability depending on which end of the continuum one occupies. She extends the linguistic meaning of animacy to the multiple ways that humans assert superiority over inorganic nature. The implications of this for disability lie in the relational potential of bodies regarded as inanimate (on life-supports), subhuman (dependent on others), or disabled (lacking full complement of physical and cognitive potential): "What if nonhuman animals, or humans stereotyped as passive, such as people with cognitive or physical disabilities, enter the calculus of animacy: what happens then?" (3). What she calls her "feral research" involves a strong critique of biopolitical theory insofar as it has been limited to human populations and not to the categories that *divide* humans from other species.

As if in defiance of the animacy principle, Sinha's title inverts the usual relationship of human to animal (people's animals) by stressing the solidarity between "Animal" and his "people." This inversion contradicts the conventional interrelationship by which animals are thought to be the possession of people—pets, livestock, food— and places the emphasis on alliances across species. The novel's narrative premise reinforces this inversion of the animacy principle by posing as a transcription of recordings by Animal to an Australian journalist as part of a book he intends to write about Khaufpur (Bhopal).[10] Animal "talks back" to the tape and, by extension, the journalist whose Western values and ableist presumptions are the subject of Animal's wry humor ("You told me that sometimes the stories of small people in this world can achieve big things, this is the way you buggers always talk" [3]). Animal isn't sure what language to use when speaking to what he imagines are thousands of Western readers who will read his story; his apostrophe throughout is to our "eyes":

> I think of this awful idea. Your eyes full of eyes. Thousands staring at me through the holes in your head. Their curiosity feels like acid on my skin. "What am I to tell these eyes?" I demand of Chunaram. "What can I say that they will understand? Have these thousands of eyes slept even one night in a place like this? Do these eyes shit on railway tracks? When was the last time these eyes had nothing to eat?"   (7–8)

This is a statement as much about the disequilibrium between rich and poor, as it is about disability. It links the voyeuristic gaze of the Western outsider with that of the able-bodied person whose prurient interest in physical impairment enables detachment while posing as sympathetic interest. Animal's opening remark, "I used to be human once. So I'm told," suggests that being "human" is a discursive rather than

---

[10] Sinha's novel is, in fact, based on interviews with Sunil Kumar, a Bhopal survivor. The journalist gives Animal a pair of his shorts in which there is a lighter with the name "Phuoc Tuy" inscribed. Animal thinks this is the journalist's name which could mean either that he is Vietnamese or else, more likely, that he served in the military during the Vietnam War. Either way, it brings the context of US involvement in foreign wars into line with its investment in other types of foreign disasters.

natural fact (1). Animal's species identity as human is "told" to him by others, and it is against this telling that Animal conscripts his own version by imagining—and undercutting—what the journalist and other well-meaning outsiders imagine him to be.

Animal's disabled perspective, as someone who walks on hands and feet, allows him a degree of second sight. As he ruefully observes, "The world of humans is meant to be viewed from eye level. Your eyes. Lift my head I'm staring into someone's crotch" (2). By asking the reader to read through *his* eyes at "crotch" level, he challenges the single-point narrative perspective of able-bodiedness: "If you want my story, you'll have to put up with how I tell it" (2). His friend Chunaram upbraids him for his brutal honesty, saying that he needs to tell the journalist "what's wanted" if he's to make money from these tapes, whereas Animal tells his story through a good deal of foul-mouthed, irreverent banter. Animal's insistence that he is not human is challenged by various characters in the novel whose humanitarian interests in helping the dispossessed, sick victims of the Kampani's neglect require a human subject to defend. One of these figures is Zafar, an activist pursuing legal and financial compensation from the Kampani. He deploys a disability rights rhetoric to convince the protagonist that he's not an animal but "especially abled," that is "you don't walk on two legs like most people, but you have skills and talents that they don't . . . you should not allow yourself to be called Animal. You are a human being, entitled to dignity and respect" (23). But Animal insists on his difference: " 'My name is Animal,' I say. 'I'm not a fucking human being. I've no wish to be one' " (23). Nor does he accept the victim status that legal remediation demands: "I hated all that talk of 'poison victims,' I don't want to be pitied, I refuse to be some fucking bhonsdi-ka [fart-born] victim" (27). He challenges fate by living inside the factory where the disaster occurred, a "haunted" place yet an appropriate place "for an animal to make its lair" (29). By adopting the derisive label, "animal," that children use to mock him, he turns negative interpellation into antinomian refusal.

The novel's plot is reminiscent, in at least one respect, to the endlessly deferred closure of *Jarndyce v. Jarndyce* in *Bleak House*. The Kampani's ability to use the law to defer reparation to its victims and families and to cleanse the factory of residual chemicals allows generations to be exposed, disabled, and die, thereby extending the disaster well beyond "that night," as everyone calls the disaster. Because of the complicity of the Kampani with the government and medical profession, all humanitarian interventions are subject to intense scrutiny by the activists. The American doctor, Elli, who opens a free clinic in the distressed area is shunned by the community because she is perceived to be an agent of the Kampani, sent to provide data that would exonerate it from responsibility. Animal admires her, but he also respects the tenacity (and belligerence) of Zafar and his followers who pursue justice, even if it means boycotting Elli's well-intentioned efforts. As we will see with NourbeSe Philip's *Zong!* legal "protections" require subjects who are considered human. When those subjects—African slaves in the case of *Zong!*, denizens of a toxic site in *Animal's People*—are deemed sub-human, legal remedy is eviscerated.

My subject is the missing body in the aesthetic. Sinha provides a global perspective on this phenomenon by creating a character who is, to all intents, invisible. As a poor orphan, injured by an industrial malfeasance, he is invisible to the company. As someone who claims his abjection as a point of pride—refusing to be "human"—he is invisible to liberal humanitarian efforts at restitution. But as a disabled person he is literally invisible to justice, a fact vividly illustrated by a story Animal tells about his appearance at a court hearing against the Kampani:

> —*Case against boy known as Animal, section chaar sau bees.*
> —*Where is the accused?*
> —*Your honour he is here.*
> —*Where? I don't see him.*
> —*Right here, your honour, in the dock.*
> —*Don't be silly. I am looking at the dock, there's no one there.*
> —*Your honour, accused is of unusual stature.* (51)

Zafar laughs at the story, "Such a fool," but his lover, Nisha, understands that Animal's invisibility to the court of justice is a metaphor for their own difficulty as powerless poor people in obtaining justice in legal terms. Animal may be "of unusual stature," but "Empty dock's our problem too" (52).

MISSING PERSONS: AMANDA BAGGS' "IN MY LANGUAGE"

Before discussing Amanda Baggs' video I want to situate her work in relationship to disability studies more generally and its critique of embodied personhood. In an attempt to move beyond a medical model toward a social constructionist version, disability studies may have inadvertently disappeared the body it sought to represent. While it is important to think of the ways social stigma, medical science, and the physical environment reinforce disability, we must remember the ways it is embodied. Disability activists who got out of their wheelchairs to crawl up steps of the US Capitol in support of federal legislation such as the ADA made visible the social barriers to access, but it seems churlish to assume from such acts that their bodies are *merely* and *only* constructed by those barriers. The simple binary of "impairment" and "disability" to mark physiological/cognitive and social conditions of non-traditional bodies tends to generalize the specific complexities of, say, blindness, HIV/AIDS, chronic disease and bipolar disorder into a one-size-fits-all body. This also diminishes the specific medical regimes, therapies, institutional support, and activism that apply to each condition. As Tom Shakespeare and others have noted, the social model of disability does not represent the broad spectrum of persons with disabilities, nor is it able to describe "the complex interplay of individual and environmental factors in the lives of disabled people" (Shakespeare, 220).

By studying disability through such binaries as impairment and disability, we forget the degree to which disability is a matter of subject positioning. Tanya Titchkosky notes that within Western cultures, "disability is typically taken for granted as the end of an expected form of functionality, voided of normalcy, and transposed into the end of human legitimacy" (82). Debates over fetal personhood or end-of-life ethics tend to focus on whether a fetus with a severe disability or a person on life support is actually a person and should, thereby, be guaranteed the protection and rights of so-called healthy people. Providing person-first language, venues for independent living, and accommodations through legal means reinforce the idea that "disability is *lived* and is lived as something other than a negative add-on to personhood" (84).

Despite cultural and legal changes in public attitudes, persons with cognitive disabilities have often been left out of discourses of independent living and accommodation. Persons with bipolar, developmental, or spectrum disorders often remain in a limbo realm, somewhere between medicalization and institutionalization while being removed—until recently—from the rainbow coalition formed around disability rights. Considering cognitive disability raises the question of whether disability studies hasn't placed too much emphasis on physical and sensory impairments to the exclusion of large constituencies of functioning individuals. Stuart Murray observes that representations of autism often presume that such individuals live in "a world of their own" or that they are "locked away" inside themselves. Foundational writings on the subject by Kanner and Asperger use phrases like "he just is there" or "the autist is only himself." Murray comments that if the "'just' or 'only' is seen in a pejorative way, then the character is barely present, a prosthetic figure in the margins used only to make other aspects of the narrative work" (32). It is precisely this question of the presence of the person within autism that dominates Amanda Baggs' video work.

Amanda Baggs is a high-functioning person with autism, neurodiversity activist, and performance artist who stopped speaking in her early twenties.[11] In the first part of her video, "In my Language," she gestures, scratches, hums, and fidgets with various objects—a piece of paper, a necklace, a slinky toy. There is no voiceover to "interpret" her gestures. Rather, she vocalizes in a sustained, pitched hum that serves as a complement to the scratching, knocking, and scraping of objects against hard surfaces. We see her typing at her keyboard and rocking back and forth in front of a window. We glimpse her body fitfully, mostly in terms of body parts—hands, lips, ears—but seldom through a frontal image. Nor does her video provide narrative links between different repetitive actions. Rather we inhabit *her* narrative of significant interactions with objects, spaces, and her own body.

In the second half of the video she provides a "translation" of her performance, speaking, as she says, in her "native language," through a DynaVox VMax computer that transforms her typed words into speech and captions.[12] Baggs' decision to use an audio track based on a digital surrogate for her voice creates an alternative

[11] There has been some controversy over the authenticity of Baggs' representation of herself as autistic. In a series of posts on the Disability in the Humanities Listserv (DS-HUM) and other blogs people who knew Baggs in earlier days declare that she has never been autistic, that she is, as one post complains, a "disability faker." Against this claim are a number of responses that note, as Ralph Savarese says, "this campaign represents an attack on the competence of those whom the medical community would describe as 'severely autistic'." Savarese goes on to say, "there's a long and spiteful history of doubting those with disabilities." DS-HUM@LISTSERV.UMD.EDU, posted Friday October 21, 2011.
[12] Faye Ginsburg provides an excellent overview of Baggs' use of social media and user-generated video in "Disability in the Digital Age."

form of presence that embodies the speaker's intelligence and critical understanding while signifying on their presumed acoustic sources. When individuals are deemed "non-productive" or "non-verbal," interventions such as Baggs' video rewrite the ableist script in different terms. In her commentary, she is explicit about how her work rearticulates a presumed linguistic normalcy:

> It is only when I type something in your language that you refer to me as having communication. I smell things. I listen to things. I feel things. I taste things. I look at things. It is not enough to look and listen and taste and smell and feel. I have to do those to the right things, such as look at books, and fail to do them to the wrong things, or else people doubt that I am a thinking being, and since their definition of thought defines their definition of personhood so ridiculously much, they doubt that I am a real person as well.

Baggs' defiant apostrophe to her viewers addresses the presumed link between language and personhood, between representation and its putative forms of embodiment. Her repetitions and humming *are* the form that language assumes for a bi-cultural person; her electronic "translation" signals her awareness of neurotypical expectations about what language constitutes and whom it interpellates. In an NPR interview, Baggs notes "many of us have a lot of trouble with face to face interaction and are also extremely isolated…A lot of us have trouble with spoken language, and so a lot of us find it easier to write on the Internet than to talk in person" (qtd. Ginsburg, 102). Her use of video, computer, and digital interface illustrates the importance of new assistive technologies in providing communication among physically and cognitively disabled populations. Such technologies also enable her to create an alternate identity through an avatar as part of the virtual community known as Second Life. Through Second Life and social media platforms, people with severe disabilities create community and social networks that would be otherwise difficult or inaccessible.

"In my Language" demonstrates a form of critical embodiment that questions normative ideas about the body and its relationship to language. Baggs makes the relationship explicit by *not* exposing her body, *not* speaking, and by challenging viewers to see her body on her own terms. She claims that her gestures and repetitions are a form of language yet recognizes that her access *to* language is vastly different from what most of us regard as communication. If the ideal of an "embodied language" is the unmediated expression of feelings through speech, Baggs' form of embodiment exists as a ventriloquized interface that mirrors her internally distanced relationship to neurotypical life. In this respect, far from illustrating her difference from "our language," she illustrates her contingent relationship to everyone's signifying body.

EXTENDING HOSPITALITY: RACHEL ZOLF, *NEIGHBOUR PROCEDURE*

In his "Philosophical Sketch" for "Perpetual Peace," Kant imagines a federation of nation-states operating under principles of international right that would bind everyone—including monarchs—to common values and moral principles: "But this natural, right of hospitality, i.e., the right of strangers, does not extend beyond those conditions which make it possible for them to attempt to enter into relations with the native inhabitants" (106). Peace among nations is only possible if states extend hospitality toward their neighbors, lest they revert to what Kant regards as the self-interested state of nature. He decries the idea that nations can assure their survival through sheer military deterrence, nor is he interested in the utopian possibility of a global or transnational state. The glue that will cement a post-Westphalian society of independent nations is an ideal of hospitality, regarded not as a form of philanthropy or kindness but as a right belonging to everyone. Cosmopolitan hospitality refers to "the right of a stranger not to be treated with hostility when he arrives on someone else's territory" (105). As Seyla Benhabib says, for Kant hospitality "entails a claim to temporary residency on the part of the stranger who comes on our land. This cannot be refused, if such refusal would involve the *destruction . . .* of the stranger" (22). Although such claims are not legally binding, they are the principle upon which political asylum is based and as such represent a liminal zone "between the rights of humanity in our person and the rights that accrue to us insofar as we are citizens of specific republics" (22). The problem, as Benhabib develops it, is that the right of hospitality, as a moral imperative, is not bound by law and thus exists only as a horizon in the "absence of an overwhelming sovereign power with the ultimate right of enforcement" (23).

What Kant could not imagine and what is increasingly the face of global society are forms of flexible citizenship, refugee communities, and stateless subjects—the new cosmopolitans of globalization.[13] The occupied territories in Israel pose an especially complex version of this situation—a nation within a state, a host, to adapt Kant, who has become the stranger. In her text, *Neighbour Procedure*, Rachel Zolf takes issue with Jewish intellectuals like Emmanuel Levinas and Martin Buber whose theoretical systems are based on the mutual constitution of self/other, I/thou, but who, in practice regard the Palestinian other as "enemy."[14] To this extent, Zolf not only indicts forms of Zionism but philosophies that draw from Hegel's theories of recognition and Kant's political philosophy of hospitality yet fail to particularize the figure who is *not* acknowledged, whose body becomes collateral damage.[15] She notes that critical theory conflicts with practice; she observes, for instance, that the Israeli Defense Force (IDF) has developed training maneuvers derived from Situationism and Deleuze/Guattari (82). To what extent is the legacy of Enlightenment thought, embodied in such intellectual traditions, complicit in the exclusions of Palestinians from full citizenship? What form of hospitality can

[13] Aiwa Ong defines "flexible citizenship" as "the strategies and effects of mobile managers, technocrats, and professionals seeking to both circumvent *and* benefit from different nation-state regimes by selecting different sites for investments, work, and family relocation" (112).

[14] In her Coach House interview Zolf remarks, "it bugs me that Martin Buber, he of I and Thou, and originally in favour of the binational state in Palestine, took Edward Said's family home in Jerusalem because he could; and that ethical philosopher Emmanuel Levinas called the Palestinian the enemy not the 'other' or even neighbour because he could." She also includes in this group the Dadaist Marcel Janco, who became a "settler-colonialist" in Israel.

[15] What I earlier referred to as the ghostly body in political discourse is reinforced by the fact that the Israeli government often refers to Palestinians as "present absentees."

exist between Palestinians and Israelis that would respect cosmopolitan right? Would a two-state solution "solve" decades-old tension between the two communities? Who is the host and who is the stranger in what Salman Rushdie calls "Palimpstine"?[16] The expropriation of Palestinian lands and displacement of peoples thwarts any hope for peace and complicates Kant's ideal of cosmopolitan hospitality.

The title of Zolf's multi-genre book, *Neighbour Procedure*, offers a variant of what we have been calling "hospitality," a "concept of the neighbour as a potentially liberating 'third' space between friend and enemy—an acknowledgement of proximity and cohabitation" (Zolf, Coach House interview).[17] But the very principle of neighborliness is vitiated by the policy developed by the Israeli army called "neighbor procedure," the tactic of "using Palestinians as human shields and forcing them to break walls inside their neighbours' homes, so that the army can move literally through the interior walls from house to house in urban warfare" (82). As a violation of hospitality the neighbor procedure performs militarily what *Neighbour Procedure* as an aesthetic practice reverses by redrawing the map of Palestinian communities, replacing names of Palestinians killed in uprisings, renaming streets with their original Arab names, returning former Arab names to Jewish settlements built on Palestinian lands:

> Nahal arose in the place of Mahalul
> Kibbutz Gvat in the place of Jibta
> Kibbutz Sarid in the place of Huneifis
> Ein Houd turned into Ein Hod   (19)

With its allusion to Old Testament catalogues, passages such as this illustrate the importance of naming as a central political issue throughout the book, whether it is the de-Arabization of the Hebrew language or the renaming of towns and communities. "Ein Houd," the Palestinian village mentioned above, became the site of a Dadaist community formed by Marcel Janco, renamed in Hebrew, Ein Hod, the former inhabitants exiled to refugee camps and new settlements. Zolf quotes Moshe Dayan, speaking of Palestinian villages destroyed in 1948, " 'you do not even know the names of these Arab villages, and I do not blame you, because those geography books no longer exist' " (81). And she juxtaposes this to Hobbes' definition of power: " 'capacity to give names and enforce definitions' " (81). To some extent Zolf's book attempts to revive names and correct definitions and in the process imagine a more complex and dialogic society in Israel-Palestine.

If *Neighbour Procedure* is a book that returns those missing from history, its voice is a heteroglossia of other texts, joining my other examples in structuring speech out of appropriated or mediated materials. Newspaper accounts of the 2009 war in

---

[16] Rushdie uses the term, "Palimpstine," in *The Moor's Last Sigh*. As Zolf quotes Rushdie it is a place "where worlds collide, flow in and out of one another...Under World beneath Over World, black market beneath white" (83).

[17] Erin Mouré speaks of *Neighbour Procedure* as an "Infection Procedure: one that invades the known borders of Genre, Copyright, Citation, Book, Ethics, houses of language, languages, pages in order to attach names to deaths, in order to name houses, all in crossing and residing at the overlapping border between Israel and Palestine" (242).

Gaza, overheard conversations, lists of Hebrew and Arabic place names, quotations from Arendt and Benjamin, philological entries, books on the Intifada, chatlist posts, all provide texts and intertexts that Zolf weaves through the book's four sections. Where previous avant-garde writers used collage as an aesthetic ordering of dissimilar materials, Zolf's appropriations pointedly address the rhetorics in which national narratives are formed. Her missing authorial voice is replaced by the legal, journalistic, and media voices that become the many-layered condition of Palimpstine, her role being, as she says, "more as medium than as author" (Coach House interview). But unlike earlier forms of poetic mediumship—from William Blake to the Surrealists—Zolf's role is less a "receiver" of the poem than a translator who must adjust one social idiolect to another socio-political imaginary.[18]

The central theme of *Neighbour Procedure* is provided by Judith Butler whose meditation on post-9/11 political conditions, *Precarious Life*, asks, "Who counts as human? Whose lives count as lives? What makes for a grievable life?" (20). Butler's questions inform much of *Neighbour Procedure* in her focus on the uses of the sovereign exception in global warfare and the indefinite suspension of rights in the name of national security. In order to grieve the loss of such individuals, it is first necessary to imagine them as human—to grant them names, agency, and culture. Zolf refuses to indulge in a simple act of recovery by turning Palestinians into martyrs or heroes, but instead displays the substitutive processes by which the "other" becomes "enemy":

> We who are live also always killing Hey you!
> The poem already exists before it is written   (67)

The emphasis here is on the preemptive structuring of subjectivity through speech acts that subordinate the citizen subject to official power. In the first line, the enemy is interpellated in its address by the figure of authority, the one who kills by shouting "Hey you!" The second line suggests that the poem of witness is never present to the events it chronicles; like Minerva's owl that flies at dusk, it is written after the events it attempts to understand.

We can see Zolf's emphasis on such interpellative speech acts throughout the book, whether this involves translation (the shift of Hebrew to Arabic characters), catalogues (naming the dead), rules (censorship protocols), comparisons, or syllogistic thinking. The latter is prominently featured in the opening section, "Shoot and Weep," drawn from print and online sources. The phrase "shoot and weep" is used by Israelis to justify violence against Palestinians during the Gaza conflict by suggesting, "we are a moral army" and thus feel for our neighbors in Gaza (*Jacket* interview). As if to capture the oxymoronic quality of the slogan, Zolf adds to each phrase the conjunction, "if":

> If the Sabbath is a form of constraint
> If jihad is the first word learned

---

[18] Perhaps one reason for the extensive and at times chaotic mixtures of languages and idiolects stems from Zolf's visit to Israel in 2009 during the war in Gaza. Zolf regards *Neighbour Procedure* as a kind of travel narrative. She titles one section of the book "Innocent Abroad," referring to Mark Twain's account of visiting the Holy Lands (Coach House interview).

> If Elie Wiesel is the Holocaust
> If one must expropriate gently
> If messianism licks at the edges of thought
> If the truth does not lie in silence   (8)

By adding the conjunction Zolf turns each statement into the first part of a dependent clause. Lacking a corresponding "then" clause, we can only imagine an alternative result for each claim. As a statement, "one must expropriate gently" might describe humanitarian justifications for appropriating Palestinian lands, but when it is preceded by "if," it becomes a hypothesis that presumes such appropriation. This particular section is called "a priori," and each of the statements appears to describe a foundational condition for subsequent actions. Hence the following: "If we shoot and weep / If Israel is not in Israel / If the treasure house of well-worn terms is laden with explosives" (9). Read as a sequence, each phrase impinges on the next as a justification for continuing to suppress rights: "if we shoot and weep, then Israel is not in Israel"; if this is the case, then, "the treasure house of well-worn terms is laden with explosives." It is an unending spiral of causality that splits Israel against itself, neighbor against neighbor.

We can see this form of false causality vividly in a brief reference to the Sbarro pizzeria bombing in 2001 in Jerusalem that killed fifteen people and wounded many others. Hamas and Islamic Jihad in Palestine claimed responsibility for a blast that, for many, turned the tide against the possibility of Palestinian–Israeli peace. Zolf refers to the bombing as follows:

> If cruel history repeats itself as its own cure
> If it happens inside the Sbarro pizzeria
> If there is an invasion of the order of the border
> If the animal is discomforted during slaughter   (10)

The conditional structure qualifies the ascription of blame and focuses it instead on history: if cruel history repeats itself...then "it happens inside the Sbarro pizzeria." And if slaughter "happens inside the Sbarro pizzeria," then retaliation is inevitable. The slaughter of patrons in a restaurant stands in contrast to kosher laws regarding the humane slaughtering of animals ("If the animal is discomfited during slaughter"). Zolf does not exonerate the Palestinian terrorists who exploded the bomb but, rather, indicts the ineluctable process of substitution, the unending product of a "cruel history" that appears as its own cure.

While "if" clauses dominate the first section, adverbial phrases dominate the subsequent section. Here Zolf presents a catalogue of those "grievable citizens" who, as her section title indicates, "[did] not participate in hostilities." She locates Palestinians who became collateral damage in the places where they were killed or injured:

> When she approached the barrier
> While flying a kite at the beach
> When he picked grass for his flock
> While sitting in the tin-covered dīwān
> When she crossed the street
> While on the way to buy candy   (12)

These individuals whose deaths occurred in everyday activities are recorded in "Grievable" and further evacuated in a subsequent section, "Nominal," where they are indicated simply by a bare presentation of numbers representing their ages:

14
13
33
17 (28)

These are followed by another series; this time the numbers are spelled-out:

seventeen
twenty five
thirty five
eighteen
fifteen (29)

Zolf strips persons of their identity, first by the hypothetical if/then logic by which they may be killed, then through the places where they are killed, then through their names, and finally in abstract numbers, each stage a memorial for the numberless dead.

In "A failure of hospitality" Zolf hints at the travestied nature of cosmopolitan empathy to which I have referred:

Future collapsed in present execution and mourning
Duty of guest and host a torn native
Narratives compete for a sacred hair lying where it shouldn't
Stoked button the key to distilled water living a quiet way
This unbearable intimacy a purity of arms suturing
Chocolate cake with coconut flecks none of us taught to see
Besieged body a piece of metal we will offer all our children
This permanent remembrance slaughtered and we promise a pleasant life   (25)

Remembering that these are all quoted materials, we might see how discrete statements in combination problematize a future that is not haunted by "permanent remembrance." The violation of hospitality—the enlistment of neighbors against themselves—creates an "unbearable intimacy." Moreover, each phrase in some way implicates the others. When the body is "Besieged," it becomes "a piece of metal"; when "remembrance" is slaughtered, the promise of a pleasant life" is also slaughtered. "Duty of guest and host a torn native" evokes the moral obligation that Kant describes as hospitality that, in the context of Palestine, creates a "torn native" caught between twin identities and contested borders.

Zolf's multi-genre process is difficult to categorize, as befits the unsettled nature of Middle East politics. The writing procedure throughout is one of substitution: Hebrew word for Arab word, number for person, grammatical structure for semantic content, terrorist for neighbor. It is a counter-narrative to the national version provided by AIPAC and other lobbying groups on behalf of Israel, but it is by no means a one-sided polemic. It insinuates itself within debates about sovereignty, where, as she says at one point, "Ethics [are] suspended at the border crossing" (67). Zolf's language of erasure, as Nava Et Shalom says, repeats "the blank spaces also produced by violence." As a contribution to biopoetics, *Neighbour Procedure* draws on the specific languages of identification and naming that control and enforce some bodies while erasing others.

LIVING SOCIAL DEATH: M. NOURBESE PHILIP, *ZONG!*

My final example, the Tobagonian/Canadian poet M. NourbeSe Philip's *Zong!* (2008), is a long poem based on a law case from 1783 concerning a massacre of slaves on a British slave ship.[19] Through navigational errors, overcrowding, and bad weather, a voyage that was supposed to take a few weeks ended up taking months as the ship traversed the Caribbean, missing or misidentifying islands along the way. When a large number of slaves began to die the captain decided that if death from so-called "natural causes" continued, the ship's owners would not be able to claim insurance for lost cargo. Hence, the crew began throwing living slaves into the sea, massacring 150 by the week's end.[20] Upon arriving in Jamaica, the ship's owners filed an insurance claim to recover their losses, leading to a trial, *Gregson v. Gilbert*, whose formal language provides the basis for Philip's poem. The trial was ultimately decided in favor of the owners, but no charges were ever prosecuted against the officers or crew. The case was subsequently reopened and decided in favor of the insurers who claimed that throwing 150 slaves overboard was unnecessary and avoidable, due to the fact that at the time of the massacre there was water aplenty on board against the owner's claim of necessity. As Philip observes, in her afterword:

> even if the courts had found against the owners of the *Zong* and ruled that they could not claim insurance compensation, given the law at that time, neither [the Captain] nor those who had helped in the massacre could be charged with murder, since what was destroyed, being property, was not capable of being murdered. (191)

In Giorgio Agamben's terms, slaves in a circuit of economic exchange and legal debate are reduced to "bare life"; they become those "who may be killed and yet not sacrificed," drowned but not murdered (8). Agamben is thinking here of institutions like the prison camp and detention center, and it is worth pondering the difference between slave ship and camp and the differing levels of control governing

---

[19] The Zong massacre is the subject of J. M. W. Turner's painting *The Slave Ship* (1840) that depicts the ship in a stormy sea in the background with a number of black, chained bodies floating in the water in the foreground. The painting is in the Museum of Fine Arts, Boston. The *Gregson* case was widely known in its day. Olaudah Equiano helped to fund an appeal of the verdict, and it has been the subject of works by Fred D'Aguiar, Derek Walcott, Edouard Glissant, and others. On representations of the Zong massacre, see Ian Baucom, "Specters of the Atlantic."

[20] The figure of 150 deaths is derived from *Gregson v. Gilbert*, but as Philip indicates in a footnote to the book, other accounts list 130, 131, and 132 lost. "The exact number of African slaves murdered remains a slippery signifier of what was undoubtedly a massacre" (208, n. 3).

each. The 1933 decree that suspended personal liberties, the freedoms of expression and assembly in Nazi Germany involved a governmental decision "for the protection of the people and State" (Agamben, 168). The state of exception on the slave ship would seem to be governed less by governmentality than by the exigencies of capital exchange, of which the actuarial element and market forces become the form that sovereignty takes. Although Agamben does not refer extensively to slavery, one could say that his description of the "logic of sovereignty" as a biopolitical matter applies to the governmentality of the State since it legitimates capital exchange in the form of bodies. Aboard the Zong, the slaves' status as property denies them a voice, but as Sarah Dowling says, *Zong!* returns a level of speech—broken, fragmented, partial—to the non-person. Philip creates "the impression of myriad voices moaning, stuttering, and working to sing" against the juridical voice that consigns them to the status of chattel (43). As a lawyer, Philip is especially positioned to understand the close proximity of the aesthetic to the legal in producing subjects—and non-subjects. Philip uses the *Gregson* case to indict the structural violence of the slave trade within the official document that sustains it. If the court case is the "true" rendering of the facts of the massacre, then *Zong!* the poem is the unraveling or interruption of the truth. As she says in an interview, "It is a text of silence (of the ocean and the Middle Passage) and silencing (as in the historical silencing of this and similar stories) that is interrupted, fractured and fragmented by the human voice" (Philip, Preziuo interview).

Philip's decision to use the precise words of the trial in the opening section of *Zong!* is reminiscent of earlier documentary poems such as Charles Reznikoff's *Testimony* or Muriel Rukeyser's *Book of the Dead*, both of which are based on court cases and legal transcripts. Unlike these prior poems, Philip establishes kinship with her lost African slaves by creating an ethnographic surrogate to whom her tale is told. Her interlocutor, "Setaey Adamu Boateng," is explained in her book blurb as an ancestral voice "revealing the submerged stories of all who were on board the Zong." Her personal stake in these ancestral voices was reinforced during a trip that the author took to Ghana in 2006 where, while visiting a shrine in a slave port of the Ewe people, she is told by a tribal elder that "none of [her] ancestors could have been among those thrown overboard…If that were the case, he continues, I would not be there" (202). Since she *is* there—since this story has, as she indicates, "chosen" her—she must have some connection to those ancestors and thus dictates her poem to one of them. The fact that the poem is dictated transforms the monological court case into a call and response in which the listener/reader is enjoined to participate by reading, quite literally, between the lines and across historical temporalities. The exclamation mark following the name of the ship, *Zong!* indicates that the poem is a shout, an exclamation, and the pun of "song" in "Zong" suggests the lyric possibilities of that response. Like Amanda Baggs and Rachel Zolf, Philip rearticulates an official view of language and submits it to deformation and mediation while retaining elements of the original in fragmented or broken form.

This first section, *Os*, as its Latin name implies, is the "bones" of the work, the material upon which the rest of the poem will be made just as Latin is, as Philip indicates by her section titles, the "father language of Europe" (209 n. 45). Words from the trial are splayed across the page, disconnected from each other and from their original occurrence. The function of such appropriation is to reinforce the degree to which African bodies, like other forms of chattel, are disappeared in an actuarial calculus. "Zong #5" like many other passages deals with water—that which the slaves were denied and that into which they were thrown (Fig. 7.3).

The gaps between words ("of months / of / weeks / of days / of / sustenance lying / dead") provide a textual representation of the *duration* of deprivation; the words beneath the line at the bottom of each page, "Mwita Muhammad Mulogo Becktemba Hadiya," mark the dead whose Yoruba names were never recorded (9). In the subsequent section, "Dicta," the black line remains, but the names no longer

&

water

(three butts good)

of

sea and

perils

of water

(one day)

water —

day one . . .

of months

of

weeks

of

days

of

sustenance

lying

dead

Fig. 7.3. From "Zong 5" of *Zong!* page 9. Excerpts from *Zong!*

appear below, providing a textual representation of their absence. Given that the term "dicta" suggests authoritative pronouncements, one might feel that the erasure of these names is a direct outcome of such official speech or, as the root of "dictation," as the products of power ventriloquized. As Dowling summarizes this usage, "The legalistic and actuarial language of the *Gregson v. Gilbert* source text negates the possibility of the slaves' personhood and accordingly their names vanish, just like their bones" (49).

The next five sections of the book are Philip's responses to the language of the trial. Fragments of words are widely spaced across the page, phonemes and morphemes enjambed or separated from each other, creating what Juliana Spahr in her book blurb calls the poem's "stutter." In public readings of *Zong!*, Philip provides an oral transcription of the fragmented words followed by a performance of the page, the latter of which reinforces the multiple valences that a given element may have. Take for example the following: "*re* ruth a fe /ast we had *mis /e en scè* / *ne* a shi / p or v / esse / l the s /ea man /y negroes a ran /t of rains the /y ring they sin /g they b /eat u /pon the d /eck ho /ld the e /ar ring fast…" (150).

In my transcription of this page in Fig. 7.4, I have punctuated each space by a slash mark, without regard to whether a line is enjambed or, indeed, is even a line, to illustrate the way that poetic elements disturb a linear reading. The opening "re" is a continuation of the greeting, "ma chère," on the previous page. If we gather the limbs of this scattered textual body, it might read as follows: "my chère Ruth, a feast we had *mise en scène* a ship or vessel the sea many negroes a rant of rains they ring they sing they beat upon the deck hold the earring fast" (9). In its rather broken form, the mixture of French, English, and Caribbean patois, the division of words into individual syllables or letters, and enjambments and indentations create the acoustic "mise-en-scène" of a chaotic shipboard environment.[21]

Once these elements are transformed into sentences, the passage appears to be part of a letter written by a crew member to one of the "women who wait" listed in the "Manifest" at the end of the book.[22] A passage begins, "I / write / to / you / of / mortality s /lien on l /ife" (69). That lien on life—the proximity to his captives—fuses the sailor's voice to the slaves. His proprietary attitudes toward them as animals and objects contrasts with his attempt to rationalize shipboard violence to the Ruth figure: "my plea is negligence / to her I / say *te amo* / her name / she smiles / will be es / se to be / I smile / and i / am / fall / am / falling / am *sum* / into / of all / murder" (69–70). It is hard to know whether he is referring to a slave woman or to

[21] In her afterword, Philip speaks of her fragmented language as a kind of authorial violence: "I murder the text, literally cut it into pieces, castrating verbs, suffocating adjectives, murdering nouns, throwing articles, prepositions, conjunctions overboard, jettisoning adverbs: I separate subject from verb, verb from object—create semantic mayhem, until my hands bloodied, from so much killing and cutting, reach into the stinking, eviscerated innards, and like some seer, sangoma, or prophet who, having sacrificed an animal for signs and portents of a new life, or simply life, reads the untold story that tells itself by not telling (194).

[22] The "manifest" is normally the ship's record of cargo, including names of crew members, food and drink, yet in Philip's rendering, it also includes "body parts" and "African Groups and Languages" along with the "Women [presumably the wives of sailors] who Wait" at home (185).

re ruth a fe   ast we had *mis*

 e en scè   *ne* a shi

        p or v   esse

   l the s   ea man

        y negroes a ran

  t of rains the   y ring they sin

     g they b   eat u

          pon the d   eck ho

   ld the e   ar ring fast bo   y *so*

 me neg   *roes had pil*

       es leahy pile   *ı* the saint of tro

   y and the de   ad city ro

       me app   ears to me

 at night *l ang*   e de me   r noir nig

    er afer her s   ex we

  t her p   aps leak p   rop them u

    p *ilé*   *ifè i*   *lé if*

è il   *é ifè* se   w the lin

   en slip sh   ut we ro   t in this ves

      sel from s   in sin

 g by rot   e a stir   ring son

    g their dy   ing grist & g   ift to u

        s *tō se*   *cure a pro*

  fit we u   *se man*   *y ruse st*

     heir swe   at the sce

        nt we stu   n the su

 n with o   ur act it

    veers off i   ts way we

       let win   ter s frost fr

 om her urn no *a*   *ve s* or *sal*

    ve s only sla   ves *às*

       e àse so b

      e it the so   und of the o

   ud on e   id fa

        lls on u   s on tu

 nis a st   ring of n   egroes on t   nd the m

   he qu   ay no sou   nd the m

      an from f   ez wa

        its to se   ll to ma

   ke a de   al *the sti*

Fig. 7.4. From "Ferrum" of *Zong!* page 150. Excerpts from *Zong!*

Ruth here, whether he is "falling" into moral decay by raping slave women or expressing his love for Ruth at home.

The voice of the slave is similarly fused with her captors: "notwithstanding we / seek the *ratio* / in Africa negroes / too / *de men* / *dem cam fo mi* / for me for / *yo* for je / *pour moi* & *para* / *mi* flee / the fields / *gun bam* / *bam* / it was / oh oh / a falling" (66). In this interrupted speech we hear the voice of the slave, undergoing the violence of capture through the multiple languages (trading dialect, French, Spanish, English) of the Middle Passage. Philip indicates that the slave trade seeks the "ratio" in and through "African negroes." For the European traders and slave-owners, "ratio" or rationality is purchased through slavery, yet the mixing of slave and trader here—with multiple versions of the first person pronoun—suggests that the speaking Subject is inextricably connected to the human commodity. Her "mi" becomes his "je" or "*yo*." What the West fantasizes as a fall into Cartesian self-knowledge, the slave suffers as a literal fall into the ocean, "a falling / my fate / & murder / come to term / grounds justice / in lies" (66). On the page, these separate phrases and broken words vividly recreate the broken interchange between black and European subject, between the languages of power and the contact languages of entrepreneurial trade.

As *Zong!* progresses, Philip occasionally changes the font to script, perhaps to reinforce the epistolary element just mentioned, and in the last section in a "ghost" or grey font with multiple overstrikes and crossings-out. This final section is called *Ebora*, a Yoruba word meaning "underwater spirits." All of these material qualities of the book stress the role of language in making bodies visible, bringing erased meanings to the surface while honoring those that have been drowned. By fore-grounding the graphic inscriptions of voice and language, Philip connects the materiality of language with the materiality of bodies doomed to suffer the fate of words over which they have no control. This recuperation of the voice is by no means an assertion of the liberal subject but, as Sarah Dowling says, is an imagina-tion of "poetic voice as a bodily emission, but one that neither connotes nor corre-sponds to personhood" (44). To re-inscribe the "oral," divination tradition out of which the African diaspora emerges, Philip provides a fugal counterpoint in the form of words taken from Yoruba, Ewa, and other West African languages. The opening of "Sal" suggests a ritual chant or mourning song based on the word, if à (divination) that blends the second syllable of the Yoruba word with the iconic English word "fall": "there is / creed there is / fate there is / oh / oh oracle / there are / oh oh / ashes / over / *ifà* / *ifà* / *ifà i* / *fa* / fa / fa / fall / ing over /& / over the crew / touching there / is fate / there is / creed" (60). The merging of West African and English language, the movement between divine apostrophe and Western fate, the contrast of "creed" and "fate"—all of these elements anticipate that "double consciousness" that W. E. B. Du Bois would ultimately describe as the African American condition. Here, the lyrical repetition of the "fa" and "oh" provide a lyric voice to a poem constructed around juridical definitions of what it means to speak.

By the last section, these earlier passages are repeated only in what I have called a "ghost script" full of overstrikes and crossings-out—as if we are seeing Philip's early draft now as the work's completion. In her afterword Philip explains that in printing out the first draft of an earlier section, her printer superimposed several pages on top of one another. Rather than correct the printer error, she decides to retain them as a "translation that has a life of its own" (206). Returning to Avery Gordon's idea of "ghostly" absence of women in modern culture, we could see this final section, "Ebora," as intimating beginnings (of the manuscript) and also the endings, *arche* and *telos*, now rendered fully as a typed or printed document. Oral and textual traditions vie for speech, marking their claims of presence against the (literal) erasures of words and phrases that stand for missing bodies. One of the repeated phrases, "The oba sobs," refers to the Yoruba word for "king or ruler," as Philip's glossary states, a phrase that appears to be a funeral dirge for lost West Africans on the ship. The fact that at the end of the poem, this phrase of mourning is rendered through light font and multiple overstrikes suggests the complicated way that the history of structural violence is written. This fact is reinforced by Philip's inclusion of the literal court testimony from *Gregson v. Gilbert*. It is the "last word" of the book, concluding with the phrase, "Rule absolute on payment of costs." Here is the legal "dead end" for Africans in the Middle Passage, but the poem, in its open form and fragmented language, its multiple voices and languages, says otherwise.

MISSING BODIES

At the outset I invoked those bodies missing through detention, exception, and social neglect. These historical contexts may seem distant from Sinha's novel, Baggs' video, Zolf's catalogues of names, and the appropriated language of *Zong!*, yet each work, in different ways, understands the limits of embodiment as a self-evident term for identity among populations whose bodies do not exist or are not accorded equal rights with others. The use of appropriated or electronically modified language complicates the voice that has dominated an expressivist poetics since the 1960s. For these authors and many other recent writers working in the wake of the linguistic turn "voice" is not an unmediated extension of a prior body but a set of discursive frames within which bodies are defined and described, excluded and counted. What interests me about these examples is their realization not only of how poor, subaltern, neurodiverse, Palestinian and African bodies have been absented but how the representation of those bodies cannot be recuperated through an unproblematic "I" or narrative frame. The form that each artist chooses incorporates—quite literally in each case—the rule of law, the protocols of description and categorization, the bio-technologies of audition and transcription—and at the same time evacuates them of their performative power. Thus we are forced to learn a "new language" of testimony, a broken language of jurisprudence, a visual language of absence in order to re-inhabit bodies that have been lost to history.

What is the connection between this story of bodies missing from history and that of the aesthetic? Although any such linkage may seem tenuous, it is important to think of the role that aesthetics has played in shoring-up attitudes toward the body in history. For Kant, as summarized by J. M. Bernstein, a judgment of taste is a "reflective assertion of the pleasure one takes in a particular object or state of affairs which, without the mediation of concepts, lays claim to intersubjective validity" (18). It is this aesthetic social contract that cements private sensory pleasure to public validation, and just as the laborer's body is effaced in the commodity, so the experiential, libidinally invested body is erased in acts of disinterested contemplation. Writers seeking to situate the body in its imbricated relationship to social relations of power have developed ways—as my initial example of Simon Starling suggests—of reclaiming missing bodies from the visual, acoustic, and legal landscapes in which they are represented and thus contained. By indirect means, the disabled victim of an environmental catastrophe speaks as an animal; the poet who *does* not speak speaks in "her own language"; the "ungrievable" civilians in a war zone are given names; the slave without a voice is re-articulated through the shards of a court brief. In NourbeSe Philip's oxymoron that governs these works, "There is no telling this story; it must be told."

8

Cleavings
Critical Losses in the Politics of Deaf Gain

"I COULD NOT SEE TO SEE—"

I heard a Fly buzz—when I died—
The Stillness in the Room
Was like the Stillness in the Air—

Between the Heaves of Storm—
The Eyes around—had wrung them dry—
And Breaths were gathering firm
For that last Onset—when the King
Be witnessed—in the Room—

I willed my Keepsakes—Signed away
What portion of me be
Assignable—and then it was
There interposed a Fly—

With Blue—uncertain—stumbling Buzz—
Between the light—and me—
And then the Windows failed—and then
I could not see to see—   (270)[1]

"I could not see to see—." The final line from Emily Dickinson's famous poem, "I heard a Fly buzz—when I died," is about the transition from consciousness to unconsciousness, framed through the metaphor of sight. What is powerful about the poem is Dickinson's understanding of the gap between sight as something one *has* and something one *is*. For sighted persons to see is to be able to organize the world into a coherent mass, to differentiate and parse passing phenomena into coherent patterns. The eyes become a transparent window onto the world. In Dickinson's account, when one cannot see, it does not mean that she has lost consciousness but that she can no longer organize visual sensations, leaving the impression that the windows, not the eyes, have failed. In this moment she is permitted to see, as it were, through a glass darkly; rather than conform the world

---

[1] Throughout this chapter I am using Cristanne Miller's recent edition of Dickinson's poems which eliminates the numbering systems of both Thomas Johnson and Ralph Franklin and places poems in the fascicles or groupings that Dickinson used to preserve them. Subsequent references to this edition will be included in the text by page number. I am grateful to Cristanne Miller, Maren Linnett, Chris Krentz, Peter Middleton, and Jeff Brune for their comments on early drafts of this chapter.

to recognizable patterns and codes, she confronts raw consciousness itself. Her repetition of "see" helps emphasize the filament-thin boundary between these two functions: doing and being, having and existing, seeing and knowing. In the opening of the poem Dickinson imagines herself in a funeral setting, experiencing the "Stillness in the Air— / Between the Heaves of Storm," while mourners pay their last obeisance. She consigns her physical being—her "Keepsakes"—to oblivion and anticipates the appearance of some divine "King" that will transport her. But her genius is to understand that all of these rituals are for that portion of her that is "Assignable" by others, and in her transition into unconsciousness she has become the sign, not the keeper of the Sign, the seer not the possessor of sight.

Dickinson had her own concrete experiences with temporary blindness as a young woman. We know that she had several eye treatments in 1864 in Cambridge under Dr. Henry Willard Williams.[2] These extended treatments were apparently painful, requiring the resting of eyes, eye-drops, and perhaps the puncturing of the cornea to reduce the accumulation of fluid. Many of her poems are about non-sighted experience ("The Soul has Bandaged moments—" and "Like eyes that looked on waste—" being the best known), and although metaphors of blindness are common in all poetry, Dickinson had an especially acute awareness of what we might call the "agential" understanding of sensory experience.[3] That is, she thought hard about what is *gained* from losing sight, not from the tragedy that it implies. She experiences what Mel Chen calls an "incredible wakefulness" that one experiences while living with illness or trauma (1).[4] Rather than bemoan her fate, writing as many female poets of her generation did about the tragedy of death and dying, she probed the loss of sensation for what it could teach her about what is most familiar—and thus invisible.[5]

I've been thinking a lot about these lines during the past years as I have gone progressively deaf.[6] Even though I have taught Dickinson's lines many times in classes, I've never had such a powerful understanding of her insight until my hearing

---

[2] Richard Sewall reports that Dickinson visited an eye doctor in Cambridgeport, Massachusetts (Cambridge) for eye treatment in 1864 and 1865 (325). On Dickinson and illness see Norbert Hirschhorn and Polly Longsworth, "'Medicine Posthumous': A New Look at Emily Dickinson's Medical Conditions."

[3] For example:

> Before I got my eye put out—
> I liked as well to see
> As other creatures, that have eyes—
> And know no other way   (177)

[4] "I realized that in the most containing and altered moments of illness, as often occurs with those who are severely ill, I came to know an incredible wakefulness, one that I was not paradoxically losing and could only try to commit to memory" (Chen, *Animacies*, 1).

[5] Cristanne Miller notes that "I heard a fly buzz" seems to refer to lines from Elizabeth Barrett Browning's *Aurora Leigh* in which, as Miller says, "a dying woman claims that 'something came between' her and the man she loved, 'catching every fly of doubt / To hold it buzzing at the window-pane'" (761 n. 244).

[6] My colleagues Carol Padden and Tom Humphries would probably say that as a culturally hearing person I have become increasingly hard-of-hearing, although from a Deaf cultural perspective, as they point out, my severe hearing loss might be seen as "a little hard-of-hearing" since it approaches total deafness. What counts as the ability to hear occupies what they see as a "different center" for hearing and deaf persons. See Carol Padden and Tom Humphries, "A Different Center," in *Deaf in America: Voices from a Culture*.

in my one functioning ear began to fade and silence descended on me like a fog. I have bilateral tumors on each auditory nerve, the result of neurofibromatosis 2, a genetically inherited disease. An operation some years ago removed one of the tumors, leaving me with no hearing on the left side, and subsequent operations and radiation on the right side have left me with virtually no hearing at all. Apparently the tumor that was treated with radiation came back to life, and the result has been several years of decreased hearing to the point that I can only make out the most basic sounds. Conversations have become difficult, requiring elaborate use of voice-to-text software on my smart phone, and I live in what I experience as a padded world where everything is quiet and smooth, framed by a dull drone of tinnitus. My own voice is a monotone of nasals without significant distinctions, a semantic hollow whose dynamics are out of my control. I will discuss the ramifications of this experience momentarily, but I simply wanted to offer my own understanding of what it might mean to say, "I could not hear to hear."[7]

And I need to capture this moment *now* since, as Dickinson indicates, when one sees, *with* the eyes one is not quite alive but living in the illusion that sight and hearing give us. The present tense sustains and elaborates a condition that a retrospective view consigns to a disparaged, transitory past. When we live in the full privilege of embodied life—when the body functions "normally," and we say we are in "good health"—the windows seem to be working, and we describe variant conditions as some defect or flaw to be remedied. Temporary or late onset disabilities upset the coherence of time and space and, most important, our relations to others. Social relationships are confirmed by representation and repetition, reinforced by the material forms (texts, images, poems) through which consensus is achieved and cited. As I have written in previous chapters, achieving consensus is a key function of the aesthetic in Kant's third critique: one has an opinion about the coherence of an object or scene that is subjective and unique which we then ascribe to others. The idea of the beautiful is tied to what we imagine others would find similarly beautiful and thus constitutes our larger sense of self, projected from the local body to the social body. When that illusion is broken, when the beautiful object is missing an arm, wears a brace, limps in spastic motion, one's sense of bodily coherence is challenged and social forms based on such coherence become fragmented. For the larger purpose of aesthetic judgment is to confirm representation on others, to assume that we are "like them" and that they mirror what our bodies perform. When the body fails to perform in a representational regime it becomes, in Dickinson's terms, "assignable" and can be made to "do" something "for" someone "as" something.

I want to pursue what it means for a body to "fail," not as a sign of loss or decline but as constituting a moment of critical awareness, a moment that Heidegger

---

[7] Dickinson's poem is not only about sight but also about the transition between a moment of intense hearing ("I heard a Fly buzz—when I died") to one of sight ("And then the Windows failed—and then / I could not see to see—"). It is as though the sound of the fly's buzz ("With Blue—uncertain—stumbling Buzz / Between the light—and me—") enables vision, interrupting the ritual of dying, with its anticipatory transformation of the flesh, and returning the body to the body. The fly is both a metaphor for corruption and decay and a sudden—if provisional—instance of liveliness.

characterizes as ontological "disturbance" leading to an understanding of being-in-time. This temporal aspect of discovery has been the focus of a good deal of philosophical inquiry concerning the primacy of temporality or spatiality. Philosophers, since Plato, have weighed the hierarchical advantages of one sense over another in establishing the superiority of, as in Plato, sight to Idea or, in the case of Heidegger, sound to Being. Arguing against a logocentric metaphysics based on vision from Plato to Husserl, Heidegger in *Being and Time* and developed more fully in his later writings vaunts sound and hearing as constitutive of *Dasein*. "*Dasein* hears, because it understands" (206). Participating in discourse—the "sounding" of language—involves an activity of unfolding truth through time; we talk *to* someone in anticipation of a response and in the process discover—not invent—truth as process. Being does not exist prior to discourse; Being is discovered *in* discourse. We may hear isolated sounds—"the creaking wagon, the motor-cycle"—but these things are "springboard[s] from which the subject leaps off and finally arrives at a 'world' " (207).

What has happened in the modern era, according to Heidegger, is that that "world" has become representation, "conceived and grasped as picture" ("Age," 129). Sight for Heidegger reifies knowledge in an image that precludes the temporal uncovering of Being through discourse. He does not imagine the importance of sight for deaf persons whose discursive relations through sign language rely on the eye. Nor, given his strictly acoustic sense of discourse, does he imagine that persons who do not hear could still be human. He anticipates postmodern theorists like Jean Baudrillard in understanding the world as a set of simulacra or copies, but he is aware that when we "get the picture" we apprehend the totality of something as represented. When Emily Dickinson says, "I could not see to see" she seems to understand the futility of prioritizing sight over sound by bringing them together in a poem—a form of discourse, after all—that is about an emergent conscious-ness. She recognizes the gap between sight and knowledge reveals vision in two modalities, one dependent on the object of sight and the other on the insight gained thereby. One might say that in the loss of sensation she sees space anew, hears a fly buzz as a component of her own mortality, differentiates the time experienced by mourners from the time experienced by the Subject. By differenti-ating and prioritizing sound and vision, Heidegger loses the opportunity to reflect on what late onset hard-of-hearing people often learn about space—that it is something heard as much as seen.[8]

I remember vividly the first time I realized the extent to which space is an acoustic phenomenon. I was in Paris for a summer after my first operation and had lost my

[8] Rebecca Sanchez has explored the debate about sight versus sound in her book, *Deafening Modernism*. She usefully questions what it might mean to explore modernism's "embodied language" through what she calls "deaf epistemology." She is less interested in studying deaf authors or novelists who represent deaf characters than in testing literary innovation against models of language provided by manual signing. She asks what it would be like to situate, say, the poetics of impersonality or objec-tivist poetics not through their debts to Symbolism or psychoanalysis, but against the backdrop of linguistic and biopolitical standardization? How does the embodied aspect of American Sign Language challenge instrumental reason and technological rationality? How do canonical modernist works implicitly anticipate aspects of sign language into experimental narrative forms?

hearing on the left side. My brain had not adjusted to the hearing loss, and I was very unstable on my feet, even when walking on solid sidewalks. I remember stepping off a curb, having looked to my right without seeing any cars coming, but was almost run over by a driver on the left whose car I couldn't hear approaching. From that time on, I had literally "to look both ways" and not rely on audial location. Balance was also a problem. I found walking on curved or bumpy roads very difficult and tended to hug the walls of buildings, trailing my fingers along the wall to steady myself. I learned to sit on the left of people I wanted to talk with (and to the right of those I didn't). As I get older, I notice that spatial positioning of the hard-of-hearing person in social situations is a common topic and subject of much senior-moment levity. Positioning, balance, judgment, walking—these are pro-prioceptive experiences that condition the body to the world, and to find them out of joint is to find oneself, to adapt Hamlet, out of time.

Being "out of time" rhymes with what Alison Kafer and Margaret Price, drawing from queer theory, have called "crip time" to refer to the variable temporalities of disability.[9] Kafer notes how persons with disabilities require different modalities of time (to move between appointments, take tests, facilitate captioning and sign language interpretation), but she speculates on how such thinking might "lead to more expansive notions of both time and futurity" (27).[10] To crip time is radically to rethink terms like "development," "cure," "progress," "health," and "incidence," and to include those who can't, for various reasons, "make it on time." Kafer's remarks about biofuturity are important in the context of Deaf Culture, although many members of the Deaf community do not identify with the term "crip" and its association with physical disabilities. At the same time and with the current debates about cochlear implants, medical interventions, and genomics, futurity for deaf persons is being redesigned around an insidious return of neo-eugenic oralist ideology, masked as progress. Mainstreaming in education, a byproduct of section 504 of the 1973 Rehabilitation Act and the Americans with Disabilities Act, has contributed perhaps even more to this trend. The Deaf community is rightly worried about the loss of a vital cultural heritage, forged through sign language. Yet seeking to retain that heritage through a monolithic deaf nationalism based on signing places the struggle in an earlier minority model and doesn't address the multiple constituencies of a post-nationalist Deaf Culture that benefits from new technologies, social networks, and intersectional alliances.

A qualification here: by "post-nationalist" I don't mean to imply, as Lennard Davis does, that we have come to a "post-deafness" moment.[11] Deaf Culture is alive and well, spurred by a growing political movement around protests at Gallaudet

---

[9] Anna Mindness discusses a parallel version for deaf people that she refers to as "Deaf Standard Time." *Reading between the Signs: Intercultural Communication for Sign Language Interpreters*, 53–4.

[10] See also Margaret Price, *Mad at School: Rhetorics of Mental Disability and Academic Life*, 1–24.

[11] Lennard Davis in "Postdeafness" makes a convincing case for seeing the limits of understanding through "categories of ethnicity, minority status, nationhood (including 'world' and 'culture') when one might do better to use the category of 'one-generation' identities to redefine the nature of social identity" (323). At the same time, some Deaf activists are concerned that the phrase "post-deafness" ignores the continuing material and social barriers that deaf people face.

University, first in 1988 and more recently in 2006, and by increased involvement in and accommodations to the public sphere. I would, however, suggest that we need a more nuanced approach to d/Deafness that recognizes the material conditions and cultural histories of capital 'D' Deaf persons while expanding small 'd' deafness to include the wide spectrum of people living on a deaf continuum. The latter would include congenitally deaf, CODAs (children of deaf adults), late-deafened, hard-of-hearing, persons with cochlear implants, aging and disabled persons, and persons whose deafness is a component of other medical problems. Among these constituencies lies the large, unexamined question of affect: how it feels to live in a world where deafness is defined through loss as silence.

"A PLANK IN REASON"

As all the Heavens were a Bell,
And Being, but an Ear,
And I, and Silence, some strange Race
Wrecked, solitary, here— (179)

Dickinson brings the funeral inside—where, as she says elsewhere "the Meanings are" (153), Instead of hearing the tolling bells *through* her ears, she *becomes* the bell; instead of *not hearing*, she *becomes* the Silence. There is no separation of sound and sensory organ; both are conjoined in the awe-filled word, "Being." And where silence had marked the space between one peal and the next, it is now one with the sounds that give it form. Silence becomes her companion—Friday to her Crusoe wrecked on his island. But whereas Crusoe treats Friday as his cannibal servant and subaltern, she and Silence are joined in the same "strange Race." What the non-racialized Subject experiences as an orderly funeral, with mourners "treading-treading—till it seemed / That Sense was breaking through," Dickinson experiences as auditory exile. All distinctions by which Reason, language, and race are constituted dissolve into silence:

And then a Plank in Reason, broke,
And I dropped down, and down—
And hit a World, at every plunge,
And Finished knowing—then— (179)

Surely one of the most vivid representations of what it means to "lose consciousness," "I felt a Funeral in my Brain," rehearses the stages through which sounds can no longer be organized around discrete pitches, meaning portioned between one phoneme and the next. The final, tentative "then" with its enclosing dashes enacts linguistically the end of knowing while leaving the syntax open to knowledges yet unimaginable ("And finished knowing [but] then..."). Dickinson embodies this tension between finality and unknowability by her slant rhyme, "down— / then—," as if recognizing that the descent from Reason cannot be configured around a rhetoric of closure.

These lines are, among other things, about the sounds within silence or we might say the impossibilities of silence as an organizing metaphor for the absence of Reason. As Carol Padden and Tom Humphries say, being deaf has less to do with silence than with negotiations with hearing people's expectations of what sounds are supposed to do.[12] It is worth remembering that deaf persons until recently were often thought to be without reason because, presumably, without speech. Nor do all deaf people lack significant ranges of sound, and for partially deaf persons, there is always a residue of some acoustic material. In my present state of hearing loss, the sounds I hear involve a dull roaring that stems from bodily circulation of blood and nerves. Tinnitus, which I used to have sporadically, is now a dominant drone, invading my consciousness at all times. Sounds have no pitch; listening to someone playing the piano, I hear only the rhythm. There is no variation in tonality from note to note; C might as well be F♯. Timbre is swallowed into a version of John Cage's prepared piano, a shattered, fuzzy pulse. An ascending motif sounds the same as downward run. I suspect that Beethoven faced these barriers every time he banged away at the piano in his later years, "hearing" the theme in his head, unable to reproduce it in his sensorium. But the harmonic and tonal complexities of the late quartets and piano sonatas were, to some extent, *enabled* by the cleaving produced by incipient deafness:

> I felt a Cleaving in my Mind—
> As if my Brain had split—
> I tried to match it—Seam by Seam—
> But could not make them fit—
>
> The thought behind, I strove to join
> Unto the thought before—
> But sequence raveled out of Sound—
> Like balls—upon a Floor—   (423)

Once again, Dickinson articulates this productive quality of the Defamiliar. She experiences a "Cleaving" of consciousness that demands to be sutured, "Seam by Seam" (as someone who sewed her poems into fascicles or pamphlets, this metaphor links her compositional process to a specifically gendered form of consciousness). She tries to link the prior condition—before the cleaving—to the next, but "sequence raveled out of sound— / Like balls—upon a Floor." Whatever is splitting Dickinson's "Mind" could be as simple as a migraine headache or as profound as a spiritual crisis, but she figures it as a loss of sequence, of temporal organization, through a metaphor of randomly moving orbs. What she represents as her cognitive disability—and here I want to insist on the relationship of sensory loss to embodiment generally—provides her with a special insight into the meaning of temporality as a "space" one inhabits.

Dickinson's sense of temporality as spatial ("the thought behind" . . . "the thought before") may have something to do with her much-discussed agoraphobia, her unwillingness to leave her father's home later in life and her subsequent retirement to her upstairs room. Although there is considerable debate about the extent of her later reclusiveness, it seems clear that she avoided most large social encounters.

---

[12] Carol Padden and Tom Humphries, *Deaf in America: Voices from a Culture* (91–109).

Some have suggested a correlation between her experiences of temporary blindness and her subsequent isolation—as if she feared that her "bandaged moments" would recur in public and threaten her antinomian resistance: "What I see not, I better see— / Through Faith—" (424). Once again, she could not "see to see" within the public gaze, but in understanding this she was able to control aspects of her life that did not conform to the austere Protestantism of mid-century Connecticut Valley. One might concur with many feminist critics of Dickinson that her refusal was her form of creativity. To reject Victorian expectations of gendered, religious, and domestic proprieties was her way of living, as Adrienne Rich says, "on [her] own premises" (70–1). But we cannot advance her politics by excising cognitive and sensory issues. Or we need to read refusal through both a disability and feminist perspective to respect the terms that embody her refusal. Her room may have been a sanctuary from women's social roles; her cedar box of fascicles may have contained her textual body. But she inhabited these bodies through periods of blindness, cognitive disability, and (perhaps) late in life, Bright's disease.

"INTERNAL DIFFERENCE"

In what has preceded I have been speaking about the ways that temporary disability— sudden injury, blindness, illness—offers a critical position on the integrity of the impaired body. Temporary or chronic conditions complicate the usual way of thinking of disability as somehow stabilized around a condition rather than as a mobile, variable identity throughout the life course. We should be cautious about phrases like "temporarily able bodied" (TAB) or "able disabled" that universalize the disability experience around a putatively normal body in transition. Yet there must be room to consider temporary, transitional, and recurrent states of impairment as part of a continuum. Susan Wendell has observed that the standard division between impairment and disability, "the medically defined condition of a person's body/mind, and disability as the socially constructed disadvantage based upon impairment [tends to] downplay the realities of fluctuating impairment or ill health" (165). As I've indicated earlier, in an attempt to place the onus of responsibility upon social institutions and legislation that create barriers to equal access, a constructionist version of disability may have marginalized the variable body in the process.[13]

Or the variable sensorium. Thus far I've been speaking, autobiographically, of "hearing loss," but I'm aware of what H. Dirksen Bauman and Joseph Murray have

---

[13] Sharon L. Snyder and David T. Mitchell offer a useful cultural model by stressing disability as a "site of phenomenological value that is not purely synonymous with the processes of social disablement. Such an emphasis does not hide the degree to which social obstacles and biological capacities may impinge upon our lives, but rather suggests that the result of those differences come to bear significantly on the ways disabled people experience their environments and their bodies." Sharon L. Snyder and David T. Mitchell, *Cultural Locations of Disability* (6).

called "deaf gain."[14] They are speaking of how, in the wake of protests at Gallaudet University and the emergence of Deaf Nation, a new consciousness has arisen around what it means to be culturally Deaf. The politics of deaf gain shifts the representations of deafness "from sensory lack to a form of sensory and cognitive diversity that offers vital contributions to human diversity" (246). I agree with this sentiment as it applies to deafness as a cultural rather than audiological form, but I want to retain something of the critical potential of "loss" for the purposes of gain.[15] With the increased visibility of queer, mixed-race, sight-impaired, trans-gendered, disabled, and deaf people into the field of cultural diversity we may miss the more invisible elements of embodied change that affect most people during their lives. As a culturally hearing person with a basic knowledge of sign language I know that I could never, even as a fluent signer, be a member of the Deaf community. Nor would I presume to so-identify. At the same time I am troubled by the phrase "hearing loss"—its implication of inadequacy or weakness—and the medical and prosthetic culture that is growing around intervention.

This rather interstitial position with regard to deafness/hearing loss has been an advantage to me as a person in the humanities with one foot firmly established in the hearing world but one foot testing the waters of Deaf World. The aesthetic tradition in which most of us in the humanities have been trained is based on the assumption that we "read" texts on pages; we inherit an "oral" culture; we analyze poems based on terms like "voice," "rhythm," "rhyme," and "line" and watch plays that feature richly embroidered spoken dialogue based on a written script. The idea of literary production signed on the body unsettles the very idea of literariness and the archival and philological traditions upon which much scholarly discourse is based. Including ASL as a second language for a literature requirement often requires defending sign language *as* a language and not a primitive gestural system, tied to English. Including ASL as a humanities requirement means defining literary production through technologies that include video, deaf clubs, performance, and film. This exercise, which is becoming increasingly common in academic environments, is a "gain" for students, but it also advances the university's goals of inclusiveness and diversity beyond the narrower frames of race, gender, and sexuality. When I use captioners in class, my students "see" disability as a relational condition, one in which communication is shared and produced by two persons. And when that captioning is reproduced on a screen, the entire class benefits from having better access to our group conversation, one enabled by provisions of the ADA. Once deaf gain is extended to broader fields of experience and pedagogy, then literacy takes on new meanings. As Bauman and Murray show, bringing d/Deaf cultural forms into the larger conversation about diversity redefines language,

---

[14] The phrase, "deaf gain," was originally used by the British performance artist, Aaron Williamson, who has on several occasions rejected the idea that he has "lost" his hearing so much as "gained" his deafness. See Bauman and Murray, "Deaf Studies in the 21st Century (255 n.1), and Michael Davidson, *Concerto for the Left Hand: Disability and the Defamiliar Body* (33).

[15] In a recent unpublished paper, Rosemarie Garland-Thomson has adapted the phrase to refer to "disability gain."

expands visual learning, revises academic and scholarly discourse, reinvents ideas of space and the built environment, and forges alliances transnationally.

At the same time, for late-deafened persons, the gains of "deaf gain" are muted by experiences of isolation and confusion within a new cultural identity:

> Heavenly Hurt, it gives us—
> We can find no scar,
> But internal difference—
> Where the Meanings, are—   (153)

While recognizing the limits of configuring deafness as audiological loss, I'd like to make a pitch for the inclusion of loss into the politics of deaf gain that expands the cultural diversity Bauman and Murray propose. Here, I am taking a page from Jack Halberstam's work on queer failure and those "ways of being and knowing that stand outside of conventional understandings of success" (2). Halberstam notes that in a heteronormative, capitalist economy, failure is not an option and that goals must include personal responsibility, independence, and self-reliance. For queers, "failure can be a style" which stands "in contrast to the grim scenarios of success that depend upon 'trying and trying again' " (3). Drawing on "low theory," Halberstam explores vernacular, avant-garde, zany, and subcultural realms that upset or carnivalize normative understandings of success. Most importantly, he notes that while failure "comes accompanied by a host of negative affects, such as disappointment, disillusionment, and despair, it also provides the opportunity to use these negative affects to poke holes in the toxic positivity of contemporary life" (3). These "negative affects" prompt my qualification of the more utopian rhetoric of deaf gain since it (gain) may marginalize aspects of disability where interactions with able-bodied expectations are experienced as failure or error. In seeking a utopian inclusiveness, the politics of gain may avoid strata of emotional life on the spectrum of cultural inclusion.

The recent turn toward affect in critical theory offers a promising arena for considering the positive *effects* of negative *affects*. Partly as a response to the critique of identity and subjectivity posed by post-structuralism, studies of affect have attempted to return the body to cultural theory, not as the origin of emotional attachment but as part of a social matrix of other bodies and interdependencies. The writings of Brian Massumi, Sianne Ngai, Lauren Berlant, Patricia Clough, Eve Sedgwick, Silvan Tomkins, and others, explore a variable, mobile quality of affect, loosed from the psychoanalytic body and its drives and distributed among varying "forces of encounter" and intensities.[16] Most pertinent, given my remarks about queer failure, is the focus on "minor affects" or what Sianne Ngai calls "ugly feelings"—attachments and relations that fly under the radar of more familiar realms of aesthetic emotion (pity, terror)—which she defines as "a bestiary of affects...one filled with rats and possums rather than lions" (7). Applied to disability, affect theory offers an (as yet unrealized) opportunity to extend the meaning of

---

[16] Gregory J. Seigworth and Melissa Gregg, "An Inventory of Shimmers," in *The Affect Theory Reader* (2).

embodiment into a relational, transactional, and interdependent area. "[No] one has yet determined what the body can do...from the laws of Nature alone."[17] Baruch Spinoza's formulation, often regarded as a founding statement of affect theory, offers an important challenge to the unitary Subject and the biologically configured body.

As I suggest in Chapter 6, for all of its emphasis on embodiment and sensation, affect theory has paid scant attention to disability, nor to the many ways that disability theory has addressed the emotional registers that attend physical and cognitive impairment.[18] Eve Sedgwick's influential discussion of queer shame, to take one example, queries what would happen if an "unwashed, half-insane man" might wander "into the lecture hall mumbling loudly, his speech increasingly accusatory and disjointed, and publicly urinate in the front of the room then wander out again" (*Touching Feeling*, 37). Such an event, as Sedgwick frames it, would "call the members of her audience into burning awareness of their own individual skin," while being able at the same time "to stanch the hemorrhage of painful identification with the misbehaving man" (37). As Tobin Siebers says of this example, shame as stigma produces a "queer emotion by which we put ourselves in the place of others" and is hence "ethically useful because it legitimates the question of identity without giving identity the status of an essence" (*Disability Theory*, 158). Yet, as Siebers concludes, "Sedgwick interrogates neither the shame nor the identity of the disabled man" (158). The use of a disabled body to illustrate a subaltern, abject, or sexually subversive identity is hardly unique to affect theory, but it is disturbing that a theoretical field dedicated to questions of attachment, relationality, and biomediation should assume an able-bodied model as the inevitable site for affective disruption.

All of which pertains to my qualification of "deaf gain," a phrase that, to some extent, restricts the affective realm surrounding deafness to a forward looking, positive agenda. Somewhat lost in this vision is the embodied experience of populations for whom loss of hearing poses a challenge, even trauma, to the lived reality of community, work, family, and solidarity. I come to this conclusion not out of any objection to the value of deaf gain but through an interest in adapting it to the kinds of intersectional alliances being formed through disability studies, a field in which the claims of gain and loss are often negotiated on more common ground.

Let me be more specific with reference to how deaf gain applies to disability gain more generally. In many disability memoirs, pivotal moments of negative affect often interrupt narratives that are otherwise inspiring testimonies to endurance and triumph. Tales of frustration with care-givers, insensitive doctors, short counters, poor signage, narrow bathroom stalls, intolerant merchants, and staring bus passengers are the very stuff of disability life writing. Rather than see such moments

---

[17] Baruch Spinoza, *The Ethics*, in *A Spinoza Reader* (155).

[18] The term "disability" is used once in *The Affect Theory Reader*. In their introduction, editors Gregory Seigworth and Melissa Gregg say that Eve Sedgwick's work "has been just as significant for demonstrating affect's place in *disabling* as much as accompanying intellectual practice" (23). Here, disability is used as the negative complement of "intellectual practice" rather than a condition whose affective implications are treated in their own right.

as diversions from a trajectory toward fulfillment and self-reliance, I'd like to see them as fissures—cleavings—that are constitutive aspects of the disability experience. In Harriet McBryde Johnson's memoir, *Too Late to Die Young*, the disability activist and lawyer describes a moment when her electric power chair breaks down, and she needs a passerby to push her to where she can phone someone to fix it. Someone else pushes her home. "Every time my chair conks, I go absolutely nuts. I can't do anything on my own. I'm stuck. Like a helpless cripple! Whatever plan I've made—and I've always made some plan—gets derailed" (28). Or consider Nancy Mairs speaking of her frustration in public spaces:

> In airports I break down and weep. Other venues provoke me to passion of various disagreeable sorts: indignation when someone without a handicapped license plate has taken a reserved space; frustration when a shop crowds in so much merchandise that I can't get my wheelchair down the aisles without risk of smothering in racks of finery or knocking down elaborate displays of fragile items; impatience when I'm trapped on the wrong side of an unautomated door that nobody else in the world seems inclined to go through; panic and ironically, loneliness when large gatherings of people in enclosed spaces, like theatre audiences, mill around me, waving and calling out to each other, without ever glancing down.   (190)

Finally, in Georgina Kleege's *Blind Rage* she writes an epistle to Helen Keller, remembering that, as she says, "I grew up hating you. Sorry to be so blunt, especially on such short acquaintance, but one of the advantages of writing to a dead person is there's no need to stand on ceremony…I hated you because you were always held up to me as a role model, and one who set up such an impossibly high standard of cheerfulness in the face of adversity. 'Why can't you be more like Helen Keller?' people always said to me" (1). Going nuts, weeping in airports, hating Helen Keller— these are hardly shouts of independent assertion or solidarity so much as recognitions of contingency and vulnerability, embarrassment and frustration.

  Such moments of affective disruption occur when the ontological meets the social, when resolve and intention butt into the built environment, when a plank in reason breaks and the body is revealed in all its clunky vicissitudes. Dickinson represents such moments as spiritual pain, "heavenly hurt," but we could extend her religious rhetoric to what happens when a kind of social consensus can no longer be presumed and must be portioned out through senses of inadequacy. If these affective states become ancillary to an emancipatory narrative of progress and independence, they lose their ability to illustrate contingency. Moreover, they become detached from their political role that relates "internal difference" to political resistance. I am not saying that disability studies needs to return to a model of dependence and pathos but to acknowledge the lived experiences of loss, frustration, pain, and embarrassment in a politics of gain.

SIDE EFFECTS

I want to conclude with a reflection on "side effects." When I visited my audiologist about hearing loss, I could not "hear to hear" his diagnosis about whatever was causing the condition. I was thus within and without the medical structure of deafness, given directions without the ability to fulfill what J. L. Austin calls the "felicity criteria" of a speech act.[19] I was *in* a speech act situation without portfolio—a condition that goes by the felicitous term, "patient." The steroids he prescribed have had little effect, as it turns out. But steroids produce side effects that anyone who has taken them will recognize—sleeplessness, irritability, water retention, hunger, weight gain. They also give one enormous energy and stimulus. Think of this chapter as a side effect of steroid stimulation.

I mention side effects to suggest that disability is never a unitary function—that each condition is a complex or spectrum of effects over the life course. A person with diabetes may also be obese, may have heart problems or blindness. A person with hemophilia often lives with severe orthopedic problems, and many severe bleeders are HIV+. Persons with MS move in and out of exhaustion, pain, and normal mobility over their lives. They often take steroids for long periods of time that significantly alter behavior, mood, and sleep patterns. Many persons become deaf as a result of diseases (meningitis, mumps, rubella), accidents, or other forms of trauma. As I said earlier, in our rejection of the medical model of disability into a purely social version we may have forgotten the body that is rendered inert in the process. And we may avoid the degree to which prosthetics like medications, signage, captioning, wheelchairs, hearing-aids, braces, and public transportation are part of the body, not excrescences. In my own case, voice-to-text software is my link to all social intercourse. To see assistive technologies as mere appurtenances is to maintain the illusion of a biological phantom, a once-whole body being propped up by scaffolding. I was once at a conference where a speaker attacked the evils of medicalization in cognitive disabilities and how Big Pharma was getting rich on prescriptions, doctors prescribing increasing amounts of anti-depressants and keeping everyone in a state of permanent medicosis. Everyone in the room nodded approvingly, but a woman spoke up in the Q&A and said "that's all very well for you to say, but if I weren't on my meds, I couldn't be here to hear you say that!"

By "side effects" I mean the residual aspects of disability that inform its core and that often play cameo roles in the disability memoirs mentioned earlier. Side effects of medication and medical procedures are components of that disability gain I have alluded to. They are considered the "bad consequences" of cure or remediation, but they need to be treated as part of the condition of cleaving, just as the tinnitus drone is part of my experience of deafness. We can rail against the medical profession, psychoanalysis, and rehabilitation science, but in doing so we may deny experiential elements of complex embodiment that define the condition of disability. In this context I would include care-givers, family members, friends, and, yes, medical professionals who make the private body a social body. It would be insensitive to call a care-giver a "prosthesis," yet such persons, as Eva Feder Kittay and others have said, become part of the person with a disability, marginalized

---

[19] J. L. Austin in describing performative utterances speaks of what happens when "something *goes wrong* and the act—marrying, betting, bequeathing, christening, or what not—is therefore at least to some extent a failure: the utterance is then, we may say, not indeed false but in general *unhappy*." This condition he describes as "the doctrine of the *Infelicities*." J. L. Austin, *How to Do Things with Words* (14).

economically and culturally but also a component of a collateral dependency condition. Recognizing what Alasdair MacIntyre calls the "virtues of acknowledged dependence" is necessary if disability studies is to intervene in a political reorganization of the body (8).

In this concluding chapter I have merged aesthetics and disability, personal anecdote and public statement hoping to contribute to an intersectional understanding of disability studies. I've also retained the present tense, despite the fact that my hearing has deteriorated from when I first wrote this text. Personal memoirs like those of Nancy Mairs, Harriet McBryde Johnson, Georgina Kleege, Simi Linton, and others have been foundational documents for disability studies not because they provide heart-warming stories of triumph and self-reliance but because they particularize the meaning of disability around specific conditions—cognitive, structural, juridical, and ethical. They provide exemplary cases by which public policy and understanding must proceed. At the same time, the fields of affect theory, queer theory, science studies, rights discourse, and new materialisms are expanding the meaning of disability beyond the social model. Finally, the current turn to the aesthetic, far from offering a retreat from the body into disinterested judgment, provides narratives of bodily and affective difference—a certain slant of light—at variance to those of pathos and triumph that often dominate public perception of disability. Emily Dickinson felt a "funeral" in her brain whose medical etiology we cannot know, but she left a record of what it felt like to become a social body falling through the body.

Works Cited

Adams, Rachel, Benjamin Reiss, and David Serlin, eds. *Keywords for Disability Studies*. New York: New York University Press, 2015.

Addison, Joseph. "Geneva and the Lake." In *Remarks on Several Parts of Italy etc. in the years 1701, 1702, 1703*. 1773 edition, printed for T. Walker. 261. Google Books. Accessed August 2, 2017.

Adelson, Betty M. *The Lives of Dwarfs: Their Journey from Public Curiosity toward Social Liberation*. New Brunswick, NJ: Rutgers University Press, 2005.

Adorno, Theodor. *Aesthetic Theory*. Trans. Robert Hullot-Kentor. Minneapolis, MN: University of Minnesota Press, 1997.

Adorno, Theodor. "Trying to Understand *Endgame*." In *Samuel Beckett's Endgame*. Ed. Harold Bloom. New York: Chelsea House Publishers, 1988.

Adorno, Theodor. "Vers une musique informelle." In *Quasi una fantasia: Essays on Modern Music*. Trans. Rodney Livingstone. London: Verso, 1994.

Adorno, Theodor. "Zemlinsky." In *Quasi una fantasia: Essays on Modern Music*. Trans. Rodney Livingstone. London: Verso, 1992.

Adorno, Theodor and Max Horkheimer. *The Dialectic of Enlightenment*. Trans. John Cumming. New York: Continuum, 1993.

Agamben, Giorgio. *Homo Sacer: Sovereign Power and Bare Life*. Stanford, CA: Stanford University Press, 1998.

Agnew, Jean-Christophe. "The Consuming Vision of Henry James." In *The Culture of Consumption*. Ed. Richard Wightman Fox and T. J. Jackson Lears. New York: Pantheon, 1983. 65–100.

Ahmed, Sara. *The Promise of Happiness*. Durham, NC: Duke University Press, 2010.

Ahmed, Sara. *Queer Phenomenology: Orientation, Objects, Others*. Durham, NC: Duke University Press, 2006.

Alaimo, Stacy. *Bodily Natures: Science, Environment, and the Material Self*. Bloomington, IN: Indiana University Press, 2010.

Apollinaire, Guillaume. *The Breasts of Tiresias*. In *Modern French Theatre: The Avant-Garde, Dada, and Surrealism*. Ed. Michael Benedikt and George E. Wellwarth. New York: Dutton, 1964. 55–92.

Appadurai, Arjun. *Modernity at Large: Cultural Dimensions of Globalization*. Minneapolis, MN: University of Minnesota Press, 1996.

Armstrong, Tim. *Modernism: A Cultural History*. Cambridge: Polity Press, 2005.

Armstrong, Tim. *Modernism, Technology and the Body: A Cultural Study*. Cambridge: Cambridge University Press, 1998.

Arnold, Matthew. "The Scholar Gypsy." In *The Norton Anthology of Poetry*, 4th ed. Ed. Margaret Ferguson, Mary Jo Salter, and Jon Stallworthy. New York: Norton, 1970.

Austin, J. L. *How to Do Things with Words*. Ed. J. O. Urmson and Marina Sbisà. Cambridge, MA: Harvard University Press, 1975.

Baggs, Amanda. "In my Language." YouTube Video, 2007. <http://www.youtube.com/watch?v=JnylM1hI2jc>. Accessed September 12, 2012.

Barnes, Djuna. *Nightwood*. New York: New Directions, 1961.

Bataille, Georges. "The Sacred Conspiracy." In *Visions of Excess: Selected Writings, 1927–1939*. Ed. Allan Stoekl. Minneapolis, MN: University of Minnesota Press, 1985. 178–81.

Baucom, Ian. "Specters of the Atlantic." *South Atlantic Quarterly* 100.1 (Winter, 2001): 61–82.

Baudelaire, Charles. "À une passante" ("To a Passer-By"). Trans. Rodney Livingston and Harry Zohn. In Walter Benjamin, *The Writer of Modern Life: Essays on Charles Baudelaire*. Cambridge, MA: Harvard University Press, 2006. 76.

Baudelaire, Charles. *The Painter of Modern Life and Other Essays*. Trans. and ed. Jonathan Mayne. New York: Phaidon, 1965.

Bauman, H-Dirksen L., ed. *Open your Eyes: Deaf Studies Talking*. Minneapolis, MN: University of Minnesota Press, 2008.

Bauman, H-Dirksen L. and Joseph J. Murray. "Deaf Studies in the 21st Century: 'Deaf-Gain' and the Future of Human Diversity." In *The Disability Studies Reader*, 4th ed. Ed. Lennard J. Davis. New York: Routledge, 2013. 246–60.

Baynton, Douglas. "Disability and the Justification of Inequality in American History." In *The New Disability History: American Perspectives*. Ed. Paul K. Longmore and Lauri Umansky. New York: New York University Press, 2001. 33–57.

Baynton, Douglas. *Forbidden Signs: American Culture and the Campaign against Sign Language*. Chicago, IL: University of Chicago Press, 1996.

Beatie, Thomas. "Labor of Love." *The Advocate* (March 23, 2008). <http://www.alternet.org/sex/80450/>.

Beaumont, Anthony. *Zemlinsky*. Ithaca, NY: Cornell University Press, 2000.

Beckett, Samuel. *Endgame*. New York: Grove Press, 1958.

Beckett, Samuel. *Happy Days*. New York: Grove Press, 1961.

Beckett, Samuel. *Rough for Theatre I*. In *The Collected Shorter Plays of Samuel Beckett*. New York: Grove Press, 1984. 65–73.

Beckett, Samuel. *Three Novels of Samuel Beckett: Molloy, Malone Dies, The Unnamable*. New York: Grove Press, 1958.

Beckett, Samuel. *Waiting for Godot*. New York: Grove Press, 1982.

Bederman, Gail. *Manliness and Civilization: A Cultural History of Gender and Race in the United States, 1880–1917*. Chicago, IL: University of Chicago Press, 1995.

Benhabib, Seyla. *Another Cosmopolitanism*. New York: Oxford University Press, 2006.

Benjamin, Walter. "On Some Motifs in Baudelaire." In *The Writer of Modern Life: Essays on Charles Baudelaire*. Ed. Michael Jennings. Cambridge, MA: Harvard University Press, 2006. 170–212.

Benjamin, Walter. "Theses on the Philosophy of History." In *Illuminations*. Ed. Hannah Arendt. New York: Schocken, 1969. 253–64.

Berger, James. *The Disarticulate: Language, Disability, and the Narratives of Modernity*. New York: New York University Press, 2014.

Berlant, Lauren. *Cruel Optimism*. Durham, NC: Duke University Press, 2011.

Bernstein, J. M. *The Fate of Art: Aesthetic Alienation from Kant to Derrida and Adorno*. Cambridge: Polity Press, 1992.

Bixby, Patrick. *Samuel Beckett and the Postcolonial Novel*. Cambridge: Cambridge University Press, 2005.

Blake, William. "The Human Abstract." In *Songs of Innocence and Experience: The Poems of William Blake*. Ed. W. H. Stevenson. London: Longman, 1971. 216.

Bolaño, Roberto. *2666*. New York: Picador/Farrar, Straus, 2009.

Boone, Joseph. *Libidinal Currents: Sexuality and the Shaping of Modernism*. Chicago, IL: University of Chicago Press, 1998.

Bragg, Lois and William Sayers. "Proust's Prescription: Sickness as the Pre-condition for Writing." *Literature and Medicine* 192 (2000): 165–80.

Brennan, Teresa. *The Transmission of Affect*. Ithaca, NY: Cornell University Press, 2004.

Brown, Richard Maxwell. "Violence." In *The Oxford History of the American West*. Ed. Clyde A. Milner II, Carol A. O'Connor , and Martha A. Sandweiss. New York: Oxford University Press, 1994. 393–425.

Bürger, Peter. *Theory of the Avant-Garde*. Trans. Michael Shaw. Minneapolis, MN: University of Minnesota Press, 1984.

Burke, Edmund. *A Philosophical Enquiry into the Sublime and Beautiful*. Ed. David Womersley. London: Penguin, 1998.

Butler, Judith. *Bodies that Matter: On the Discursive Limits of "Sex."* New York: Routledge, 1993.

Butler, Judith. *Precarious Life: The Powers of Mourning and Violence*. London: Verso, 2004.

Cachia, Amanda. "Disabling Surrealism: Reconstituting Surrealist Tropes in Contemporary Art." In *Disability and Art History*. Ed. Ann Millett-Gallant and Elizabeth Howie. New York: Routledge, 2017. 132–54.

Cachia, Amanda. "What Can a Body Do?" Catalogue for exhibition at Cantor Fitzgerald Gallery, Haverford College, October 26–December 16, 2012.

Calinescu, Matei. *Faces of Modernity: Avant-Garde, Decadence, Kitsch*. Bloomington, IN: Indiana University Press, 1977.

Callahan, John F. *In the African American Grain: Call-and-Response in Twentieth-Century Black Fiction*. Urbana, IL: University of Illinois Press, 1988.

Cartwright, Lisa. "A Cultural Anatomy of the Visible Human Project." In *The Visible Woman: Imaging Technologies, Gender, and Science*. Ed. Paula A. Treichler, Lisa Cartwright, and Constance Penley. New York: New York University Press, 1998. 21–43.

Casper, Monica J. and Lisa Jean Moore. *Missing Bodies: The Politics of Visibility*. New York: New York University Press, 2009.

Cavell, Stanley. "Ending the Waiting Game: A Reading of Beckett's *Endgame*." In *Samuel Beckett's Endgame*. Ed. Harold Bloom: New York: Chelsea House Publishers, 1988. 59–78.

Chen, Mel. *Animacies: Biopolitics, Racial Mattering, and Queer Affect*. Durham, NC: Duke University Press, 2012.

Childs, Donald J. *Modernism and Eugenics: Woolf, Eliot, Yeats, and the Culture of Degeneration*. Cambridge: Cambridge University Press, 2001.

Clark, Kenneth. *Looking at Pictures*. Boston, MA: Beacon Press, 1960.

Claussen, Detlev. *Theodor Adorno: One Last Genius*. Trans. Rodney Livingstone. Cambridge, MA: Harvard University Press, 2008.

Clough, Patricia. "The Affective Turn: Political Economy, Biomedia, and Bodies." In *The Affect Theory Reader*. Ed. Melissa Gregg and Gregory J. Seigworth. Durham, NC: Duke University Press, 2010. 206–25.

Colker, Ruth. *Pregnant Men: Practice, Theory, and the Law*. Bloomington, IN: Indiana University Press, 1995.

Connor, Steven. *Samuel Beckett: Repetition, Theory, and Text*. Oxford: Basil Blackwell, 1988.

Cross, Susan. "The Nanjing Particles." In *The Nanjing Particles*. Ed. Susan Cross. North Adams, MA: MASS MoCA, 2009. 43–51.

Davidson, Michael. "Aesthetics." In *Keywords for Disability Studies*. Ed. Rachel Adams, Benjamin Reiss, and David Serlin. New York: New York University Press, 2015. 26–30.

Davidson, Michael. "Cripping Consensus: Disability Studies at the Intersection." *American Literary History* 28.2 (Summer, 2016): 433–53.

Davidson, Michael. *Concerto for the Left Hand: Disability and the Defamiliar Body*. Ann Arbor, MI: University of Michigan Press, 2008.

Davis, Lennard. *Bending over Backwards: Disability, Dismodernism, and Other Difficult Positions*. New York: New York University Press, 2002.

Davis, Lennard. *Enforcing Normalcy: Disability, Deafness and the Body*. London: Verso, 1995.

Davis, Lennard. "Postdeafness." In *Open your Eyes: Deaf Studies Talking*. Ed. H-Dirksen Bauman. Minneapolis, MN: University of Minnesota Press, 2008. 314–26.

de Man, Paul. "Literary History and Literary Modernity." In *Blindness and Insight: Essays in the Rhetoric of Contemporary Criticism*. New York: Oxford University Press, 1971. 142–65.

Deleuze, Gilles and Félix Guattari. *A Thousand Plateaus: Capitalism and Schizophrenia*. Trans. Brian Massumi. Minneapolis, MN: University of Minnesota Press, 1987.

Derrida, Jacques. "The Pharmakon." In *Dissemination*. Trans. Barbara Johnson. Chicago, IL: University of Chicago Press, 1981. 98–118.

Derrida, Jacques. *Specters of Marx: The State of the Debt, the Work of Mourning, and the New International*. New York: Routledge, 1994.

Detloff, Madeleine. *The Persistence of Modernism: Loss and Mourning in the Twentieth Century*. Cambridge: Cambridge University Press, 2009.

D., H. [Hilda Doolittle]. *H.D.: Collected Poems, 1912–1944*. New York: New Directions, 1983.

Dickinson, Emily. *Emily Dickinson's Poems: As She Preserved Them*. Ed. Cristanne Miller. Cambridge, MA: Harvard University Press, 2016.

Dostoevsky, Fyodor. *Notes from Underground*. Trans. Richard Pevear and Larissa Volokhonsky. New York: Vintage Classics, 1994.

Dowden, Stephen D. *A Companion to Thomas Mann's Magic Mountain*. Rochester, NY: Camden House, 1999.

Dowling, Sarah. "Persons and Voices: Sounding Impossible Bodies in M. NourbeSe Philip's *Zong!*" *Canadian Literature* 210/211 (Autumn/Winter, 2011): 43–59.

Eagleton, Terry. *The Ideology of the Aesthetic*. Oxford: Basil Blackwell, 1990.

Edelman, Lee. *No Future: Queer Theory and the Death Drive*. Durham, NC: Duke University Press, 2004.

Eliot, T. S. "Hamlet." In *Selected Essays of T. S. Eliot*. New York: Harcourt, Brace & World, 1960.

Eliot, T. S. "The Waste Land." In *The Complete Poems and Plays, 1909–1950*. New York: Harcourt, Brace & World, 1962. 37–55.

Ellmann, Maud. "More Kicks than Pricks: Modernist Body-Parts." In *A Handbook of Modernism Studies*. Ed. Jean-Michel Rabaté. London: John Wiley, 2013. 255–80.

Englebert, Tine. "Mad, Scarlet Music." *Oscholars*. Special issue on "The Birthday of the Infanta." <http://oscholars-oscholars.com/special-issues/infanta/> (September, 2002).

Et Shalom, Nava. "'The Family Playing Host to the Missile': A Review of Rachel Zolf's *Neighbour Procedure*." *Zeek* (October, 2010). <http://zeek.forward.com/articles/117015/>. Accessed July 28, 2013.

Fanon, Frantz. *Black Skin, White Masks*. New York: Grove Press, 1967.

Feder Kittay, Eva. *Love's Labor: Essays on Women, Equality, and Dependency*. New York: Routledge, 1999.

Felski, Rita. *The Gender of Modernity*. Cambridge, MA: Harvard University Press, 1995.

Finger, Anne. "The Artist and the Dwarf." In *Call Me Ahab: A Short Story Collection*. Lincoln, NE: University of Nebraska Press, 2009. 39–60.

Fitzgerald, F. Scott. *The Great Gatsby*. New York: Scribner's, 2004.

Flatley, Jonathan. *Affective Mapping: Melancholia and the Politics of Modernism*. Cambridge, MA: Harvard University Press, 2008.

Flynn, Catherine. "'Circe' and Surrealism: Joyce and the Avant-Garde." *Journal of Modern Literature* 34.2 (Winter, 2011): 121–38.

Foster, Hal, ed. *The Anti-Aesthetic: Essays on Postmodern Culture*. Port Townsend, WA: Bay Press, 1983.

Foster, Hal. *Prosthetic Gods*. Cambridge, MA: MIT Press, 2006.

Foucault, Michel. *The History of Sexuality: An Introduction*. Volume 1. Trans. Robert Hurley. New York: Random House, 1990.

Foucault, Michel. *The Order of Things: An Archaeology of the Human Sciences*. New York: Pantheon, 1970.

Frank, Arthur. *The Wounded Storyteller: Body, Ethics, and Illness*. Chicago, IL: University of Chicago Press, 2013.

Frank, Joseph. *The Widening Gyre: Crisis and Mastery in Modern Literature*. Bloomington, IN: Indiana University Press, 1963.

Frawley, Maria H. *Invalidism and Identity in Nineteenth-Century Britain*. Chicago, IL: University of Chicago Press, 2004.

Freud, Sigmund. *Three Case Histories*. New York: Collier Books, 1963.

Freud, Sigmund. "The Uncanny." In *The Uncanny*. Trans. David McLintock. New York: Penguin, 2003. 123–61.

Fussell, Paul. *The Great War and Modern Memory*. Oxford: Oxford University Press, 2000.

Garland-Thomson, Rosemarie. *Extraordinary Bodies: Figuring Physical Disability in American Culture and Literature*. New York: Columbia University Press, 1997.

Garland-Thomson, Rosemarie. *Staring: How We Look*. New York: Oxford University Press, 2009.

Garner, Stanton B. "The Gas Heart: Disfigurement and the Dada Body." *Modern Drama* 50.4 (Winter, 2007): 500–16.

Gettleman, Jeffrey. "A New Wave of 'Lost Boys' in Sudan War." *New York Times*, July 1, 2012.

Gilbert, Sandra M. and Susan Gubar. *No Man's Land: The Place of the Woman Writer in the Twentieth Century: Volume 2, Sex Changes*. New Haven, CT: Yale University Press, 1989.

Gilman, Charlotte Perkins. "Birth Control, Religion and the Unfit." *The Nation*, January 27, 1932. <http://www.thenation.com/article/154433/birth-control-religion>. Accessed July 15, 2015.

Gilman, Charlotte Perkins. *Herland, The Yellow Wall-Paper, and Selected Writings*. Ed. Denise K. Knight. New York: Penguin, 1999.

Gilman, Sander. *The Jew's Body*. New York: Routledge, 1991.

Gilman, Sander. *Making the Body Beautiful: A Cultural History of Aesthetic Surgery*. Princeton, NJ: Princeton University Press, 1999.

Gilroy, Paul. *The Black Atlantic: Modernity and Double Consciousness*. Cambridge, MA: Harvard University Press, 1993.

Ginsburg, Faye. "Disability in the Digital Age" In *Digital Anthropology*. Ed. Heather A. Horst and Daniel Miller. London: Berg, 2012. 101–26.

Gordon, Avery. *Ghostly Matters: Haunting and the Sociological Imagination*. Minneapolis, MN: University of Minnesota Press, 1997.

Gordon, Jan. "The 'Talking Cure' (Again): Gossip and the Paralyzed Patriarchy." In *The Body and Physical Difference: Discourses of Disability*. Ed. David T. Mitchell and Sharon L. Snyder. Ann Arbor, MI: University of Michigan Press, 1997. 202–22.

Greene, Vivien, ed. *Italian Futurism, 1909–1944*. New York: Solomon R. Guggenheim Museum, 2014.

Halberstam, Judith. *The Queer Art of Failure*. Durham, NC: Duke University Press, 2011.

Halberstam, Judith. *Skin Shows: Gothic Horror and the Technology of Monsters*. Durham, NC: Duke University Press, 1995.

Hanson, Ellis. "The Languorous Critic." *New Literary History* 43.3 (Summer, 2012): 547–64.

Hardt, Michael. "Foreword: What Affects Are Good For." In *The Affective Turn: Theorizing the Social*. Ed. Patricia Ticineto Clough. Durham, NC: Duke University Press, 2007. ix–xiii.

Heidegger, Martin. "The Age of the World Picture." In *The Question concerning Technology and Other Essays*. Trans. William Lovitt. New York: Harper & Row, 1977. 3–35.

Heidegger, Martin. *Being and Time*. Trans. John Macquarrie and Edward Robinson. New York: Harper & Row, 1962.

Heinrich, Ari Larissa. *Chinese Surplus: Biopolitical Aesthetics and the Medically Commodified Body*. Durham, NC: Duke University Press, 2018.

Herndl, Diane. *Invalid Women: Figuring Feminine Illness in American Fiction and Culture, 1840–1940*. Chapel Hill, NC: University of North Carolina Press, 1993.

Herring, Scott. *Queering the Underworld: Slumming, Literature, and the Undoing of Lesbian and Gay History*. Chicago, IL: University of Chicago Press, 2007.

Hewitt, Andrew. *Fascist Modernism: Aesthetics, Politics, and the Avant-Garde*. Stanford, CA: Stanford University Press, 1993.

Hirschhorn, Norbert and Polly Longsworth. "'Medicine Posthumous': A New Look at Emily Dickinson's Medical Conditions." *The New England Quarterly* 69.2 (June, 1996): 299–316.

Huyssen, Andreas. *After the Great Divide: Modernism, Mass Culture, Postmodernism*. Bloomington, IN: Indiana University Press, 1986.

James, Henry. *The American Scene*. Ed. Leon Edel. Bloomington, IN: Indiana University Press, 1968.

James, Henry. "The Beast in the Jungle." In *Selected Tales*. Ed. John Lyon. London: Penguin, 2001. 426–61.

James, Henry. "The Jolly Corner." In *Selected Tales*. Ed. John Lyon. New York: Penguin, 2001. 550–76.

James, Henry. *The Portrait of a Lady*. Ed. Jonathan Bamberg. New York: Norton, 1975.

James, William. "The Emotions." In *The Principles of Psychology*, vol. II. New York: Dover, 1950. 442–85.

Jameson, Fredric. *Fables of Aggression: Wyndham Lewis, the Modernist as Fascist*. Berkeley, CA: University of California Press, 1979.

Jameson, Fredric. *Postmodernism: Or, the Cultural Logic of Late Capitalism*. Durham, NC: Duke University Press, 1991.

Jay, Martin. "Drifting into Dangerous Waters." In *Aesthetic Subjects*. Ed. Pamela R. Matthews and David McWhirter. Minneapolis, MN: University of Minnesota Press, 2003. 3–27.

Joyce, James. *Selected Letters*. Ed. Richard Ellmann. London: Faber, 1975.

Joyce, James. *Ulysses*. New York: Random House, 1986.

Kafer, Alison. *Feminist, Queer, Crip*. Bloomington, IN: Indiana University Press, 2013.

Kant, Immanuel. *The Critique of Judgment*. Trans. James Creed Meredith. Oxford: Oxford University Press, 1952.

Kant, Immanuel. "Perpetual Peace: A Philosophical Sketch." In *Kant: Political Writings*. Ed. Hans Reiss. Cambridge: Cambridge University Press, 1991. 93–130.

Kaplan, Alice. *Reproductions of Banality: Fascism, Literature, and French Intellectual Life*. Minneapolis, MN: University of Minnesota Press, 1986.

Kellner, Douglas. *Critical Theory, Marxism and Modernity*. Baltimore, MD: Johns Hopkins University Press, 1989.

Kelly, Michael. *A Hunger for Aesthetics: Enacting the Demands of Art.* New York: Columbia University Press, 2012.

Kenner, Hugh. *The Pound Era.* Berkeley, CA: University of California Press, 1971.

Kevles, Daniel J. *In the Name of Eugenics: Genetics and the Uses of Human Heredity.* Cambridge, MA: Harvard University Press, 1985.

Kierkegaard, Søren. "Repetition." In *Fear and Trembling and Repetition.* Ed. Howard V. Hong and Edna H. Hong. Princeton, NJ: Princeton University Press, 1983, 274–330.

Kim, Jim Yong, Joyce V. Millen, Alec Irwin, and John Gershman. *Dying for Growth: Global Inequality and the Health of the Poor.* Monroe, ME: Common Courage Press, 2000.

Kim, Myung Mi. *Commons.* Berkeley, CA: University of California Press, 2002.

Klaren, Georg. Libretto for Alexander Zemlinsky, *Der Zwerg.* James Conlon, dir. EMI Classics, 1996. Digital recording.

Kleege, Georgina. *Blind Rage: Letters to Helen Keller.* Washington, DC: Gallaudet University Press, 2006.

Knadler, Stephen. "Dis-abled Citizenship: Narrating the Extraordinary Body in Racial Uplift." *Arizona Quarterly* 69.3 (Autumn, 2013): 99–128. Web. Project Muse, September 22, 2015.

Knapp, James. *Literary Modernism and the Transformation of Work.* Evanston, IL: Northwestern University Press, 1988.

Knowlson, James. *Damned to Fame: The Life of Samuel Beckett.* New York: Simon & Schuster, 1996.

Kontje, Todd. *The Cambridge Introduction to Thomas Mann.* Cambridge: Cambridge University Press, 2011.

Kontje, Todd. "Modern Masculinities." In *Thomas Mann's* The Magic Mountain*: A Casebook.* Ed. Hans Rudolf Vaget. New York: Oxford University Press, 2008. 71–94l.

Kontje, Todd. *Thomas Mann's World: Empire, Race, and the Jewish Question.* Ann Arbor, MI: University of Michigan Press, 2011.

Laughlin, Harry Hamilton. *Eugenical Sterilization in the United States.* Chicago, IL: Psychopathic Laboratory of the Municipal Court of Chicago, 1922.

Lawlor, Clark. *Consumption and Literature: The Making of the Romantic Disease.* Basingstoke: Palgrave Macmillan, 2006.

Lawrence, Karen R. "Orlando's Voyage Out." In *Virginia Woolf: An MFS Reader.* Ed. Maren Linett. Baltimore, MD: Johns Hopkins University Press. 327–54.

Le Bon, Gustave. *The Crowd: A Study of the Popular Mind.* Mineola, NY: Dover Publications, 2002.

Lee, Anthony. "Trace." In *The Nanjing Particles.* Ed. Susan Cross. North Adams, MA: MASS MoCA, 2009. 17–25.

Lee, Sherry D. "The Other in the Mirror, or, Recognizing the Self: Wilde's and Zemlinsky's Dwarf." *Music and Letters* 91.2 (May, 2010): 198–223.

Lessing, Gotthold. "Laocoön, or On the Limits of Painting and Poetry." In *German Aesthetic and Literary Criticism: Winckelmann, Lessing, Hamann, Herder, Schiller and Goethe.* Ed. H. B. Nisbet. Cambridge: Cambridge University Press, 1985. 58–133.

Levinas, Emmanuel. *Totality and Infinity: An Essay on Exteriority.* Trans. Alfonso Lingis. Pittsburgh, PA: Duquesne University Press, 1969.

Lewis, Wyndham. *Time and Western Man.* Ed. Paul Edwards. Santa Rosa, CA: Black Sparrow Press, 1993.

Linker, Beth. "On the Borderland of Medical and Disability History: A Survey of the Fields." *Bulletin of the History of Medicine* 87.4 (Winter, 2013): 499–535.

Linton, Simi. *Claiming Disability: Knowledge and Identity*. New York: New York University Press, 1998.

Longmore, Paul K. and David Goldberger. "The League of the Physically Handicapped and the Great Depression: A Case Study in the New Disability History." *Journal of American History* 87.3 (December, 2000): 888–922.

Longmore, Paul K. and Lauri Umansky, eds. *The New Disability History: American Perspectives*. New York: New York University Press, 2001.

Love, Heather K. "Forced Exile: Walter Pater's Queer Modernism." In *Bad Modernism*. Ed. Douglas Mao and Rebecca L. Walkowitz. Durham, NC: Duke University Press, 2006. 19–43.

Loy, Mina. *The Lost Lunar Baedeker: Poems*. Ed. Roger L. Conover. New York: Farrar, Straus, 1996.

Lucey, Donnacha Seán. "'These Schemes Will Win for Themselves the Confidence of the People': Irish Independence, Poor Law Reform and Hospital Provision." *Medical History* 58.1 (2014): 46–66.

Luciano, Dana. "Invalid Relations: Queer Kinship in Henry James's *The Portrait of a Lady*." *The Henry James Review* 23.2 (2002): 196–217.

Lukács, Georg. *Realism in our Time*. New York: Harper, 1964.

Lunn, Eugene. *Marxism and Modernism: An Historical Study of Lukács, Brecht, Benjamin, and Adorno*. Berkeley, CA: University of California Press, 1982.

Lutz, Tom. *American Nervousness: 1903, an Anecdotal History*. Ithaca, NY: Cornell University Press, 1991.

Lyon, Janet. "Carrington's Sensorium." In *Leonora Carrington and the International Avant-Garde*. Manchester: Manchester University Press, 2017. 163–76.

Lyon, Janet. *Manifestoes: Provocations of the Modern*. Ithaca, NY: Cornell University Press, 1999.

Lyon, Janet. "On the Asylum Road with Woolf and Mew." *Modernism/modernity* 18.3 (September, 2011): 551–74.

McBryde Johnson, Harriet. *Too Late to Die Young: Nearly True Tales from a Life*. New York: Holt, 2005.

MacIntyre, Alasdair, *Dependent Rational Animals: Why Human Beings Need the Virtues*. Chicago, IL: Open Court, 1999.

McRuer, Robert. *Crip Theory: Cultural Signs of Queerness and Disability*. New York: New York University Press, 2006.

Maher, Jane Maree. "Prone to Pregnancy: Orlando, Virginia Woolf and Sally Potter Represent the Gestating Body." *Journal of Medical Humanities* 28 (2007): 19–30.

Mahlstedt, Andrew. "Animal's Eyes: Spectacular Invisibility and the Terms of Recognition in Indra Sinha's *Animal's People*." *Mosaic* 46.3 (September, 2013): 59–84.

Mairs, Nancy. "Into the Wider World." In *Waist-High in the World: A Life among the Nondisabled*. Boston, MA: Beacon Press, 1996. 190–210.

Mann, Thomas. *The Magic Mountain*. Trans. John E. Woods. New York: Vintage, 1996.

Mao, Douglas and Rebecca L. Walkowitz, eds. *Bad Modernisms*. Durham, NC: Duke University Press, 2006.

Marcus, Jane. "Laughing at Leviticus: *Nightwood* as Woman's Circus Epic." In *Silence and Power: A Reevaluation of Djuna Barnes*. Ed. Mary Lynn Broe. Carbondale, IL: Southern Illinois University Press, 1991. 221–50.

Marcuse, Herbert. "The Affirmative Character of Culture." In *Negations: Essays in Critical Theory*. Boston, MA: Beacon Press, 1968. 88–133.

Marinetti, F. T. *Mafarka the Futurist: An African Novel.* Trans. Carol Diethe and Steve Cox. London: Middlesex University Press, 1998.

Marinetti, F. T. *Selected Writings.* Ed. R. W. Flint. New York: Farrar, Straus & Giroux, 1972.

Memmi, Albert. *Dependence.* Boston, MA: Beacon Press, 1984.

Miller, Cristanne, ed. *Emily Dickinson's Poems: As She Preserved Them.* Cambridge, MA: Harvard University Press, 2016.

Mindness, Anna. *Reading between the Signs: Intercultural Communication for Sign Language Interpreters.* Yarmouth, ME: Intercultural Press, 2006.

Mitchell, David T. and Sharon L. Snyder. *The Biopolitics of Disability: Neoliberalism, Ablenationalism, and Peripheral Embodiment.* Ann Arbor, MI: University of Michigan Press, 2015.

Mitchell, David T. and Sharon L. Snyder. *Narrative Prosthesis: Disability and the Dependencies of Discourse.* Ann Arbor, MI: University of Michigan Press, 2000.

Mitchell, David T., Sharon L. Snyder, and Linda Ware. "'[Every] Child Left Behind': Curricular Cripistemologies and the Crip/Queer Art of Failure." *Journal of Literature and Cultural Disability Studies* 8.3 (2014): 295–313.

Morris, David B. *Illness and Culture in the Postmodern Age.* Berkeley, CA: University of California Press, 1998.

Mouré, Erin. "On Zolf's *Neighbour Procedure.*" *Canadian Literature* 210/211 (Autumn/ Winter, 2011): 241–8.

Murray, Stuart. *Representing Autism: Culture, Narrative, Fascination.* Liverpool: Liverpool University Press, 2008.

Ngai, Sianne. *Ugly Feelings.* Cambridge, MA: Harvard University Press, 2005.

Nieland, Justus. *Feeling Modern: The Eccentricities of Public Life.* Urbana, IL: University of Illinois Press, 2008.

Nietzsche, Friedrich. "Nietzsche contra Wagner." In *The Portable Nietzsche.* Ed. Walter Kaufmann. New York: Penguin, 1985. 661–83.

Nietzsche, Friedrich. *Thus Spoke Zarathustra.* Trans. R. J. Hollingdale. Baltimore, MD: Penguin, 1969.

Nixon, Nicola. "'Prismatic and Profitable': Commerce and the Corporate Person in James's 'The Jolly Corner.'" *American Literature* 76.4 (2004): 807–31.

Nixon, Rob. "Neoliberalism, Slow Violence, and the Environmental Picaresque." *Modern Fiction Studies* 55.3 (Fall, 2009): 443–67.

Nordau, Max. *Degeneration.* New York: D. Appleton & Co., 1895.

Norris, Frank. *The Octopus.* New York: Penguin, 1986.

Norris, Frank. "Zola as a Romantic Writer." In *McTeague.* Ed. Donald Pizer. New York: Norton, 1977. 273–4.

Norton, Rictor, ed. "Of the Mollies Club, 1709–10." *Homosexuality in Eighteenth-Century England: A Sourcebook.* Updated July 23, 2018. <http://rictornorton.co.uk/eighteen/>.

Nossiter, Adam. "Ohio Bill Would Ban Abortion if Down Syndrome Is Reason." *New York Times*, August 23, 2015, National ed.: A1+.

Nussbaum, Martha C. *Frontiers of Justice: Disability, Nationality, Species Membership.* Cambridge, MA: Harvard University Press, 2006.

O'Connor, Flannery. *Mystery and Manners: Occasional Prose.* Ed. Sally Fitzgerald and Robert Fitzgerald. New York: Farrar, Straus & Giroux, 1961.

Old San Francisco. Dir. Alan Crosland. Warner Bros. 1927.

Olson, Charles. "Letter 5." In *The Maximus Poems.* Berkeley, CA: University of California Press, 1983. 21–9.

Ong, Aiwa. *Flexible Citizenship: The Cultural Logics of Transnationality.* Durham, NC: Duke University Press, 1999.

Ouellette, Alicia. *Bioethics and Disability: Toward a Disability-Conscious Bioethics.* Cambridge: Cambridge University Press, 2011.

Padden, Carol and Tom Humphries. *Deaf in America: Voices from a Culture.* Cambridge, MA: Harvard University Press, 1988.

Parsons, Deborah. *Djuna Barnes.* Horndon, UK: Northcote House, 2003.

Pearson, Nels. "'Outside of here it's death': Co-dependency and the Ghosts of Decolonization in Beckett's *Endgame.*" *ELH* 68.1 (2001): 215–39.

Pernick, Martin S. "Defining the Defective: Eugenics, Aesthetics, and Mass Culture in Early Twentieth-Century America." In *The Body and Physical Difference: Discourses of Disability.* Ed. David T. Mitchell and Sharon L. Snyder. Ann Arbor, MI: University of Michigan Press, 1997. 89–110.

Philip, M. NourbeSe. Interview with Marika Preziuo. *Latineos* (September, 2010). <http://latineos.com/en/articles/literature/item/46-m-nourbese-philip-zong.html>. Accessed July 28, 2013.

Philip, M. NourbeSe. *Zong! As told to the author by Setaey Adamu Boateng.* Middletown, CT: Wesleyan University Press, 2008.

Plato. *The Collected Dialogues Including the Letters.* Ed. Edith Hamilton and Huntington Cairns. Princeton, NJ: Princeton University Press, 1973.

Plumb, Cheryl J. *Djuna Barnes* Nightwood*: The Original Version and Related Drafts.* New York: Dalkey Archive Press, 1995.

Poe, Edgar Allan. "Maelzel's Chess-Player." In *Essays and Reviews.* New York: Library of America, 1985. 1253–76.

Poore, Carol. *Disability in Twentieth-Century German Culture.* Ann Arbor, MI: University of Michigan Press, 2007.

Pound, Ezra. *The Cantos of Ezra Pound.* New York: New Directions, 1973.

Pound, Ezra. "Date Line." In *Literary Essays of Ezra Pound.* New York: New Directions, 1968. 74–88.

Pound, Ezra. "Hugh Selwyn Mauberley." In *Personae: Collected Shorter Poems.* New York: New Directions, 1971. 185–204.

Pound, Ezra. "In a Station of the Metro." In *Personae: Collected Shorter Poems.* New York: New Directions, 1971. 109.

Pound, Ezra. "Portrait d'une femme." In *Personae: Collected Shorter Poems.* New York: New Directions, 1971. 61.

Pound, Ezra. "A Retrospect." In *Literary Essays of Ezra Pound.* New York: New Directions, 1968. 3–14.

Pound, Ezra. "The Serious Artist." In *Literary Essays of Ezra Pound.* New York: New Directions, 1968. 41–57.

Price, Margaret. *Mad at School: Rhetorics of Mental Disability and Academic Life.* Ann Arbor, MI: University of Michigan Press, 2011.

Proctor, Robert N. "The Destruction of 'Lives Not Worth Living.'" In *Deviant Bodies: Critical Perspectives on Difference in Science and Popular Culture.* Ed. Jennifer Terry and Jacqueline Urla. Bloomington, IN: Indiana University Press, 1995. 170–96.

Quayson, Ato. *Aesthetic Nervousness: Disability and the Crisis of Representation.* New York: Columbia University Press, 2007.

Quayson, Ato. *Calibrations: Reading for the Social.* Minneapolis, MN: University of Minnesota Press, 2003.

Rabaté, Jean-Michel. "Loving Freud Madly: Surrealism between Hysterical and Paranoid Modernism." *Journal of Modern Literature* 25.3/4 (Summer, 2002): 58–74.

Rancière, Jacques. *Aesthetics and its Discontents.* Trans. Steven Corcoran. Cambridge: Polity Press, 2009.

Rasula, Jed. *Destruction Was my Beatrice: Dada and the Unmaking of the Twentieth-Century.* New York: Basic Books, 2015.

Ravenscroft, Janet. "'Who Are You Looking At?' Picturing Difference in Early Modern Spain." Unpublished paper.

Reyes, Alvaro. "On Fanon's Manichean Delirium." *The Black Scholar* 42.3–4 (November, 2015): 13–20.

Rich, Adrienne. "I Am in Danger—Sir—." In *The Fact of a Doorframe: Poems Selected and New, 1950–1984.* New York: Norton, 1984. 70–1.

Robbins, Bruce, ed. *The Phantom Public Sphere.* Minneapolis, MN: University of Minnesota Press, 1993.

Rogin, Michael. *Blackface, White Noise: Jewish Immigrants in the Hollywood Melting Pot.* Berkeley, CA: University of California Press, 1998.

Rosenberg, Charles. *Explaining Epidemics and Other Studies in the History of Medicine.* Cambridge: Cambridge University Press, 1992.

Sahn, Sarah. "Between Friends: Disability, Masculinity, and Rehabilitation in *The Best Years of our Lives.*" Unpublished manuscript.

Salisbury, Laura and Andrew Shail, eds. *Neurology and Modernity: A Cultural History of Nervous Systems, 1800–1950.* Basingstoke: Palgrave Macmillan, 2010.

Sanchez, Rebecca. *Deafening Modernism: Embodied Language and Visual Poetics in American Literature.* New York: New York University Press, 2015.

Savoy, Eric. "The Queer Subject of 'The Jolly Corner.'" *The Henry James Review* 20.1 (1999): 1–21.

Schaffer, Talia, *The Forgotten Female Aesthetes: Literary Culture in Late-Victorian England.* Charlottesville, VA: University Press of Virginia, 2000.

Schaffer, Talia and Kathy Alexis Psomiades, eds. *Women and British Aestheticism.* Charlottesville, VA: University Press of Virginia, 1999.

Scheper-Hughes, Nancy. *Saints, Scholars, and Schizophrenics.* Berkeley, CA: University of California Press, 1979.

Schweik, Susan. "Kicked to the Curb: Ugly Law Then and Now." *Harvard Civil Rights– Civil Liberties Law Review Amicus* 46 (2011): 1–16.

Schweik, Susan. *The Ugly Laws: Disability in Public.* New York: New York University Press, 2009.

Sedgwick, Eve. *The Epistemology of the Closet.* Berkeley, CA: University of California Press, 1990.

Sedgwick, Eve. *Tendencies.* Durham, NC: Duke University Press, 1993.

Sedgwick, Eve. *Touching Feeling: Affect, Pedagogy, Performativity.* Durham, NC: Duke University Press, 2003.

Seigworth, Gregory J. and Melissa Gregg. "An Inventory of Shimmers." In *The Affect Theory Reader.* Ed. Melissa Gregg and Gregory J. Seigworth. Durham, NC: Duke University Press, 2010. 1–25.

Seitler, Dana. "Queer Physiognomies; Or, How Many Ways Can We Do the History of Sexuality?" *Criticism* 46.1 (Winter, 2004): 71–102. Web. Project Muse. May 1, 2016.

Serlin, David. "At Your Fingertips: Toward a Synthetic History of Tactile Modernity." Unpublished talk at Princeton University, February 10, 2014.

Serlin, David. *Replaceable You: Engineering the Body in Postwar America*. Chicago, IL: University of Chicago Press, 2004.

Sewall, Richard B. *The Life of Emily Dickinson*. New York: Farrar, Straus & Giroux, 1980.

Shakespeare, Tom. "The Social Model of Disability." In *The Disability Studies Reader*, 4th ed. Ed. Lennard Davis. New York: Routledge, 2013. 214–21.

Showalter, Elaine, *Daughter of Decadence: Women Writers of the Fin-de-Siècle*. London: Virago Press, 1993.

Siebers, Tobin. *Disability Aesthetics*. Ann Arbor, MI: University of Michigan Press, 2010.

Siebers, Tobin. *Disability Theory*. Ann Arbor, MI: University of Michigan Press, 2008.

Silverman, Kaja. *Male Subjectivity at the Margins*. New York: Routledge, 1992.

Simmel, Georg. "The Metropolis and Mental Life." In *On Individuality and Social Forms*. Ed. Donald Levine. Chicago, IL: University of Chicago Press, 1971. 324–39.

Singer, Peter. *Practical Ethics*. Cambridge: Cambridge University Press, 2011.

Sinha, Indra. *Animal's People*. New York: Simon & Schuster, 2007.

Smith, Shawn Michelle. *Photography on the Color Line: W. E. B. Du Bois, Race, and Visual Culture*. Durham, NC: Duke University Press, 2004.

Smith-Rosenberg, Carroll. *Disorderly Conduct: Visions of Gender in Victorian America*. New York: Oxford University Press, 1985.

Snyder, Sharon L. and David T. Mitchell. *Cultural Locations of Disability*. Chicago, IL: University of Chicago Press, 2006.

Sontag, Susan. *Illness as Metaphor and AIDS and its Metaphors*. New York: Picador, 1989.

Spackman, Barbara. "Mafarka and Son: Marinetti's Homophobic Economics." *Modernism/modernity* 1.3 (September, 1994): 89–104.

Spinoza, Baruch, *The Ethics*. In *A Spinoza Reader: The Ethics and Other Works*. Ed. Edwin Curley. Princeton, NJ: Princeton University Press, 1994.

Stevens, Wallace. "Esthétique du Mal." In *The Collected Poems of Wallace Stevens*. New York: Knopf, 1968. 313–26.

Stich, Sidra. *Anxious Visions: Surrealist Art*. Berkeley, CA: University Art Museum, 1990.

Stone, Deborah A. *The Disabled State*. Philadelphia, PA: Temple University Press, 1984.

Strauss, Joseph. *Extraordinary Measures: Disability in Music*. New York: Oxford University Press, 2011.

Symonds, John Addington. *The Memoirs of John Addington Symonds*. Ed. Phyllis Grosskurth. London: Hutchinson, 1984.

Tajiri, Yoshiki, *Samuel Beckett and the Prosthetic Body: The Organs and Senses in Modernism*. Basingstoke: Palgrave Macmillan, 2007.

Tanitch, Robert. *Oscar Wilde on Stage and Screen*. London: Methuen, 1999.

Taylor, Julie. "Introduction: Modernism and Affect." In *Modernism and Affect*. Ed. Julie Taylor. Edinburgh: Edinburgh University Press, 2015.

Terada, Rei. *Feeling in Theory: Emotion after the "Death of the Subject."* Cambridge, MA: Harvard University Press, 2001.

Thomson, Stephen. "'La justice, c'est la femme à barbe!': the Bearded Lady, Displacement and Recuperation." In *Apollinaire's Les Mamelles de Tirésias. The Last Taboo: Women and Body Hair*. Ed. Karin Lesnik-Oberstein. Manchester: Manchester University Press, 2006. 83–102.

Tibol, Raquel and Frida Kahlo. *Frida by Frida: Selection of Letters and Texts*. Trans. Gregory Dechant. Mexico: Editorial RM, 2006.

Tiedemann, Rolf. "Historical Materialism or Political Messianism." In *Benjamin: Philosophy, Aesthetics, History*. Ed. Gary Smith. Chicago, IL: University of Chicago Press, 1989. 175–209.

Titchkosky, Tanya. "The Ends of the Body as Pedagogic Possibility." *Review of Education, Pedagogy, and Cultural Studies* 34.3–4 (2012): 89–93.

Tomkins, Silvan. *Shame and its Sisters: A Silvan Tomkins Reader.* Ed. Eve Kosofsky Sedgwick and Adam Frank. Durham, NC: Duke University Press, 1995.

Toomer, Jean. *Cane.* New York: Liveright, 2011.

Tzara, Tristan. "The Gas Heart." In *Theater of the Avant-Garde, 1890–1950.* Ed. Robert Knopf. New Haven, CT: Yale University Press, 2015. 246–56.

Vaget, Hans Rudolf. "The Making of *The Magic Mountain.*" In *Thomas Mann's* The Magic Mountain: *A Casebook.* Ed. Hans Rudolf Vaget. Oxford: Oxford University Press, 2008. 13–30.

Valente, Joseph. "Modernism and Cognitive Disability: A Genealogy." In *A Handbook of Modernism Studies.* Ed. Jean-Michel Rabaté. London: John Wiley & Sons, 2013. 379–98.

Velasco, Shirley. *Male Delivery: Reproduction, Effeminacy, and Pregnant Men in Early Modern Spain.* Nashville, TN: Vanderbilt University Press, 2006.

Verlaine, Paul. "Languor." In *An Anthology of French Poetry from Nerval to Valery.* Ed. Angel Flores. New York: Doubleday, 1958.

Viramontes, Helena Maria. "Cariboo Café." In *The Moths and Other Stories.* Houston, TX: Arte Público, 1985. 61–75.

Vrettos, Athena. *Somatic Fictions: Imagining Illness in Victorian Culture.* Stanford, CA: Stanford University Press, 1995.

Wald, Priscilla. *Contagious: Cultures, Carriers, and the Outbreak Narrative.* Durham, NC: Duke University Press, 2008.

Weigand, Hermann J. "Disease." In *Thomas Mann's* The Magic Mountain. Ed. Harold Bloom. New York: Chelsea House, 1986. 7–22.

Weininger, Otto. *Sex and Character.* London: William Heinemann, 1907.

Wells, H. G. *The Island of Doctor Moreau.* London: Penguin, 2005.

Wendell, Susan. *The Rejected Body: Feminist Philosophical Reflections on Disability.* New York: Routledge, 1996.

Wilde, Oscar. "The Birthday of the Infanta." In *The Complete Shorter Fiction of Oscar Wilde.* Ed. Isobel Murray. Oxford: Oxford University Press, 1979. 185–202.

Wilde, Oscar. *The Picture of Dorian Gray.* New York: Oxford University Press, 2008.

Williams, Raymond. *Marxism and Literature.* Oxford: Oxford University Press, 1977.

Williams, William Carlos. *The Collected Poems of William Carlos Williams. Vol. I: 1909–1939.* Ed. A. Walton Litz and Christopher MacGowan. New York: New Directions, 1986.

Wilson, Edmund. *The Wound and the Bow.* New York: Oxford University Press, 1947.

Winckelmann, Johann Joachim. "Thoughts on the Imitation of the Painting and Sculpture of the Greeks." In *German Aesthetic and Literary Criticism: Winckelmann, Lessing, Hamann, Herder, Schiller and Goethe.* Ed. H. B. Nisbet. Cambridge: Cambridge University Press, 1985. 29–54.

Wood, Ann Douglas. " 'The Fashionable Diseases': Women's Complaints and their Treatment in Nineteenth-Century America." In *Clio's Consciousness Raised.* Ed. Mary S. Hartman and Louis Banner. New York: Octagon, 1976. 1–22.

Woolf, Virginia. *On Being Ill.* Ashfield, MA: Paris Press, 2012.

Woolf, Virginia. *Orlando.* New York: Harcourt, 2006.

Woolf, Virginia. "Street Haunting." In *Street Haunting and Other Essays.* Ed. Stuart N. Clarke. London: Vintage, 2014. 225–40.

Worton, Michael. "*Waiting for Godot* and *Endgame*: Theatre as Text." In *The Cambridge Companion to Beckett.* Ed. John Pilling. Cambridge: Cambridge University Press, 2005. 67–87.

Yeats, William Butler. "Under Ben Bulben." In *W. B. Yeats: The Poems*. Ed. Richard J. Finneran. New York: Macmillan, 1983. 327.

Žižek, Slavoj. "Otto Weininger, or, 'Woman Doesn't Exist.'" *New Formations* 23 (Summer, 1994): 97–113.

Zolf, Rachel. "Coach House Books asks Rachel Zolf a few things about Neighbour Procedure." <http://www.chbooks.com/q-a/coach-house-books-asks-rachel-zolf>. Accessed July 28, 2013.

Zolf, Rachel. "Jacket Interview." *Jacket* (2009). <http://jacketmagazine.com/37/iv-zolf-ivb-bettridge.shtml>. Accessed July 29, 2013.

Zolf, Rachel. *Neighbour Procedure*. Toronto: Coach House Books, 2010.

Index

Index

Printed and bound by CPI Group (UK) Ltd, Croydon, CR0 4YY